The Tragedy of Manuel Azaña

and the Fate of the Spanish Republic

LIZARRAGA

Manuel Azaña

The Tragedy of Manuel Azaña

and the Fate of the Spanish Republic

By Frank Sedwick

Ohio State University Press

To Alice
sine qua nihil

FOREWORD

PROFESSOR SEDWICK's life of Azaña is a welcome addition to the already impressive corpus of scholarly books published in the United States on the Spanish Republic and the Civil War which consumed it. Azaña was one of the founders and by far the most significant of the leaders of the Republic. The Republic lived while he lived, and when he died it died.

I had known Azaña for years before he became a national, indeed a world figure. He was then secretary of the Ateneo, an honorary and elective post. He already had his typical *cara de pocos amigos*, his face of (a man with) but few friends, as we say in Spain, meaning by it not that such a man lacks, but that he does not want, many friends. He was standoffish, short-tempered, and, if by no means taciturn, certainly not talkative. His countenance was complex: the lower part of the face, sulky; but in his eyes and eyebrows there lurked an almost pathetic appeal for sympathy.

This enigmatic façade covered a warm and even affectionate heart, slow to open out to others less out of intellectual superiority than out of downright shyness. Whether this feature had grown in him from his consciousness of being less than handsome (though he was too intelligent to strike one as plain) or for some other reason, the fact is that the warmth in him was of all his secrets the one he tried hardest to guard but succeeded least in guarding.

This explains that a man with a face of few friends could have so many. Of course he was chary of the profuse forms of friendliness of which Spaniards, for all their vaunted introversion, are rather prodigal. No smiles, no shouts of pleasure, no embracements. But if he was sparing in the forms of friendship, he was generous in the substance of it.

He was very much a Castilian, straight up as well as straight, and too fond of liberty to sacrifice even a scrap of it to mere comfort or well-being. In those early days of our acquaintance, he was a Reformist, a follower of Don Melquiades Alvarez, the Asturian republican who was leading a clever maneuver to bring the moderate and free-thinking republicans into the fold of the monarchy, in exchange for guarantees of a progressive policy on the part of the Crown. Azaña seemed to detect in this attitude of his chief a softening of his fighting spirit due to a desire to live comfortably, and he uttered this thought to me with the utmost contempt. I knew that Don Melquiades, by Paris or London standards, lived an almost austere life, and I admired the more his Castilian critic born and bred in the tradition of a bread-and-water sort of life.

Azaña was very much like a Castilian tree, rather solitary, deep-rooted (for water is scarce and hidden below), rough-barked, many-branched, but somewhat neglectful and sparing of its foliage, which it is apt to think of as too rhetorical and effusive for the bare lands and skies of central Spain. And yet, warm and vital within, and ready to vibrate in the wind and yield quiet music just for itself and the wide space and the sunset. But no birds.

A pessimist, of course. If Lamennais thought that *il faut un minimum de bien-être pour la vertu,* we are free to think that a minimum of rainfall is necessary for optimism. Yellow Spain, two thirds of it, including all of Castile, is the driest land in Europe. How could it give forth crops of juicy optimists? No. Remember Sancho. "Every man is as God made him, and at times worse." That saying, and its sudden spurt of pessimism at the end is in fact true to Azaña's own style. But then, both Azaña and Cervantes were born in Alcalá.

So let us guard against being misled by this or that of his public utterances into mistaking Azaña for a naïve revolutionist who expected the millennium to blossom out of his next budget. His disillusionment with the Republic ripened at the end of the Civil War, but it is safe to surmise that the seed of it was already in him on the very day he took office as the first War Minister of the new regime. For a man of letters who had never owned a weapon in his life, was not the very choice of ministry a sure sign of pessimism? He knew only too well that the history of Spain is beset with the same pair of opposites which time and again used to occupy Don Quijote's imagination: arms versus letters.

But in Don Quijote this was just fancy. In Azaña, it was stark reality. He knew that in Spain the slow growth of institutions had always been, is, and shall always be threatened by the military and by the militant, who are just another kind of military. And out of aversion for the military, he did not perhaps see clearly enough the danger from the militant.

For he made mistakes, of course. Personally, I believe he was wrong in ousting Alcalá Zamora from the Presidency in connivance with Indalecio Prieto. Wrong in substance and wrong in form. For that maneuver implied a deed of injustice towards the president and an irreparable blow to the stability and good name of the Republic. Of this and of other of his shortcomings, I am fully aware. Yet, since too many small men have tried to denigrate him since his death, let one man who owed him no allegiance say that Azaña was the biggest mind and the noblest heart among the leaders of the Republic.

SALVADOR DE MADARIAGA

Oxford, England
June 19, 1963

PREFACE

THE SPANISH REPUBLIC of 1931-1939 was a house built mostly upon the sand. Its structure rested, in part, on a number of writers converted into statesmen *ad hoc*. Moderates like Unamuno, Ortega y Gasset, Madariaga, and Azaña could not withstand the steady erosion from the Left, on top of which came the sudden deluge from the Right. After the fanatics of both these extremes had undermined the foundations, the storm of civil war then demolished the Republican edifice, whose exiles are the wreckage that still floats around the world.

Many of the writer-statesmen disappeared from the Spanish scene in the first year of the Civil War. On the last day of 1936, death relieved Miguel de Unamuno from further despair of seeing Spaniards kill one another. He died in his home in Salamanca. Having moved about Europe and South America since 1936 in self-imposed exile, José Ortega y Gasset returned to Spain in 1945. There he was to live ten more years, reconciled to the durability of the Franco state, although by no means to its political philosophy. Salvador de Madariaga left Spain at the outbreak of the Civil War and never returned, a voluntary exile from his native land like numerous other first-class Spanish scholars and statesmen, who had good reason to leave. Among those who did not leave was Manuel Azaña, twice Prime Minister and the last President of the Spanish Republic. Dutifully he remained in Spain until the Civil War was irremediably lost for the Republic, and then he died obscurely in France in 1940.

"Why write a book on Azaña?" a colleague inquired of me; "Europe has forgotten him and America never knew him." Precisely so, and all the more reason for light on the life and works of this intellectual, this Spanish Kerensky (Azaña met Kerensky once in 1931 and was unimpressed), who was undoubtedly the principal political figure of the Second Spanish Republic, but Spain's most neglected literary personality during his productive years as a writer between two World Wars. Until now, no one has bothered to study Azaña's works to see how they reflect the rise and fall of his political star.

The author is well aware that while some sections of this book may be microscopic in their analysis, others are telescopic. To find reliable data on Azaña was not an easy task; to give complete details on certain periods of his life was impossible. The surviving relatives and friends of Azaña in Spain and in the Americas were co-operative, but: (1) Most of Azaña's own generation is dead. Only one childhood companion, now an octogenarian, remains alive. (2) Azaña was, by nature, a solitary. Few people really knew him well. (3) Although Azaña died in 1940, neither his complete memoirs nor his complete works have yet been published. (4) From the lips of the still-embittered exiles from Spain, facts are distorted by passions. (5) The Civil War generations still in Spain are reluctant to comment freely on pre-1939 events or personalities. (6) Many of the Republic's documents were scattered to the four winds in the chaos of defeat. More important, the post-1939 Spanish government has either confiscated the remaining documentary and other factual data or has in many subtle ways intimidated librarians and custodians to withhold such references from writers lacking an established proper point of view vis-à-vis the regime. These difficulties become particularly apparent to an objective biographer of any Republican personality, and especially to the biographer of Manuel Azaña, who was the man most hated by the rebellious and still-governing Right wing.

It is with gratitude to the American Philosophical Society (Penrose fund) and to Ohio Wesleyan University, for their research and travel funds, that I present the first sketch in English of this unknown man, imperfect though it may be. Moreover I hope that my detachment from specific religious and political affiliations may have led to an interpretation of the causes of the Spanish Civil War free from the usual biases, though possibly for this very reason the book may not please most of the people whom it principally concerns—Spanish Republicans-in-exile, Spanish Francoists, Catholics, Monarchists, Communists, Anarchists, Socialists, and Azaña's surviving relatives in Spain and Mexico, some of whom have become my close friends. To the latter I can repeat only what I learned from Manuel Azaña: compassion is not a condiment sprinkled upon justice according to taste and circumstance; rather justice is of itself compassionate (else it is not justice), and one should hope for no more.

FRANK SEDWICK

Rollins College
Winter Park, Florida

CONTENTS

ILLUSTRATIONS

xvii

Lo que importa es tener razón, y después de tener razón,
importa, casi tanto, saber defenderla; porque sería triste cosa
que, teniendo razón, pareciese como si la hubiéramos perdido
a fuerza de palabras locas y de hechos reprobables.

—Manuel Azaña

*The important thing is to be right, and, after being right,
it is nearly as important to know how to defend what is right;
because it would be a sad thing if it seemed that we, being
right, had lost our rightness by dint of mad words and re-
proachable deeds.*

FLAT on the high plain of Castile lies Alcalá de Henares, tethered to Madrid by thirty-one kilometers of highway. A sleepy town, just as it was a century ago, and physically unimpressive, its historical importance must be sought down the back streets, a zigzag seldom ventured by the few tourists who pause in Alcalá en route to Guadalajara. Nowadays Alcalá does not even boast a hotel worthy of the name, although a good meal can be had at the quaint Hostería del Estudiante. Bugles of the Spanish military detachments stationed in Alcalá sometimes resound down the arcades that shelter much of the main street, while from the sky comes the scream of U.S. jet airplanes which have just taken off from the nearby Torrejón air base. But the citizens of Alcalá remain impassive, like the storks in their rooftop nests, secure in the permanence of their ancient town.

The city which under the Arabs came to be known as Alcalá de Henares was founded by the Romans as Complutum or Compluvium, whose etymology probably has to do with water. The inhabitants are still sometimes referred to as *complutenses,* and the original name of the famous University of Alcalá was Universidad Complutense, established by the equally famous Cardinal Cisneros in 1508 and closed in 1836 when it gave way to the University of Madrid. Of course Alcalá has a patron saint. She is the *Virgen del Val* (contraction of *valle*, or valley), whose supposedly miraculous image appeared in 1184 on a bank of the Henares river, and part of whose name appears —though quite unrelated to Alcalá—in the title of a posthumous and unfinished novel by a *complutense* named Manuel Azaña.

Esteban Azaña, father of Manuel, recorded the history of Alcalá and its people up to 1882 in a work of two volumes which he published in that year and entitled *Historia de Alcalá de Henares (antigua Compluto)*. Ten years earlier, the elder Azaña had also founded a school for the working class known as the Colegio para Obreros, which opened its doors in January of 1873. Not because of a scarcity of students (there were about 200), but through the apathy of its professors, the school lasted only two years. Because of these and many other services unselfishly rendered to Alcalá by the civic-minded Esteban Azaña, a street was named after him, the Calle de Don Esteban Azaña. Even though this street was not named for the son, but for the father, who died January 10, 1890, since the Spanish Civil War the street has had to revert to its original designation of Calle Nueva.

Like most quiet Spanish towns, Alcalá does explode once daily during the early evening hours with café life and strollers of every description, many of them Spanish paratroopers whose oversized black-ribboned berets lend color to the noisy scene on the main square. Every Spanish town has its main square, and this one is appropriately named the Plaza de Cervantes, for Alcalá's most famous son is Spain's most celebrated writer—the creator of *Don Quijote*. The Plaza de Cervantes is not really a square but an unpaved rectangle, with several gardens at one extremity and a kiosk at the other, and double rows of sycamores standing on the two long sides like sentinels. These trees are the retainers over whom a monument to Cervantes presides from the very center of the dusty court. The inscription on the pedestal of the statue could not be simpler: "Cervantes. Año 1879." Cast in Florence, Italy, the statue is reputed to weigh 750 kilos, its bronze figure of Cervantes being one and a half times life size. In sixteenth-century garb, and girt with a sword, the standing figure of Cervantes holds a pen in his right hand and a scroll in his left. Eight months after the statue was set in place, the reigning monarchs Alfonso XII and María Cristina visited Alcalá on June 8, 1880; and to Esteban Azaña, mayor of Alcalá, fell the honor of receiving them and pointing out the historical sights of the city, including the newly erected monument to Cervantes, which arouses so little curiosity nowadays.

Earlier in that same year of 1880, on January 10, Manuel Azaña was born in Alcalá, but the previous year saw an event of nearly equal import in the life and miracles of the Azaña family: to commemorate the unveiling of the statue of Cervantes, Esteban Azaña published his first book. Already a public speaker in his capacity of mayor, the elder Azaña left his name on what is now a rare tome that bears the sonorous title of *Memoria de los acuerdos del iltre. ayuntamiento de la ciudad de Alcalá de Henares para la erección de un monumento a Miguel de Cervantes Saavedra.*[1] Without examination of the book, one could scarcely guess what it contains: minutes of sessions of the municipal government, poems mostly by local poets, and speeches eulogizing Cervantes; but mainly it is a history of the city's efforts to erect that monument to Cervantes. The long-awaited statue having finally been finished and set in place, the town council had asked Esteban Azaña to edit this book of homage to Cervantes in which the elder Azaña himself describes the statue and the ceremonies of its dedication. The

[1] This book was printed in Alcalá de Henares in 1879. One of its original 600 copies may be seen in New York City at the library of the Hispanic Society of America.

minutes of the September 22, 1879, meeting of the *Ayuntamiento* show that the cost for 600 copies of the book was voted unanimously, and that since Azaña was chairman of the group, the book was to become his literary property. The efforts of Esteban Azaña had been the chief *tour de force* in the final acquisition of the monument, which he himself unveiled on October 9, 1879, exactly one year after he had laid the first stone, and forty-six years after the statue had been first planned by the *Ayuntamiento* in 1833. In the political life of the nation, the year 1879 also marked the end of a tumultuous decade of abortive liberalism (the First Spanish Republic) and internal strife that presaged the national calamities at the end of the century.

In his speeches Esteban Azaña evidenced a certain flair for dramatic oratory that was to be reborn with more finesse in Manuel. The elder Azaña, who frequently signed his papers Esteban Azaña y Catarineu (Esteban's mother was Catalonian), always gave a good performance, notwithstanding a show of modesty and a feigned lack of talent for writing or for public speaking. This self-deprecation was merely one aspect of his style ("I, without any merit, without scientific knowledge, lacking literary forms," etc.), for he really gave evidence of broad classical and historical knowledge that belied his lack of a university education. If his style was defective in any way, it was because of his excessive allusions, but he had a genuine knowledge of *Don Quijote,* an insight which renders less tiresome the otherwise extravagant encomium of Cervantes as his city's symbol of greatness. Although he was usually speaking as a politician, and moreover as a politician of Cervantes' native city, on the whole Don Esteban wrote clearly and displayed a literary awareness not unbecoming the mayor of Alcalá de Henares. A man so intensely bound to his *patria chica,* however, could not have been the cosmopolitan that his son was destined to become when, many years later, Manuel Azaña gave his own lecture on Alcalá de Henares before an assemblage at the Ateneo of Madrid. Apart from these civic activities, Esteban Azaña y Catarineu was also a business man of some importance in Alcalá. He was descended from a line of scriveners and minor public servants of the peripheral type of nobility known in Spain as "hidalgo." Less is known about his wife, Josefina Díaz, except that she was an intelligent and reportedly exceptional woman who shared her husband's library as well as his mildly liberal ideas, but it was an otherwise bourgeois and traditionally Catholic family which he supported by an income derived from both a soap factory and extensive land holding. Several of these farms still remain in the family; a principal one is the *Finca de los Barrancos,* not far from Alcalá, and soon to be reforested under forced partnership with the state. A Catarineu soap is still manufactured somewhere in Spain, but no longer in Alcalá nor under any interests of the Azaña branch of the family. Esteban Azaña also had a fleeting interest in a chocolate factory, but the truth is that both he and his son Manuel were given far more to literature and civic affairs than to business.

Manuel Azaña had two brothers and a sister. Carlos died as a child. Gregorio, the eldest son, like Manuel studied law before he ultimately settled in Zaragoza, where he was presiding officer of the regional high court located in that city, his official title having been *Presidente de la Audiencia Territorial de Zaragoza.* As young men, both Gregorio and Manuel took an interest in local politics in Alcalá. Gregorio was once elected representative of the Alcalá-Chinchón district to the provincial congress, after having held previous municipal office in Alcalá. In 1905, the two brothers also helped edit a weekly satirical review known as *La avispa* (the wasp), one of whose stinging articles gave rise to a lawsuit against Manuel, quashed only when it was shown that he had not written that article.

Gregorio's three marriages had produced one son (also named

Gregorio) and eight daughters when he died of heart trouble in 1934, at precisely the time when Manuel, already ex-Prime Minister, was unjustly incarcerated in Barcelona and prevented even from attending his brother's funeral. Each of Gregorio's three wives predeceased him. The first wife, Cristina, died childless in 1897 after less than two years of marriage. The second marriage gave seven children: two did not survive infancy; the others are, chronologically: Concepción, Carmen, Josefa, Gregorio, and Ana, at whose birth the mother, Amparo, died in 1912. The third wife was Carmen, a victim of tuberculosis in 1927; her two children were Manuela and, the younger, Enriqueta. Gregorio's only son was assassinated by Nationalist sympathizers in Córdoba during the first days of the Civil War. Five of the six surviving sisters and half sisters still live in Spain, having returned from exile; the sixth, Enriqueta, is a nun who resides in Salinas, California. Manuela, pleasant and petite, is married to an architect and lives in Madrid, as does Carmen. Josefa, recently widowed, a most comely woman despite the Azaña trait of a very pale complexion, lives with her daughter in Lorca (Murcia). The eldest, Concepción, is unmarried, lives in Alcalá de Henares, and exercises the principal control over the family interests. Ana, whose husband was killed by shrapnel during a Nationalist air raid in Valencia in 1937, returned from exile in France in 1940 and now resides with her two sons in a *pensión* which she owns in Madrid. One of these sons is Manuel Martínez Azaña, named for his great uncle, Manuel Azaña, whose literary career this young relative is bent upon emulating. Young Manuel had his first play, *La forja de los sueños*, produced May 17, 1960, at the Teatro Goya in Madrid. A handsome and talented youth, he is undaunted by the censorship of many lines from his play, or by the fact that the second of his surnames is a disadvantage to any kind of career in Spain today. The play itself is a subtle and poetic work which I have been privileged to co-edit for its publication in Spanish (Houghton Mifflin Co., 1963) and to co-translate into English under the title *Where Dreams Are Forged*.

So much for Gregorio and his family. His and Manuel Azaña's only sister was Josefa. The childless widow of a one-time cavalry officer named Ramón Laguardia, she died on December 5, 1959, at the age of 75. Particularly in later years Josefa bore a striking facial resemblance to her brother Manuel. Although she never wholly shared Manuel's political philosophy, she feared for her life during the Civil War and had to be treated for nervous disorders. After the Civil War, it was she who restored in magnificent fashion and refurbished the Azaña house at Calle de la Imagen 3, which the Nationalists had damaged extensively when they occupied Alcalá at the end of the War. There in the family home she had lived somewhat secluded until her death.

The Azaña house was tastefully restored to reflect all of its original charm. Calle de la Imagen is a short and narrow street convenient to the old and arcaded business area of Alcalá. On the corner diagonally across the street from the Azaña home is the supposed house of Cervantes, also restored, and a national monument. Imagine the affinity to Cervantes that young Manuel Azaña must have felt when he read *Don Quijote* for the first time, an affinity which inspired him years later to publish his own critical essay on the invention of the *Quijote*. Today one of the nieces, Concepción, occupies the Azaña home. Most of the original furniture was wrecked at the end of the Civil War, and the room where Manuel was born is no longer used as a bedroom; but his original desk, chair, and lamp are still by the window in his study. Photographs of him decorate the living room and drawing room as well as the study. Numerous other photos of Manuel are treasured in a family album. Despite the changes wrought by the Civil War in

Spain, despite the stigmatization of the name Azaña, despite the Catholicism practiced in the home and formalized in its elegant little chapel, the relatives of Manuel Azaña are patently proud of him who was once President of the Spanish Republic and who fought to free state from church in Spain.

Book twenty-four, folio sixty-four, of the baptismal records of the parish of San Pedro in Alcalá de Henares reveals that on January 17, 1880, a son of Esteban Azaña and Josefina Díaz was baptized with the following given names: Manuel María Nicanor Federico Carlos, or simply Manuel Azaña Díaz. The name Azaña is uncommon. It suggests the Spanish noun of identical pronunciation, *hazaña:* a heroic deed or exploit, also used in the ironic sense to mean an ignoble action. Like his surname, the life and deeds of Manuel Azaña are liable to double interpretation. The present intention is neither to glorify the man nor to anathematize him, but to understand him. To achieve part of this understanding, one must realize that Manuel Azaña lost both of his parents early in his life.

Nothing is notable about Manuel's earliest years except the unhappy effect of the death of his parents. His mother died July 25, 1889, and his father in 1890, so Manuel became an orphan at the age of ten. He rattled about the big old house with the other children, all of whom were frequently alone despite the attempts of their paternal grandmother, Concha de Catarineu, to look after them. Thus was the great solitary intellectual of later life a logical development of the precocious but shy young Manuel, whose emotional ties were so few in his boyhood and who as an adolescent distinctly preferred things to people. Watched over by solicitous but authoritarian ecclesiastics, Manuel found an early refuge in reading. Indeed he read constantly. He was particularly fond of Jules Verne, whose then newly published works stirred his imagination. For a long time Manuel insisted that he wanted to become a sailor; but books—law books and others—were to become his career far removed from sailoring.

Though the father had remarried *in articulo mortis*, an obscure affair which made Manuel not less an orphan and which gave rise to a lawsuit filed by a maternal uncle, the patrimony was more than sufficient to underwrite the education of the children. Manuel received his early schooling in his native city at the Colegio Complutense, founded in 1850 and now defunct. Next he attended the Instituto del Cardenal Cisneros and became a *bachiller* at the age of thirteen. From there he went "to college" at the Augustinian school in the Escorial, where this young man with the morals of a believer but the temperament of a non-believer first rebelled against religious dogma. Having finished his studies at the Escorial, he went to Zaragoza, where he completed a licentiate in law. In 1897 he returned to Alcalá to see his only boyhood sweetheart (a relative named Josefa Díaz Gallo) and to undertake his first journalistic endeavor, the co-editorship of a local magazine.

This is the time to introduce José María Vicario Sanz, Azaña's best boyhood friend. José Vicario is one of the traditions of Alcalá, part of the local color. In probably his mid-eighties, he is today like the monument to Cervantes, whose pedestal alone shows wear while the essential part of the creation remains firm. A bachelor, José lives modestly at the Plaza de San Julián 2 with his niece; unlike Don Quijote's, she is niece and housekeeper in one. By comparison to Gustave Doré's drawing, Vicario's study could be that of Alonso Quijano, except for a scarcity of books on chivalry, because Vicario's shelves are lined largely with nineteenth-century authors, but not so many that the works of Manuel Azaña fail to enjoy a prominent position. Two of Vicario's prized possessions on display are a large autographed photo (with dedication to José Vicario) of his friend

11

Manolo, as Manuel's friends in Alcalá used to call him, and a bound collection—probably the only one extant—of the review, *Brisas de Henares* (Breezes from the Henares), which he and Azaña established in 1897 and published for seven months.

The pages of this aggressive political and literary magazine carry the first record in print of Manuel Azaña's latent rebellion. Published at Coches 10 (a street name which still exists) and sold for twenty *céntimos* per copy, the periodical carried all types of features: short stories, caustic editorials, jokes, poems, and résumés of the sessions of the Alcalá city council. Many of the political and literary items were signed by "Salvador Rodrigo," the first of a number of pen names that Azaña was to employ in his career as a writer. For the occasion, Vicario's nom de plume was "El Vicario de Durón." Always identifiable by the shield of the city of Alcalá that appeared at the top of the title page of each issue, the review prospered and its later issues even attracted some advertising to help defray expenses. September 2, 1897, was the date of the first number of *Brisas de Henares;* thereafter it appeared on the first, tenth, and twentieth of each month until its final issue of March 10, 1898. Then Azaña was going to go back to school, and Vicario did not want to carry on the enterprise alone.

Through the years, however, the two friends saw each other often. During the 1930's when Azaña enjoyed high political office and national prestige, he frequently felt a need to get away from the capital for a night and would go to Alcalá, where he preferred to arrive late and unnoticed. He seldom failed to visit the "Vicario de Durón" for a chat in the latter's study on these informal occasions. In official capacity, however, Azaña visited Alcalá only once or twice during his tenure of the most important posts in national government.

The year 1898 found Spain at war with the United States and Manuel Azaña enrolled as a graduate student at the Universidad

Central (University of Madrid), where he earned a doctor of laws degree in 1900. There he was privileged to study under the famous humanist Francisco Giner de los Ríos, as well as under the well-known jurists Azcárate and Posada, who provided him with sufficiently good recommendation for placement in the eminent law firm of Luis Díaz Cobeña.

Do not picture a hard-working young apprentice trying to get ahead with simple habits and frugal fare. In Madrid, Manuel had acquired a taste for elegance. He put fine clothes on his back, dined at the best restaurants, and cultivated a *tertulia* of friends as unsettled as he. His legal career was soon ended; presumably he found active law practice dull and never again returned to it. Instead he gave himself over to books, and also to desirable young ladies, an indolent life supported by income from the family estate in Alcalá.

At about this time the young man also gave his first lecture, or at least his first public address to have been published. The year was 1902, year of Alfonso XIII's assumption of the throne of a then constitutional monarchy. Azaña was only twenty-two years old when he read this speech, entitled *La libertad de asociación*,[2] before the Academy of Jurisprudence in Madrid. Behold the young jurist addressing his elders: he, squat, blond, mustachioed (at that time), with two fathomless pools for eyes set in a large head that sprouted two correspondingly large ears. Even at that age Azaña was nearsighted, and he wore the sickly pale complexion which was soon to accentuate an early obesity.

"Freedom of Association," and all the title implies, is a fitting intro-

---

[2] The speech was published in Madrid in 1902 by Imprenta de los hijos de M. G. Hernández and is a very rare pamphlet today. The University of California (Berkeley) library owns what is probably the only copy in the U.S.A. Until I told them of it, this publication was unknown to Azaña's widow and brother-in-law, who are planning to publish Azaña's complete works.

duction to the ideological pattern of Manuel Azaña. Syntactical analysis of this, his first, recorded public message reveals also the dense style of complex but orderly sentence structure representative of his prose and oratory. It is not surprising that this first speech lacks rhetorical originality in its composition; rather he reverts to a few time-worn devices. One of them is in the ending, where he does not permit the turn of his argument to announce, unsaid, a logical point of conclusion; instead he resorts to the "In conclusion, gentlemen . . ." type of leave-taking, to which he adds the final words in the form of a literary tag, a quotation without depth, moreover, or originality: "Freedom, to make association possible; association, to make freedom fecund."[3] Yet in a work even so early as this one, Azaña was dealing with some of the same specific and cardinal precepts, the same axes to grind, that were to form his often-stated personal and political credo: freedom of association as an ideal in itself, which includes freedom for the proletariat to form co-operatives ("the co-operative idea is not socialist"), freedom for statesmen to develop political parties, freedom for scholars to speak out freely; the sovereignty of the state free from clerical influence, and free from the oppression of the military caste; the creation of a citizenry who take an interest in affairs of state and public order; and the faith in one's own times and contemporary resources. As his book on French political theory will reveal, Azaña interpreted freedom as a duty (a giving), not a privilege (a taking).

In his personal life, Manuel was beginning to encounter problems less theoretical than those of citizenship. The money was running low in Alcalá. Until then, he had returned to the family home only for an occasional vacation, to see his old friend José Vicario, or to roam the fields that he knew and liked so well. Suddenly circumstances forced him to attempt a rescue of the family holdings. To this end Azaña

[3] Quoted from Piernas Hurtado, *El movimiento cooperativo.*

moved back to Alcalá, where he tried to modernize the farming properties and at the same time pay a living wage to his workers. He became restive, however, not primarily because success eluded him, but because in Madrid he had developed a cosmopolitan taste which was proving to be incompatible with rural confinement. With most of the Azaña capital dissipated, Manuel went back to Madrid in a more serious frame of mind. Still it was a valuable experience for a future statesman; and in a speech at Madrid years later, on February 11, 1934, Azaña was able to say, "I too have been a farmer."

In Madrid he took the path that has always seemed so attractive to many middle-class Spaniards. He became a respectable bureaucrat, having won a competitive examination for an administrative post in the Registry Office of the Ministry of Justice. José Vicario retains a copy of the speech that Azaña had to give as part of his *oposiciones* for the position. Azaña discharged the duties of the position competently, but since it was neither demanding nor lucrative, he found enough hours free both to continue his intellectual activities at the Ateneo and to supplement the income from other sources. He did some teaching at the Academy of Jurisprudence and was also secretary of the Institute of Comparative Law. In addition, he began to write articles for newspapers both in and out of Spain.

In 1911, at the age of thirty-one, Azaña won a grant from the Council for the Development of Studies (*Junta de Ampliación de Estudios*, created in 1907, a government-backed organization which sent Spanish scholars abroad) to go for a year to Paris and the Sorbonne. He was competent in the French language, and French politics fascinated him not less than the liberal milieu of the French capital itself. It was natural that Azaña be attracted to French ideas because basically he was a realist who moved within the practical concept of intellectual discipline which the French call *le droit*. Much at home in the literary life of Paris, Azaña sent back newspaper articles to Madrid under the pen name "Martín Pinel" and undoubtedly began to collect data for his *Estudios de política francesa contemporánea*. He admired the British as well as the French but never achieved a visit to England, nor to America.

Back at his various jobs in Madrid the following year, Azaña settled down to a routine that included late hours (and late to rise), much strolling, even more reading, an occasional *tertulia*, but a veritable haunting of the halls of the Ateneo, that haven of intellectuals and liberals where he studied, gave lectures, or spent hours in contemplative thought. Now and then he played tennis or a game of cards or chess. Occasionally he bought a lottery ticket and was known to win. He continued to take pleasure in fine cuisine, since his was a delicate palate which savored such dishes for the gourmet as *angulas*, tiny ashy-pale eels cooked intact in deep oil. Already in his early thirties Azaña had become fleshy, in fact had a paunch. In 1913 he joined the new Reformist political party *(Partido Reformista)* of Melquiades Alvarez, with whom he held meetings and gave lectures on behalf of the party, one of them held at the Teatro-Salón Cervantes in his home town of Alcalá toward the end of 1913. In the same year Azaña was elected secretary of his beloved Ateneo, a post which he held through 1919. Also in 1913 Azaña published a booklet entitled *La situación económica del Ateneo de Madrid*. In the summer of 1914 he first met Cipriano Rivas Cherif, the young intellectual who was to become Azaña's best friend and whose sister Azaña was to marry in 1929.

World War I came during that same summer of 1914, on July 28. Formally Spain remained neutral, and economically she profited by that status, but Spanish public opinion became divided. As one might have expected, Manuel Azaña declared himself with the minority in favor of France and England, countries whose achieved reality of democratic life he admired so much. He spoke vehemently in the Ateneo against Germany (one of his best lectures was "Los motivos de la germanofilia") and wrote for the liberal Madrid dailies *El imparcial* and *El liberal* with similar conviction. He even helped to organize pro-Allied demonstrations throughout Spain, like the one held in the Bull Ring of Madrid. About 1916 Azaña and his friend Rivas Cherif toured much of northern Spain, from town to town, to help in the pro-Allied propaganda campaign. It was this kind of introduction to political stump procedures that perhaps impelled Azaña to enter two unsuccessful campaigns for public office. In 1918 and again in 1923 he ran as a *Reformista* candidate to parliament from the province of Toledo and was backed by the Socialists of that region. Attributing his defeat to the deeply rooted *caciquismo* (political boss system), and taught by experience the futility of an intellectual's speeches in overcoming the influence of an opponent's wealth, later during the Republic Azaña was to introduce changes in the electoral laws designed to minimize local political corruption.

Italy had entered the Great War on the side of the Allies. In 1917 at the invitation of the Italian government, Azaña was one of five Spanish writers who toured the Italian-Austrian war front. The others of the group were Américo Castro, Luis Bello, Santiago Rusiñol, and Miguel de Unamuno, whose relations with Azaña were still cordial at that time, though Unamuno behaved boorishly throughout the trip. Earlier the French government had invited Azaña, Ramón Menéndez Pidal, and some others to tour the war areas of France. From France, Azaña had written to Rivas Cherif of his confidence in an Allied victory.

Coincident with the triumph that Azaña predicted was the publication of his first full-length book, the heart of which was three lectures that he had given at the Ateneo in January of 1918. Also about that time, the Reformist party had asked Azaña to make a report on the status of the Spanish military situation. The book on French policy bears no publication date, but Azaña signed the prologue as October, 1918, one month before the Armistice in Europe (November 11, 1918). The full title of the book is *Estudios de política francesa contemporánea*, Vol. I: *La política militar* (Studies in Contemporary French Policy [Politics], Vol. I: Military Policy), first of a projected three-volume series, the second to be entitled *El laicismo* (Laicization) and the third, *La organización del sufragio* (The Organization of Suffrage). The remaining two volumes were never published.

As Azaña explains in his prologue, the study has nothing to do with the technical preparation of an army for war. It would have been presumptuous of him to assume the role of military strategist. Instead he writes of military policy, particularly insofar as it reflects French public life of the preceding fifty years. Even though Azaña begins with the French Revolution, his specific analysis covers the 1871-1914 period, which dates from the previous armistice with Germany and includes France's total reorganization up to the start of World War I. An interesting key to French political thought of the period, and more than a history book, these over three hundred dense pages of erudition were Azaña's own private training ground for concepts of government which later he was to propose for Spain, on the French model. For example, as Minister of War of the first Republican government, he undertook a program of army reform which undoubtedly derived from what he expressed as one of the aims of his book: the search for a military policy that would render the greatest defensive efficiency without diminishing the freedom of the individual or the sovereignty of the government. Every army is potentially a threat to its own government, and nineteenth- and twentieth-century Spaniards have known what it is to live under such a threat, so often has the Spanish military seen fit to rise up in the role of savior of the state, as in 1874, 1923, and 1936. Thus Azaña's purpose in presenting this material is more didactic in nature than it would seem at first sight—instructive for Spaniards, not Frenchmen. Manuel Azaña's apprenticeship for government was much more extensive than his colleagues realized, and certainly was not confined to the gestation period of Spanish Republicanism in the late 1920's.

Azaña's political theory all lies on the bedrock of freedom for the individual. Remember that as early as 1902 he was discoursing on freedom of association. Azaña's study of French politics has likewise as its nucleus the individual and his freedom, inviolate but within well-defined social obligations. Liberty becomes equated with *patria* when the state assures its citizens that it will defend their rights, and when the citizens in turn give to the state the protection (public office, military duty, etc.) required for its efficiency and survival. But these rights of the citizen are earned rights; contrary to Article 1 of the Declaration of the Rights of Man, men are not "born free." Even though many of Azaña's thoughts on republicanism may be rooted ultimately in the French Revolution ("the French Revolution, to which most modern peoples in Europe are indebted for their political existence," as he said in the Cortes, May 27, 1932), he distilled all sentiment from the French precepts; and his critics are wrong in accusing him of nineteenth-century romantic liberalism. Azaña's concept of individual freedom is not the one of Rousseau: not the one linked to "nature" and denying to any man a "natural" authority over any other man; not the one by which a given human being is himself the best judge of his own best means of preserving his right, even his duty, of being free and autonomous. Instead Azaña interprets liberty as a collective force, a kind of mutual guarantee among men, a force whose legal authority transcends the individual's ego and lies in the common interest of citizenship, this common will to be transferred, in turn, to the leaders of state. Azaña asserted that the freedom of the individual could be maintained only through the public good, which is the limited kind of freedom called democracy. Collective freedom is an act of giving; pure "natural" freedom is an act of taking—hence the moral superiority of collective freedom. Thus Azana's concepts of freedom are highly civilized ones, unsentimental, practical, and realistic. As he so often repeated later in speeches, liberty does not make men happy; it simply makes them men.

Why did Azaña, essentially an aesthete and *littérateur*, seek the military problem among all the Spanish problems in which he might have interested himself? Antonio Ramos Oliveira supplied an answer in his book *Politics, Economics and Men of Modern Spain, 1808-1946,* which has the best chapter on Azaña that anyone has written, which has, in fact, the only accurate picture of the man and his motives. "What spurred Azaña to seek to change the face of his country was chiefly the longing for harmony and beauty, the preoccupation of the artist rather than the politician. It was natural that Azaña should choose the military question, since for a temperament like his, nothing could have been more 'noisy and disorderly' [this phrase is Azaña's] in Spain than the invasion of public life by the Army. To put it simply, the Army did not allow him to write, to fulfill himself, in a grave and noble sense; the Army was the major obstacle which prevented Spain from realizing her destiny."[4] Ramos Oliveira was probably right when he concluded that to silence and discipline the Army was Azaña's "oldest and perhaps his only aspiration in politics."

Manuel Azaña was approaching the transitional age of forty, variously described as the twilight of youth or the dawn of maturity. By

---

[4] Antonio Ramos Oliveira, *Politics, Economics and Men of Modern Spain, 1808-1946* (London, 1946), pp. 308-9.

this time he had defined himself well, even if only to men of letters, political theorists, and journalists. The masses were not to hear much of him until more than ten years later, his only "popular" activities having been the propaganda campaigns during the First World War and his several unsuccessful bids for political office. Azaña's ability to blend forensic elegance with disarming logic was earning him a reputation as a convincing speaker; on the other hand, as a writer, his obvious originality and unquestioned command of language failed to win any sizable bloc of readers to a prose that seemed dense and cold, and perhaps erudite to a fault.

He was brilliant, they said, but unapproachable. He seemed to be perpetually on guard against others, and, what is more, he had a bad temper. His physiognomy was not one to instill confidence. He was ugly, beatifically ugly! His paunch was becoming as rotund as his prose, and the stubby hands were becoming thick with flesh that fell over and under the several rings which he always wore. It was time for the moustache to come off forever, and he was balding, the remaining hair having turned grey on the square head. As the chin grew larger, so did the nose. His coloring had never been good, because the entire family shared a pale complexion. On the whole, Azaña's physical appearance was far from prepossessing.

When this "pimply-faced Mr. Pickwick," as one observer later described him, came to power in the Republican government, no other man before the public eye was subjected to more cruel and persistent caricature in the opposition's press. He was a toad, a frog, a salamander, a snake—anything slimy or untouchable, but most especially a snake—the stealthy, hissing, vengeful danger, and with the additional implication of femininity, since *snake* is a feminine noun (*la serpiente*) in Spanish. Admittedly vain, sensitive, and somewhat vengeful (womanish characteristics, reputedly), Manuel Azaña lived the solitary life of erudition that prevented him, in the estimation of some, from more normal functions like marriage. It is impossible to say who originated the rumor of his "unnatural practices," much less to verify the truth of it; but whether or not it was true, everybody heard of it sooner or later, and the story persists even today. There was even one wild tale that spread to France, to the effect that Azaña liked to dress up as a woman. Included in the calumny was bouncy, nervous little Cipriano Rivas Cherif, since he was Azaña's companion and adulator. Malicious jokes were invented about Rivas Cherif's given name. With the diphthong split, the name *Cipriano* was easily twisted into two unseemly ones. Some of the slanderers were silenced later when Azaña married Don Cipriano's sister; others found this marriage to be good reason for redoubling their vituperations.

The Great War over, Paris was becoming gay again. Azaña and Rivas Cherif spent the latter months of 1919 and early part of 1920 there, with a side trip to Alsace-Lorraine and the inauguration ceremonies of the French University of Strasbourg, to which Azaña had been invited. In France the two good friends led a carefree life and maintained themselves largely from literary translations. Among Azaña's translations, then and later, are works by Jean Giraudoux, George Borrow, and Gilbert Chesterton, as well as Voltaire's memoirs.[5] All of the numerous translations by Azaña are from either English or French. He and Rivas Cherif frequently helped each other, but their names appeared together on a title page only once: their Spanish translation of the *Mémoires* of Mlle. de Lespinasse, one of the eighteenth-century salon-leaders. Rivas Cherif was competent in Italian as well as in French and English, for he had taken his doctorate at the University of Bologna (he once told me he loved Italy the best of all places), and during this period in Paris he translated Goldoni's *La*

[5] See Azaña's translations in the Appendix.

22

locandiera, Dante's *Il convivio,* Fogazzaro's *Daniele Cortis,* Foscolo's *Ultime lettere di Jacopo Ortis,* and some short novels by Verga, along with works by Gautier *(Le capitaine Fracasse),* Rochefoucauld *(Mémoires),* and even Hans Christian Andersen. In 1913 Rivas Cherif had translated the *Fioretti* (about St. Francis of Assisi); in 1911-12 he published in two volumes the *Romances* of the Duque de Rivas; in 1921 he edited the first Clásicos Castellanos edition of poetry by Ramón de Campoamor. Then in 1928 he was the co-translator of some of Joseph Conrad's tales, and in 1944 he gave Dana's *Two Years before the Mast* to readers of the Spanish language.

In the spring of 1920 the two friends returned to Madrid, where a mutual friend, Amós Salvador, offered to underwrite the foundation of a literary journal which they called *La pluma,* its name taken from the quotation originated by Azaña and placed at the head of each volume: *"La pluma es la que asegura castillos, coronas, reyes y la que sustenta leyes"* (The pen is what preserves castles, crowns, kings, and is what maintains laws). This motto typifies Azaña's faith in the goddess Intelligence. His deity was to fail him later when the pen and the word were not enough to preserve the Spanish Republic they had created.

La pluma appeared monthly from June, 1920, to June, 1923, all issues printed by Sáez Hermanos, and wrapped, addressed, and mailed by Azaña and Rivas Cherif themselves. The first issue bore a statement of editorial policy that committed *La pluma* to independent writing, free from ties to any school of thought or literary movement, and, though disclaiming the ivory tower, in opposition to what the editors described as the present bad taste in writing. Theirs was not the usual type of crusade wherein a group of writers feel out of step with their times. All in all, *La pluma* was a good monthly, one that seemed to lack only variety.

In an uphill struggle, the editors managed gradually to attract many of the best-known liberal writers of the day, some of whom, like Valle Inclán, were already old friends from Azaña's *tertulia* at the Café Regina. Of the established writers, the most frequent contributors were Gómez de la Serna, Pérez de Ayala, and Valle Inclán, whose *esperpentos* were the feature work in many issues. They published Unamuno's three-act play *Fedra* in three installments: January, February, and March, 1921. Other well-known contributors were Juan Ramón Jiménez, Pedro Salinas, Alfonso Reyes, Jorge Guillén, Antonio Machado, Federico García Lorca, and Salvador de Madariaga. Rivas Cherif supplied poems and short stories, and also did most of the book reviews, including a review (with highest praise, naturally) of his friend Azaña's translation of George Borrow's *The Bible in Spain* (June, 1921, issue). Azaña furnished some book reviews himself but found it hard to confine his analyses to a reasonable length; even in reviewing a book, he was given to the dense long-paragraph style which characterizes nearly all of his writings as well as his oratory.

Most of Azaña's non-fictional feature contributions to *La pluma* were gathered later with others of his essays in a collection appropriately entitled *Plumas y palabras* (Madrid, 1930), which we shall examine in another place. "El secreto de Valle Inclán," Azaña's contribution to the issue of January, 1923 (a number devoted entirely to Valle Inclán), was the only one of Azaña's essays from *La pluma* included in his other collection entitled *La invención del Quijote y otros ensayos* (Madrid, 1934). When he wrote for *La pluma*, sometimes Azaña signed his own name, as in the serializing, in eight installments, of about half his *El jardín de los frailes* (discussed in the following chapter); at other times he signed his articles with one or the other of his two pen names of that time: "Cardenio" and "El Paseante en Corte."

Three fictional items stand out among Azaña's *La pluma* contributions not collected or expanded later in the volume *Plumas y palabras*, which contained all non-fiction. The first of these, part of the inaugural issue of *La pluma*, is perhaps Azaña's best short story, one which shows the expert subtle irony that typifies Azaña's writing. It is entitled "A las puertas del otro mundo" (At the Gates of the Other World). Because of its content, which by a striking coincidence anticipated some of the actual circumstances of Azana's death, comment on this story will be reserved for the last chapter. The second tale is "Auto de las cortes de Burgos, o triple llave al sepulcro del Cid y divino zancarrón," a hoax *auto* with argument, dialogue, and a pretended note on the edition at the end. Azaña's sarcasm seems always to be at its best when he gibes at the clergy. Here he mocks the church's propensities for the collection and adoration of relics. The supposed remains of the Cid are exhumed, much to the joy of a certain Latin-speaking Archbishop of Trajanópolis. When a doctor identifies the bones as those of a horse (probably Babieca!), the Archbishop is unconvinced; rather, he argues that maybe the Cid was a giant, and he kisses the bones to indicate that they are a relic. The skit terminates in mock classic style with the appearance of Fernando III and a little dance. The piece was signed by "Cardenio."

This *auto* was the second of three works that Azaña wrote under the heading *Fantasías*. The third was equally entertaining, signed also by "Cardenio" for the September, 1921, issue, along with the first installment of *El jardín de los frailes*. Entitled "Si el alarbe [sic] tornase vencedor" (If the Arab Should Return Victorious), and replete with the wildest anachronisms, it depicts an imaginary war between Spain and invading Moors from Morocco. Again, its refined wit is all satire. Two Moors are debating the advisability of invading Spain. The one who favors an attack argues that previously it took the Spaniards eight hundred years to recoup what Islam had won in a few months. The other Moor maintains that if the Spaniards are indeed rustic and backward, that is precisely what will make them good fighters. It is decided, nevertheless, to invade. In Spain the mobilized clergy bless the first stone of each fortress ordered restored by the Academy of Fine Arts. The preparations for war reveal the Spaniards' collective tendency to improvise: *"Lo improvisamos todo: un soneto, una fortaleza, un ferrocarril"* (We improvise everything: a sonnet, a fortress, a railroad). Squads of monks in a certain monastery twice as big as the Escorial work feverishly making scapularies. Another factory is making medals, their distribution assured by the women who will take them to the front. The Archbishop of Tarragona commands the right wing of the assembled army, with all the cavalry, while Alejandro Lerroux (Azaña's political opponent-to-be during the Republic), proclaimed a Maestre de Santiago, governs the left wing. The bull *(bula)* of the crusade is on sale but does not sell well since many people are expecting to get it at the last moment at a reduced price. With such preparations for war, naturally the Spaniards lose the battle and retire to prepared positions.

Throughout the 1920's Azaña attacked the church, which was growing powerful again in a period marked by total damming of the earlier tide of liberalism in government. Apparently he had the good sense to throw a smoke screen of fiction or surreptitious publication over most of his political and ecclesiastical attacks. An unfortunate lack of such precaution, by the way, sent Unamuno into exile. The last issue of *La pluma* in June, 1923, therefore, represented a voluntary cessation of publication, in order that Azaña and Rivas Cherif might take what they thought was a step forward in joining the editorial board of the better-known magazine *España*.

Founded by José Ortega y Gasset in 1915, *España* was a weekly journal dedicated to republicanism as well as to literature. Both before and after Azaña associated himself with the staff of *España*, its political messiahship kept the publication in constant disfavor with the government and the military censors, to whose unholy prerogatives every issue of *España* alluded during this period. When words or sentences and even whole paragraphs were deleted from its copy, *España* countered effectively by publishing the given article with the censored portions represented exactly by blank lines of dots. The February 16, 1924, issue bore a laconic announcement, in funereal type, of the decree exiling Unamuno (who had been a frequent contributor) and closing the Ateneo. One might suppose that even some of the advertising carried by the magazine antagonized the watchdogs, because each issue during Azaña's incumbency contained at least one and sometimes two advertisements for firearms—singular sponsorship for a literary journal! Its editors courted the enmity of the Primo de Rivera government and baited the censors until finally *España* was forced to cease publication with the March 29, 1924, issue.

The best-known contributors to the pages of *España* were largely the same writers who had lent their prestige to *La pluma*. Among them were Valle Inclán, Unamuno, Juan Ramón Jiménez, Madariaga, Ramón Gómez de la Serna (with his drawings, as usual, accompanying his literary work), Jorge Guillén, Pedro Salinas, Jaime Torres Bodet, Luis Araquistain, José Bergamín, and Antonio Espinosa. In addition to his own editorial contributions, both literary and political, Azaña had a hand in the direction and management; in 1924 the business office was transferred to his own house at Calle de Hermosilla 24 *duplicado* (*duplicado* means the second of two houses with the same number) in the district of Madrid known as the *barrio de Salamanca*. The same printer, Sáez Hermanos, published both *La pluma* and *España*. As for Rivas Cherif, he performed the same function that he had with

La pluma: he wrote a more than occasional article and was the chief literary critic and book reviewer.

On joining *España,* Azaña ceased to use his old pseudonyms, but certain unsigned editorial comment reveals his style and sentiment if not his name. Azaña later collected his best non-fictional works from both *España* and *La pluma* in a volume which will be examined in the next chapter. Present mention need be made of his few chief contributions that appeared only in *España.* There are also those which did not appear even in *España,* like one entitled "Suicidio de Pedro Crespo" (Suicide of Pedro Crespo) announced for the December 8, 1923, *España,* but suppressed by censorship along with four other articles of the same issue, one of them by Unamuno; or the one entitled "Nuevos partidos, libertades viejas" (New Parties, Old Liberties), originally announced as deleted from the November 10, 1923, issue, but which appeared later without explanation, unsigned, and perhaps cut or revised—or perhaps not—in the March 15, 1924, number. Whenever an article could not be published, which was not an infrequent occurrence, the editors of *España* inserted an ambiguous little notice about "causes contrary to our wishes," etc.

Either the censors were inattentive when the article on "Nuevos partidos, libertades viejas" was set in type, or else Azaña concluded that discretion was not the better part of valor. "Liberty is the condition of citizenship," he writes, and then goes on to censure the church, which in countries where it has lost its privileged secular position, ends by embracing the very freedom that it had sought with all its means to destroy. Also he evokes freedom of the press, historically the sire of all public liberties, and indispensable to any chance of survival for the new liberal parties seeking to organize themselves, since no group can share its own ideas without means of communication. Thus Azaña returns to his old theme of freedom of association.

The article "La vanidad y la envidia" (Vanity and Envy) in the same issue is directed against the dramatist Jacinto Benavente, a one-time Germanophile (Azaña disliked Germany instinctively) and, at that writing, a monarchist. Benavente had asserted publicly, "I am a monarchist because I am a Spaniard," words refuted by Azaña without difficulty.

In other articles Azaña reacts to the Spanish-American War (which he always considered an ill-advised and useless manifestation of Spanish "honor," except for the lessons it taught Spaniards), ruminates on Joaquín Costa (whom he always took to be a pessimist and anti-democrat who was as wrong at one extreme of prescription for Spanish regeneration as was Ganivet at the other), condemns Maurice Barrès (nationalistic French novelist, recently deceased at that time), and eulogizes Woodrow Wilson on the occasion of his death. One might well expect that the internationalist and progressive Azaña would have seen in Woodrow Wilson a kindred spirit whose labor deserved more acclaim than his actual success might have indicated. Finally, mention must be made of a little one-act dialogue with five scenes, "El fénix de las Españas," published in the March 1, 1924, España. A political satire on the Conde de Romanones, an aristocrat prominent in government circles, it is similar in form and ironic tone to the "fantasy" that Azaña had inserted in the September, 1921, La pluma. This time he exercises his satirical bent by depicting some fictitious elections in contemporary Spain. Azaña did well in this genre, the colloquy, which possibly he should have cultivated more. It will be shown that he was a failure as a dramatist, but then so was Pío Baroja, who was an expert at the non-dramatic dialogue like Paradox, Rey. Instead of writing a great work of fiction, Manuel Azaña was constantly invading the library, drawn there by a scholarly curiosity that usually prevailed over his imaginative creativity. The only time that he gave undivided effort to fiction was in his single great novel, *Fresdeval*, posthumous, unfinished, and most of it composed when he was in hiding and unable to haunt the libraries.

So it was that during his "literary 1920's" Manuel Azaña was not composing the great modern Spanish novel; instead he was collecting material to win the National Prize of Literature, in 1926 at the age of 46, for his *Life of Don Juan Valera*.

The prize did not include automatic publication of the winning manuscript. But there is another reason, not generally known, why the book never has been published *in toto*. Valera's daughter Carmen made Azaña promise not to publish the whole work until after her death. Ironically she outlived Azaña by a few months. Though the *Life of Don Juan Valera* as a complete manuscript has been lost, parts of it will be collected for the first time in Azaña's complete works, supposedly ready now for publication in Mexico.[6] Azaña did begin right away, however, to disseminate the work piecemeal. The first portion to be printed was entitled "Valera en Rusia," published as pages 5–40 of the January-February, 1926 (Año XX, Tomo LII, Nos. 200 and 201), review *Nosotros* of Buenos Aires. Valera had gone to Russia in 1856 as secretary to a diplomatic mission headed by the Duke of Osuna. Azaña's article treats of the six months that Valera remained there. Based largely on the copious correspondence of Valera, it describes and interprets Valera's love affairs. A large part of the original

---

[6] It seems ironical that with Azaña's essays on Valera finally ready for publication, another biography of Valera, also based on Valera's letters, has recently been published in Spain: Carmen Bravo Villasante, *Juan Valera* (Barcelona, 1959), 365 pp. Even though Azaña's complete works are ready for publication now, it may be some time before the volumes actually appear. Azaña died without a will, and the heirs, his widow in Mexico and his nieces in Spain, have been unable to agree on the rights. It is not really a question of royalties, but one of propriety. The complete works would have to include Azaña's memoirs, the publication of which would surely open old wounds among Republicans in exile as well as possibly create difficulties for Republicans who have by now returned to Spain, including the relatives in Madrid and Alcalá de Henares.

prize-winning study, in fact, was based on Valera's letters and personal papers, made available to Azaña by Valera's daughter. Azaña thanked her publicly in his prologue to the Clásicos Castellanos (Vol. XXX) edition of Valera's first and principal novel, *Pepita Jiménez*, published by La Lectura in Madrid, 1927. Apropos of this prologue, here is an excerpt from an unpublished letter which Azaña wrote to Miguel de Unamuno on May 25, 1928: "Me satisface que haya encontrado usted bien el prólogo de *Pepita Jiménez*. Tengo ahora para imprimir otra monografía sobre Valera, que comprende su historia personal y literaria mientras estuvo en Italia con el Duque de Rivas (1847-1849)" ("I am glad that you liked the prologue to *Pepita Jiménez*. I am now about to print another monograph on Valera, which covers his personal and literary history while he was in Italy with the Duque de Rivas"). It was through this editing of a volume in the most reliable series of edited Spanish classics that Azaña became recognized as a literary scholar. Prior to the 1926 prize, Azaña's work had been largely journalistic, aside from his study of French military policy and his translations.

In 1927 Azaña also published a book with the title *La novela de Pepita Jiménez* (Madrid: Imprenta Ciudad Lineal). While the sixty-one-page prologue that he wrote for the Clásicos Castellanos volume is a condensation from his prize-winning work, *La novela de Pepita Jiménez* represents a long section copied from the prize work almost verbatim. The mother work bore still a fourth offspring, the "monograph" mentioned in Azaña's letter to Unamuno, which is really a book entitled *Valera en Italia: Amores, política y literatura*, not published until 1929, by Editorial Páez (Madrid) as number XIV of the Biblioteca de Ensayos series. This last physically unimpressive book contains something of a reward for the curious reader: it has a youthful photograph of Azaña opposite the title page. This photo bears Azaña's autograph, one in which a graphologist might see severity, self-discipline, and straightforwardness. It is the only autographed photo ever to appear in any of Azaña's works published during or after his lifetime. The fifth and final piece on Valera, entitled simply *Valera*, forms one of the four essays in Azaña's *La invención del Quijote y otros ensayos,* published in Madrid in 1934 by Espasa-Calpe.

Why did Azaña study Valera? What drew his attention to the life and writings of that aristocratic Cordoban who lived from 1824 to 1905? For one thing, it was a question of convenience and opportunity: Valera's complete works, numbering forty-six volumes plus other papers, were being published in 1905-17, intellectually expansive years for Manuel Azaña. More important, however, it was a case of attraction to a kindred spirit, which seems perfectly obvious once it is pointed out. I refer again to the chapter on Azaña in Ramos Oliveira's book. With good reason Ramos Oliveira held that Valera and Azaña "both looked at Spain from the same angle. In essentials, their characters were the same." Even their tastes and opinions were in many ways identical. Let us hear Azaña speak on Valera; the quotation is from Azaña's essay entitled *Valera:*

> Modesty, moderation, the careful preservation of personal intimacy; purity of line, clarity, order, the perpetual appeal to good sense, simplicity, grace; with a corresponding aversion to all that is noisy and disorderly.

All of these characterize Azaña too. One might quibble about his "modesty," yet the tendency to display an unrestrainable brilliance of intellect is not really presumption or egotism. As was demonstrated in the matter of Azaña's interest in military affairs, the origin of this interest was aesthetic in nature: a wish to see the "noisy and disorderly" military curtailed in its unharmonious effect upon Spanish public and intellectual life. To quote Ramos Oliveira on Valera, "Valera felt a proud aversion from [sic] Spanish society which seemed to him primitive, coarse, presumptuous and ignorant. He perceived, above all, the aesthetic, or anti-aesthetic, aspect of Spanish things—a quality which was also prominent in Azaña. Over a long period, much the same thing happened to Azaña in politics as happened to Valera." Azaña himself noted how Valera's "mental fineness prevented him from being fanatical; his personal dignity did not permit him to mingle with the rabble and elbow his way among the throng." This should not be interpreted to mean that Azaña rejected any associations with the lower classes. To him, the mob meant all people who lacked character and substance, of whom a large portion may have been found among the upper classes. Rather he saw in "the people" fortitude, loyalty, natural courtesy and pride, and a passionate capacity for noble action—misplaced energies within the scheme of Spanish traditionalism, but useful qualities within the liberal democratic state that he envisioned.

Valera too had been a statesman, but one with far less direction and conviction than Azaña. Both were urbane cosmopolites, as opposed to the *castizo* type, and in this lies the key to Azaña's total personality. He rejected what most historians would call Spanish traditionalism, as a way of life incompatible with twentieth-century social and technical progress within a European community of nations. Azaña and Valera were men of the world, of unmistakable culture and intellect. Each was critic, translator, and linguist; neither had talent for the writing of verse. An elegant style, as unaffected as it was unemotional, characterizes their prose. *Pepita Jiménez* is as polished and at the same time as slow moving as Azaña's *El jardín de los frailes;* the characters' interior life is the thing. It is a noteworthy coincidence that the hero of each of these works is a seminarist who rebels, but the two works have nothing else in common beyond their respective yet divergent religious themes.

Azaña himself observed that the style of *Pepita Jiménez* is superior to the plot. All the action is interior, psychological. This the most renowned of Valera's novels is the story of a young man, Luis, who, while he is studying for the priesthood, unwittingly falls in love with the widow for whom the novel is named. The novel reaches its climax when Luis finally decides to renounce his projected career in order to marry her. All of the novelist's subtle art is revealed in the very gradual change in outlook of Luis, the stream of interior processes carried along by means of an exchange of correspondence between Luis and his uncle, a priest from whom Luis seeks advice. Although *Pepita Jiménez* is not really anticlerical, Azaña saw in its author a certain spirit of irreligion.

Azaña maintains that Valera "did not accept the divine origin of religion. He was not a practicing Catholic, not even a Christian, but publicly he abided by a liberal Catholicism." And Azaña also saw in Valera an "independent rationalist" who was opposed to what Azaña calls "traditional forms." Valera wrote that "barbarism, coarseness, and ordinariness are in Spain irremediable," and he objected even to copying colloquial language.

In short, Valera's spirit was one in which reason dominated. Of Valera's double passion of literature and politics, Azaña observes that "ever since he was young, Valera desired *limitless* [italics Azaña's] power, glory. Pursuing them he had misspent time in politics." His profession as a novelist came late in life. Azaña too turned late in life to fiction, too late to finish his one great work. When at the critical point in the parallel lives of both men Valera became disillusioned in politics, there was still time left to become a great writer; Azaña at that juncture forged ahead to become a great statesman, and when his star fell it was too late to become a great writer. Even some of the details of their personal lives coincided. For example, both inherited lands which did them little good. At the age of forty-three Valera married a pretty young girl of twenty-two; Azaña at forty-nine married a woman about twenty-two years his junior.

One could go on, but this is enough. Azaña and Valera were spiritual brothers whose beliefs, art, and careers were astoundingly similar in many ways. Recall, however, that Azaña was only in his mid-forties when he did his study on Valera, and that Azaña's glory was still to come. Thus he did not have the full picture of his own life to compare to Valera's, much less the objective view of his own personality. Not less than three separate but identically worded statements appear in Azaña's writings, two of them preceding the 1926 work on Valera, in which Azaña says of Valera: "He is not my type, neither in the moral nor literary realm" (*No es mi tipo, ni en lo moral ni en lo literario*). Can one surmise that Azaña underestimated his own sensitivity? More than that, "he is not my type" is a declaration of intention not to follow Valera's course, not to give up politics for letters at this crossroads in his intellectual life. To the extent that the subject of study—Valera— in the 1926 prize-winning work served as an example to its author, that manuscript was in the final analysis an unintentional political treatise, like most of Azaña's other works to come. The work on Valera also marks the end of a long apprenticeship. "He is not my type" seems to say: Bring on the Republic!

IN THE literary life of Manuel Azaña, everything prior to the 1920's was prologue. His maturation as a writer coincided with the rise and fall of the Primo de Rivera dictatorship: one might say that the mere existence of the dictatorship gave him good reason to write, for there are epochs when the oppression of free minds can provide a stimulus to intellectual activity by giving them something to protest. Then too, the suspension of Azaña's review *España* in 1924 presented both prestige and challenge to its editors, a Spanish phenomenon no more paradoxical than the value of a period of exile, or a jail sentence for political crimes, as an apprenticeship to a political career. With the fall of the dictatorship, however, new political vistas presented Azaña with new responsibilities, which, by the sheer press of time, were to restrict his literary activities.

King Alfonso XIII's generally shaky edifice of state had seen public disorder, bribes, misappropriation of state funds, labor and political unrest, a depreciation of currency, and inept government on the whole. Thirty-three separate cabinets were appointed from May, 1902, to September, 1923. As a result of this instability, although more specifically as a reaction to the Moroccan problem (which involved scandal from apparently political exploitation of military defeats of the Spanish army at the hands of insurgent Berber tribesmen), General Miguel Primo de Rivera issued at Barcelona on September 12, 1923, a manifesto addressed to the nation and to the army, a document whose immediate effect was a coup d'état.[1] It declared martial law: the expulsion of all civil governors from office, their functions to be assumed by military governors and commandants. All means of communication, banks, power stations, reservoirs, and political meeting centers were to be placed under military supervision. The next day the government of Manuel García Prieto resigned, whereupon all the ministries were taken over by the eight brigadier generals and one admiral whom Primo de Rivera had appointed to assist him. The Cortes was dissolved and the 1876 Constitution was suspended. Not until December 3, 1925, was a civilian "cabinet" reinstalled to replace the military one. The Constitution remained suspended until 1931.

A permanent military dictatorship emerged, friendly to the aristocracy and the church, with Primo de Rivera destined to exercise his nearly supreme will until early in 1930. Best described as an era of arbitrary paternalism, it was not a wholly bleak period in Spanish history; in many ways it was one of progress, for in his own way Primo was patriotic. Numerous railroads and highways were constructed. Facilities for wire communication were greatly expanded. The dictator tried to foster an economy of make-Spanish, buy-Spanish. Most important, he contrived to end the wars in Morocco. Self-characterized as a benevolent dictator, Primo did not extend his peripheral liberalism, however, to the area of free political thought. He mistrusted all political activity and liked to think of himself and his regime as apolitical.

---

[1] Soon after the coup d'état Azaña wrote a political article which appeared in Spanish in both *Nosotros* of Buenos Aires and *Europe* of Paris. He interpreted the origin and significance of the military dictatorship and predicted its long-range incapacity either to bolster or properly supplant the decadent monarchy.

His phenomenal lack of culture, coupled with an obnoxious conceit, gave him a totally military idea of government which antagonized the intellectuals, who balked at the censorship imposed upon them. Miguel de Unamuno and others made martyrs of themselves in exile. Protected by Primo's slogan of *"Patria, Religión, Monarquía,"* the church controlled education from top to bottom, much as it does unofficially in present-day Spain. When the professors began to protest and the students to riot, Primo de Rivera closed a number of the universities along with the Ateneo, haven of the intellectuals. An unmanageable spirit of opposition grew little by little into one of revolution. The disintegration of the dictatorship reached its final stage when Primo's main prop, the army, failed to respond with the vote of confidence that he requested of army chiefs in a circular letter dated January 26, 1930.

On January 28 these circumstances permitted the King to emerge from his role of puppet and receive the resignation of the dictator. Primo de Rivera did not leave Madrid until February 12, when he went to Barcelona. There he sought support for another coup, unsuccessfully, and finally traveled to Paris, where he died on March 16, 1930. The King asked General Dámaso Berenguer to form a government dedicated to a return to constitutionality, but Berenguer's progress in this direction could not offset the deep-seated resentment against the King. Consequently, by mid-1930 the republican parties were many and their meetings widespread, even if still clandestine.

Azaña saw that the old Reformist party, which he had joined in 1913, could not liberalize the monarchy. He had also concluded that his own status as a man of letters actually was a hindrance to him in the party. Therefore Azaña dissociated himself from Melquiades Alvarez, whose subordinate he had been for over ten years, attacking Alvarez in a monograph entitled *El hombre con las manos en los bolsillos* (The

Man with His Hands in His Pockets). In 1927 Azaña helped to found the political party known as *Acción Republicana* (Republican Action). He was aided in this enterprise by several other intellectuals, including his friend José Giral Pereira, who later was to hold high office in the Republic—Minister of the Navy, Minister of State, and even Prime Minister in the early months of the Civil War. A professor of pharmaceutical chemistry at the University of Madrid, Giral had a pharmacy on Atocha Street, where the group held its first meetings. *Acción Republicana* was a wholly new party, dedicated to a high code of political and moral ethics. Through this party, through the Ateneo to whose presidency he was elected in 1930—he had been its general secretary from 1913 to 1919—and through the Revolutionary Committee, Azaña was to play his part in bringing about the Republic. Much of this activity was done under cover, and later he had to go into hiding when he was sought by the police.

In April of 1927, the same year in which *Acción Republicana* was born, Azaña published in Madrid his first full-length original non-academic work, the first twelve of its nineteen chapters having been published earlier in *La pluma:* the initial installment in the September, 1921, issue, and the eighth and last in the June, 1922, issue. The book is a remarkable blend of autobiography and fiction entitled *El jardín de los frailes* (Garden of the Monks), which was, by the way, dedicated to Rivas Cherif. This work is the key to some of the concepts of state and patriotism that were to guide Azaña's actions in high political office less than five years later. Though it is generally considered to be his best work, and was his own favorite among his books, *El jardín de los frailes* was not widely read. For that matter, none of Azaña's writings has ever been widely read. Few people took this work any more seriously than another accurate projection of personality by another rising head of state was taken: Hitler's *Mein Kampf*—not that these two books had anything else in common beyond their obsessiveness, the one with the influence of the Catholic church and the other with the power of the Jews. Any such comparison reveals, moreover, that at bottom Azaña was an aesthete whose language and style were almost as important to him as the substance of his narrative. To this day *El jardín de los frailes* is looked upon as a quaint stylistic exercise, product of a period when "confessions" were in vogue: those who have studied the book have done so in the light of literature. Neglected by the historians, this work contains some of the very same phrases to be declaimed by Azaña on the floor of the Spanish Cortes; and between the lines it tells as much about the future of its author—and of the Republic—as it does of his past.

El jardín de los frailes is an objective presentation of a subjective matter—Azaña's days as a student at the Augustinian school in the Escorial. Despite his anecdotal approach to the narrative, these confessions are only mildly entertaining. As reminiscences they are neither humorous nor nostalgic, and even the title seems tongue-in-cheek; more appropriately it might have been something like "The Forging of a Rebel." From a literary point of view, the chief merit of this narrative is its impeccable prose, but its core is a commentary on religious education in Spain.

Azaña condemns as decadent a society whose educational system is bound to the church-state. As he saw it, the whole educational process there in the monastery school was a fraud, and the teachers, grotesque. The author is not afraid to paint himself in a bad light, because he implies that the school itself was responsible for turning him inward. "I loved things a lot," he writes, "but hardly ever my neighbors. . . . I loved my books, and the room in which I used to read, and its light, its smell." Azaña was not made for the solitude of a cell, yet here was where his scholarly bent announced itself (for learning is basically an asocial process), even though the development of a critical sense was discouraged and even forbidden: "We learned to refute Kant with five points, and Hegel, and Comte, and so many more. We used to oppose the erroneous assaults with good objections: 1. It is contrary to the teachings of the church; 2. it leads straight to pantheism; and other puncture-proof reasons."

So the sensitive young man, frustrated, lonesome, and bored, soon saw in those massive rocks of the Escorial a jail, and himself as the unjustly condemned. "To think nostalgically of school days," he observes, "is a mental aberration because among students, bestial instincts come to the fore." The reader learns that not the least of these "bestial instincts" was a widespread sexuality. Also Azaña affirms that all the students at the school were only lukewarm believers, and none of them saw a refuge of repose, peace, or consolation in their religious beliefs or practice. Only the landscape and the change of seasons gave any measure of direction to this young man's confused spirit. "I have dreamed of destroying all this world," he concludes. Later, as Prime Minister of the Republic, he was to have his opportunity to do so.

Undoubtedly the most explicit pages are the ones which Azaña devotes to religious doctrine. The school worked the opposite of its goal in young Manuel. There where he had time and solitude to think and to examine his religious precepts, he passed through certain spiritual crises not dissimilar to those of Unamuno at a later age; and he concluded that his own faith lacked originality. There at the Escorial he rebelled at the supernatural simplified, in order to put it within reach of human understanding, and he lost his religion along with his concept of Spain as a continuation of the Catholic monarchy of the sixteenth century. Before his days at the Escorial, he had simply gone along with the religious current, so to speak, ever since a paddle had been put in his hand at an early age. Unaware where or how he had received his fundamental notions of faith, he knew only that they manifested themselves in the form of lists committed to memory, recitable with not more nor less emotion or understanding than the lists of the Visigothic kings. Thus he began to doubt a faith that seemed prefabricated; and, even more important, he became convinced that the pure Christian—the orthodox Catholic, the ascetic, the one preoccupied with his own salvation and the hereafter—is an anti-citizen, for pure faith is unsociable. "It is not useful in the republic; it neither strengthens its sovereignty nor defends it." Let us hear him out (*El jardín de los frailes*, p. 157): "His [the pure Christian's] greatest victory is the one over himself; it is more important to him to conquer the enemies of his soul than those of the state. The simple Christian, humble and poor, a model of meekness, is not a citizen. Charity goes against the state, proud imposer of obligations. The Christian heart, self-driven to enter the realm of God, destroys civic motivation; that same Christian heart loves its neighbor even though the latter fights under another flag. The mendicant, the hermit, what society do they found? For what undertaking can they be counted on?"

Thus Azaña formulates his ideas on limiting the influence of the church in his republic. The line of thought is developed somewhat as follows: (1) human dignity exists only in a free state, a republic; (2) in order to perpetuate itself, a republic, more than any other form of government, requires good citizens; (3) responsible citizenship and patriotism are incompatible with Catholicism; *ergo* (4) in a republic, the influence of the church must be limited. Though most Christians are not so overwhelmed by their faith as is Azaña's pure Christian, still

Azaña might have found validity in Voltaire's statement that whenever one can say of any state of life that if everyone embraced it, the human race would be lost, it is demonstrated that the state is worthless, and that he who embraces it, does harm to the human race. Applied to the monastic life, in fact to Azaña's teachers at the Escorial, the argument might seem irresistible. It is not surprising that the author of *El jardín de los frailes* would one day argue in favor of Article 26 of the Republican Constitution by affirming that "Spain has ceased to be Catholic," even though this famous utterance has been misinterpreted out of context.

As an autobiography, *El jardín de los frailes* is relatively short, yet dense: taut, coldly intellectual, analytical, its dry bones of logic scraped clean of the slightest imperfection of prose. Manuel Azaña acts now as a writer who is sure of himself, contemptuous of all that is commonplace or sentimental. Yet with its learned vocabulary and complicated sentence structure, his book is too perfect an example of "fine" writing ever to have any extensive popular appeal. Its elegant prosiness rarely relieved by dialogue, chained to form and excessive pure description, with the rotund sentences where adjective is piled upon adjective and a comma is never so good as a semicolon, the narrative is lost in a jungle of eloquent discourse, almost rhetoric, of the type in which Azaña was to excel in the years to come. If the book foretells Azaña's insistence on the separation of church and state, a program whose repercussions shook the whole edifice of the Republic, it likewise presages the forensic capacities of the Republic's master orator.

Of equal autobiographical value, but of far less literary significance, is Azaña's first and only play, *La corona*. Published for the first time in 1928 in Madrid, *La corona* came in the wake of *El jardín de los frailes*.

It is a curious work, to which Azaña appended a short one-act farce entitled *Entremés*[2] *del sereno*.[3] A *sereno* in Spain is a species of public night-watchman who lets you in your own house late at night. The custom began centuries ago when keys were too large and too heavy to be carried on one's person. Honesty is the only real qualification for the position, whose perquisites are few. Frequently old and untutored, often accused of being deaf, inasmuch as he is summoned by three claps of the hands, the *sereno* has long been rendered with humor in Spanish letters. The less said about Azaña's comic endeavor, the better. Little more can be said for the obviously poetic theme of *La corona*, but, to anyone who would study the rising political star of Manuel Azaña, the political aspects of this play are just as revealing as were the religious ones of *El jardín de los frailes*.

The play is dedicated to L. R. C., the L. standing for Lola, nickname of Dolores Rivas Cherif, who was to become Azaña's wife the following year. In a still-unpublished letter dated May 25, 1928, Azaña wrote to Miguel de Unamuno: "También he caído en la tentación de escribir para el teatro, y he hecho un drama; pero hasta ahora no encuentro quien lo represente. En fin, por hacer de todo, y esto sí que es dramático, creo que voy a casarme, probablemente en el otoño! Ya es hora de que Primo de Rivera y yo, sentemos la cabeza!" ("I too have fallen into the temptation of writing for the theater, and I have

[2] For the reader who perhaps has eaten *entremeses*, a kind of Spanish antipasto, but who has never read nor seen an *entremés*, it may be well to explain that the word has two uses. In the literary sense it means a one-act interlude, usually a farce, in verse or in prose, and one which emphasizes local color. It is frequently presented between the acts of a standard-length play.

[3] This *entremés* was transplanted into Italian and in 1933 appeared under the title of *Intermezzo madrileno* in Vol. 33 of the *Collezione del teatro comico e drammatico*, published in Florence. Of incidental interest, in the same small tome is a three-act short play by Ignacio Sánchez Mejías, a Spanish bullfighter. Such unlikely company for a work by Azaña may throw some doubt upon its worth. This now rare item in Italian may be found at the New York Public Library.

done a drama; but up till now I have not found anybody to stage it. What is more, to try everything, and this really is dramatic, I think I am going to get married, probably next autumn! [Actually the marriage did not take place until February 27, 1929.] It is high time for Primo de Rivera and me to settle down!"). It will be remembered that Doña Dolores was the youngest sister of Cipriano Rivas Cherif, Azaña's long-time friend.

Inasmuch as Cipriano Rivas Cherif had become, in 1930, director of the Teatro Español in Madrid, which by the way is still in operation and state subsidized, he managed to arrange what turned out to be a short run of *La corona* at the Teatro Español. By the date of the Madrid première, April 12, 1932, the Republic was entrenched and Azaña had become a public figure.

Four months earlier *La corona* had been given a trial run at the Teatro Goya in Barcelona. Having just become Prime Minister, Azaña received an enthusiastic reception in Barcelona when he arrived to witness the first performance of his play, which he viewed from the audience rather than from the wings. The performance disappointed him, however, not because his good friend, the well-known Catalonian actress Margarita Xirgu, failed to charm as leading lady, or because Rivas Cherif lacked ardor in his duties of director, but because the theater-goers that night interpreted the play as a political rather than dramatic or poetic work.

When *La corona* came to Madrid in April, many of the chief figures of government and the Cortes were among the first nighters at the Teatro Español, which faces the little square named Plaza de Santa Ana, not far from either the Ateneo or the Cortes. This time Azaña stationed himself behind the scenes, instead of in the audience, in order that the audience focus its attention on the play rather than on him as its author and prime magistrate of the Republic. Still, he appeared on stage after the first act to acknowledge the applause, and at the end he joined Margarita Xirgu and the cast for curtain calls. After the play had run for a polite period, it was then published for a second time on May 14, 1932, minus the *entremés*. This second edition lists the names of the cast who acted the play at the Teatro Español.

La corona elicited praise from Enrique Díez-Canedo, the eminent critic, linguist, and creative writer in his own right, who at the time was the drama critic for *El sol* of Madrid, and who was later to become the Republic's ambassador to Argentina and Uruguay. Díez-Canedo had been a contributor to both *La pluma* and *España,* as well as a *contertuliano* of Azaña.[4] After the première of the play in 1932, Díez-Canedo reproduced an article that he had written for *El sol* on July 26, 1930, as a review of the first edition of the play. To this reproduction he added only that the presentation of *La corona* on the stage did not modify in any way his first and favorable impression. Other reviewers like Melchor Fernández Almagro, Luis Calvo, and Antonio Espina were equally polite, but, subsequent to the almost occasion-of-state of the first night, the public itself could hardly be enthusiastic over the long tedious scenes of *La corona;* and the play became a vehicle for much nasty derision of Azaña in publications by his political and military adversaries. With the exception of a subsequent performance organized in Mexico by the Republic's ambassador of the time, Julio Alvarez del Vayo, there is no evidence to indicate that Azaña's play was ever presented again anywhere, though Azaña tried unsuccessfully to have the French translation by Jean Cassou and Jean Camp staged

---

[4] Other prominent members of the same *tertulia,* which met in the Café Regina, were Valle Inclán (when he was in Madrid), Luis Bello, Martín Luis Guzmán (the Mexican writer), Luis Araquistain, Gregorio Marañón (cousin of the well-known physician), Sindulfo de la Fuente (well liked by Azaña), Luis García Bilbao, Ricardo Gutiérrez, Juan Echevarría, Amós Salvador (benefactor of *La pluma*), and of course Cipriano Rivas Cherif.

in Paris in 1939. Friend Rivas Cherif still insists that *La corona* is one of the best Spanish plays of the twentieth century.

Apparently Azaña was attempting a tragedy in the classic tradition but fell short of the mark. The characters are more interesting than the plot.[5] Azaña speaks through both Lorenzo and Aurelio, whose respective roles of idealist and realist are mainly a composite of the author's own interior tug of war. To begin with, Lorenzo is another ex-seminarist—Lorenzo *el Estudiante,* he is called—his idealism reminiscent of the seminarist in Valera's *Pepita Jiménez,* which Azaña had of course studied; in other ways, Lorenzo is a later portrayal of the other seminarist who passed through the *Garden of the Monks.* The blend personifies in Lorenzo an awakened, but frustrated, ambition together with an idealism run rampant.

It is seldom in complimentary fashion that a man is termed ambitious. This is wrong. Since few leaders of state attain their post by chance, a man can best be judged by his conduct after his ambitions have been realized. In spite of the accusations of his enemies, Azaña was never a tyrant, never seized the reins of absolute and undemocratic power, as he had ample opportunity to do. If he was ambitious, it was therefore a healthy, positive ambition, one of ultimate benefit to his fellow men, for all peoples need leaders. In the case of the ambitious Lorenzo, no final judgment can be cast, for he dies far short of achieving his ambitions. Still, his obsession with power is easily, though

---

[5] It is the end of a civil war, with no time nor place specified. The deposed princess and heir to the throne, Diana, is fleeing through the wild mountains with her devoted champion, Lorenzo "the student." They are trapped by the revolutionaries, headed by Aurelio, who have won the day. The price for Lorenzo's life is Diana's acceptance of the crown, at the insistence of Aurelio, who can thus become the power behind the throne. Diana adapts herself to circumstances in royal fashion, but the idealistic Lorenzo becomes increasingly morose and will accept nothing less than her elopement with him if she truly loves him. She refuses. He threatens. She, angered, summons aid. When Lorenzo draws his sword against Aurelio, Diana screams for help. Two men assail Lorenzo and kill him. Now Diana falls on the inert body of Lorenzo, but in grief, and shouting "assassins" as the final curtain comes down.

perhaps exaggeratedly, identifiable with presumably similar drives in his creator, as when in Act I, Scene II, Lorenzo rants: "I dreamed of commanding! Innumerable armies! Squadrons on the seas! And also a peaceful kingdom, new cities and great monuments erected by me." Maybe an understanding Diana might have changed all this. And in the final scene of the last act, Lorenzo says, like Don Quijote, "I know who I am," the much commented-on phrase which Azaña himself classifies in one of his essays (*La invención del Quijote*) as "the dogma of free will of one's own conscience." In Scene II of Act I, Lorenzo summarizes his status: "The soldiers gave me the nickname of Student, because they knew that I escaped from the seminary to enlist. It would be better to call me the savage." Azaña in his own way "escaped" from the Garden of the Monks and remained the perpetual student, yet one with strong military and political interests. In the final scenes of the play, Lorenzo appears to be impelled by his passion for Diana, but then maybe he is merely reacting from offended pride. This self-confessed man of action must impose his will, must dominate, for in the first scene of the play he had said: "I am not made for obedience. I only know how to command." This Lorenzo, who has shot two ministers of state, is more intransigent than compassionate—a reputation that Azaña was to acquire by reason of his own words, although a false reputation on the basis of his deeds.

If Lorenzo personifies frustrated ambition, Aurelio represents ambition fulfilled; and in Act II, Scene I, Aurelio gives his formula for success:

> War and politics are the same thing, at least in my life. War is a normal happening in politics, even though it may not be customary. I have always made war on my country when I have not been able to make politics [policy] in any other way. You know that in politics and in war our clearest thoughts, the most subtle calculations, depend

49

on the collaboration of others. The other man is stupid, and thoughts fail. My prudence, others give it an uglier name, consists of calculating the stupidity of the other man.

The real-life Azaña used to bark like this too, but his bark was more fearful than his bite. Azaña's literary strong men mirror a vicarious, but mistaken, projection of himself, for he really presented only the veneer to his own inner sensitive and yielding nature. How often on the floor of the Cortes Azaña gained his triumphs principally by means of an effective haughty disdain of the opposition! To this extent, Aurelio is a part of Azaña, the façade for deeper Lorenzo-like qualities.

Although Azaña always disclaimed having endowed the work with political meaning, much less Spanish political meaning, a neat bit of symbolism leaps from the pages of *La corona* if one wants to imagine it, as perhaps the audiences in Barcelona and Madrid did. The play can be conveniently interpreted as a symbol of the conditions against which Azaña struggled, if it is allowable that Lorenzo is Azaña: Diana represents the weak-willed King Alfonso XIII; Aurelio symbolizes the harsh and crafty Primo de Rivera, the improvised power behind the nominal throne who says that truth is impractical: ". . . I have learned that intelligence does not serve to find truth, but to lead one through life" (Act III, Scene III). Other aspects of the drama fall in line, like the mentality of the police state, personified in the conscienceless Minister of Police. Also recall Azaña's previous attempts, in *La pluma*, to write anachronistic and apocryphal political literature in the fashion of Swift. The name of the play itself is revealing and exemplifies one of the two figures of speech prominent in Azaña's prose and oratory: metonymy and synecdoche. In nearly all his many later references to the Spanish monarchy, he was to use *crown* to the almost total exclusion of *monarch* or *king* or *queen*, perhaps with some psychological carry-over from the play.

All in all, it is a stiff play, replete with commonplaces and character-istically wordy, with more mouthed dialogue than action. Not even the love scenes offer respite from the tedious dialogue, and the whole of the work seems contrived. Azaña had no more lyric gift than another old bachelor writer named Pío Baroja, who was able neverthe-less to excel in his profession, as Azaña might have done had he not been swept away by the capricious winds of politics. If women seldom appear in Azaña's works, this is all the more reason to consider Diana a symbol. One thing is certain: she is not a credible portrayal of Doña Dolores, even if Lorenzo's words of love are Don Manuel's. Obviously Azaña lacked direction in his literary endeavors. He had no talent for playwriting and little insight for the forging of dramatic characters. In a word, *La corona* is pedestrian. One does not know what the play is about until he has made his way through ten long pages. The dialogue reads as if it were oratory, and the lovers reason the nature of their love in parliamentary style. Dreams of political grandeur fill the stage. Even the vocabulary is predominantly political, with constant repetition of words like *político, revolución, legal, policía, oposición, libelos, orden, Estado, Gobierno, libertad, guerra, facciones, partido, constitución, parlamento, ley, pueblo, ministros*—and *ambición*. *La corona* is, therefore, a revealing psychological document on its author, even if it is not a good play.

Azaña and some friends, including Valle Inclán and Rivas Cherif, once formed a theatrical group which met at the house of the Baroja brothers. The members of El Mirlo Blanco, as the group was called, used to write pieces, and the group would act them out. Though for a long time Azaña did not write anything—he also preferred to watch rather than act—just before the group disbanded he had written a play, one of whose roles he was going to interpret for the members.

Almost surely this play was *La corona*, though no one knows which role he had planned to act.

As an impersonator Azaña had already made his mark with this theatrical group. The occasion yields a significant anecdote. Once Ricardo Baroja's wife, Carmen, suggested that the group give a masked ball. A ball with intellectuals like the gruff Pío Baroja and the gaunt Valle Inclán wearing masks should be amusing indeed. Plans were made, the party was held at the Baroja residence, everybody came, and the affair was a great success. Valle Inclán was dressed as a Leonese villager. Dolores Rivas Cherif arrived in early nineteenth-century formal attire. Most of the disguises were routine ones, without psychological clue to their wearers' inner preoccupations. When the dancing and gaiety were at their peak, suddenly the door opened and there entered an elegantly garbed cardinal. With an imposing air the cardinal flung back his cape to extend a hand on which shone a colossal ring. That cardinal was Azaña, with the best and most original disguise of all. Each of the ladies kissed the ring, and so solemn was the whole proceeding that for a time some of them almost believed it was a real cardinal. After the ecclesiastic had been identified and duly admired, the party resumed. Azaña chatted a long time with Doña Dolores that night while the others danced. Her saint's day came soon afterward, and he sent her a big bouquet. Subsequently they became *novios*.

Not in vain did Manuel Azaña dedicate *La corona* in 1928 to Dolores Rivas Cherif, because the marriage vows were exchanged on Wednesday, February 27, 1929, the date inscribed inside the gold band which Sra. de Azaña still (1963) wears on her right hand, in accordance with Spanish custom. It was a formal wedding at the Church of San Jerónimo in Madrid, with reception and banquet afterwards at the still-fashionable Hotel Ritz, followed by a honeymoon in

Paris. (During that honeymoon Don Cipriano himself married and soon after took a theatrical company to Buenos Aires, whence he returned to Madrid ten months later with his first born.) Born of a good family, whose now ramshackle castle still stands in Villalba de los Alcores, in the province of Valladolid, Dolores Rivas Cherif was then a short but handsome woman, very sensitive, and the baby of the family. Though she was about twenty-two years younger than her 49-year-old husband, Dolores de Azaña developed all the tact and grace befitting the social position to which Manuel Azaña was to rise. Later the eminent portrait painter López Mezquita captured her charm in a fine canvas, which today looks down from a wall in the dining room of Sra. de Azaña's tiny apartment in Mexico City, where she lives widowed and in exile. Don Manuel, unendowed with either athletic physique or pleasing physiognomy, was a fortunate man to win such an alluring young wife. Even though the marriage was not sudden—they had been engaged since the previous April—it astounded Azaña's acquaintances who had seen in him only the perpetual bachelor. The wedding ceremony was a Catholic one. The couple became very much devoted to each other despite their differences in religious outlook. To this day, Doña Dolores, wife of him who uttered on the floor of the Cortes "Spain has ceased to be Catholic," remains Catholic in her religious practices. She and her husband always respected each other's religious outlook, as the peculiar circumstances of Manuel's death in 1940 will reveal.

The couple established themselves at Calle de Hermosilla 24 *duplicado* in Madrid, and Manuel Azaña returned to his accustomed activities. In the summer of 1929, his Spanish translation, *La carroza del Santísimo,* of a play by Mérimée was presented at the Teatro Maipo in Buenos Aires (but never published, so far as can be ascertained). Then in 1930 he published two books. This was also the year in which the Ateneo elected Azaña to its presidency, a key post in the incubation of the coming Republic, which in 1930 was only a year away.

The first of these books in 1930 (it bears the date November 25) is only an oddity, another of Azaña's many translations: *Antología negra*, translated from the original French work by Blaise Cendrars and published by Editorial Cenit of Madrid. This book holds nothing of general relevance to the thought of Azaña, as for example *La Biblia en España* certainly did, nor does he give his translation any prologue, introduction, or preliminary note of comment or explanation. *Antología negra* is simply a fanciful collection of animal fables, folklore, anecdotal and moral tales, refrains or proverbs, and allegorical legends of the creation of mankind. The book is a hard-to-find item today, but one of interest principally to the folklorist.

The other work bears the attractive title *Plumas y palabras* and was published by Compañía Iberoamericana de Publicaciones in Madrid. It is a collection of essays, almost all of which had already been published in *La pluma* and *España*. These essays in *Plumas y palabras* consist mostly of critical comment, in the negative sense of the word. Azaña was wont to assume that once the negative aspects of certain problems of literature and society were exposed, positive solutions would spring from the intelligence. Manuel Azaña really believed that the intellect, and only the intellect, could solve most of the problems of civilization. In this he clashes with Unamuno. How often the words *inteligente* and *inteligencia* are to be found in these essays and in all the speeches and writings of Azaña! Man had only to be intelligent and reasonable. Six years hence, the greatest acts of unreason were to be called the Spanish Civil War.

Among these essays of *Plumas y palabras* is his review of a play, *Asclepigenia*, by Juan Valera, which was a lecture that Azaña had given in Madrid on December 27, 1928. In another essay, he speaks again of "Jorge Borrow y la *Biblia en España*," that George Borrow whom Azaña saw as a kind of Don Quijote, and whose book, he reiterates, is not only true, but revealing, and a work of art. Azaña writes also about such various matters as the Moors in literature and history; about the blameworthy Spanish custom of removing bones to other final resting places; about political bosses; about the problems of the governmental civil service (a system which he says ought to be reorganized); about his disdain of celebrities; about the death penalty; and about the institution of literary prizes, which he condemns as commercialization, even though, let it be remembered, he had won and accepted such a prize himself. To write with money as a goal, he says, is "detestable."

An underlying theme in most of the other essays is the question of individual freedom. His own intellectual and political liberty is Manuel Azaña's most insistent personal aspiration: he is a "violent democrat," inflexible within the limits of his rights and what is right. But he wonders whether Spaniards are, by temperament, naturally opposed to a freedom more general than their own haughty individual independence; that is, can the Spaniard be taught to rise above his inclination to be a spectator, in order to establish and perpetuate a liberal society in Spain? He was surely not thinking of himself when he gave the answer in *La velada en Benicarló*, that pathetic analysis which he wrote during the Civil War and wherein he concluded that the Spaniard, so jealous of his own liberty as a person, hates the freedom of his neighbor—a kind of national psychosis that was the fundamental cause of the situation which led to the Civil War. Yet, in words if not acts, it is possible that Azaña too shares the trait and hence a part of the blame. In one of the essays here, "La inteligencia y el carácter en la acción política," he characterizes himself as follows:

I am not indulgent, I do not compromise, I do not pardon. . . . I practice the Calderonian rule of upsetting the table if someone in front of me upsets a chair [slightly misquoted from Calderón] . . . .

. . . .

For me, political action is a defensive movement of intelligence, in opposition to the domination of error. Any political struggle, stripped of appearances, resolves itself into a contest between what is true and what is false . . . . Only the one who is possessed of the truth can be intransigent, fanatical . . . .

But whose truth? What is this absolute truth, what are the timeless abstract axioms for which Azaña would subjugate a thousand private liberties? To the extent that he denied compromise of conflicting truths, until it was too late, Azaña remained always a naïve politician, for compromise in political life does not necessarily eliminate either intelligence or honor from political processes; rather, it gives them the measure of practicality necessary for stability of government. Although in affairs of state Azaña was not to prove so absolutely inflexible as he wished to seem, still it is obvious from his pre-1931 writings that he at least attempted to do in government very nearly what he had studied and planned for—and he remained forever convinced that inflexibility was a product of intelligence. In these essays and elsewhere, most of Azaña's political discussions devolve to questions of ethics, rather than to the exhibition of sound knowledge of theories of political science. He believes in concepts like liberty, suffrage, constitution, citizenship, separation of church and state, and assumes that all *intelligent* people will ultimately accept them through the process of reason; meanwhile he laments that "one must go around explaining the most elementary things to the people."

The fact is that Azaña can never be said to be identified with the people, if this means the workers, the proletariat, whose increasing power he came to fear. Recall his previous failures to win any political election. The only elections he had ever won were those in the Ateneo, from whose halls he vaulted straight into those of the Ministry of War when the Republic was declared. Nor was he ever tempted by communism, whose only Marxian precept he shared was possibly the one about religion being the opiate of the people. He favored all efforts to improve the economic lot of the workers and peasants, even so far as the redistribution of lands, but his was always the larger aim of creating better citizens, rather than the specific one of filling stomachs. To Azaña republicanism stood for the orderly exercise of civil rights. With the raging waters of dissent thus well dammed by solid constitutional bulkheads of truth, with the storm clouds of militarism blown from the Spanish landscape, well-defined currents of parliamentarianism should guide an even stream of economic progress from the pacific reservoir of good will, a steady rate of flow judiciously (intelligently!) guaranteed by the ministers of state at the sluice gates. Quite unlike most reformists, who anticipate a stable citizenry to be possible only when hunger has ceased to be a major problem, Azaña expected his stabilized economy to be the result of stable civic virtues. Physically comfortable himself, Azaña clung to a republicanism which was largely an aspirant democratic state of mind reflecting his own. But intellectuals, by themselves, are never a sufficient force to carry a revolution, because comfort is not essential to them. Therefore, even if Azaña had not been comfortable, it would scarcely have occurred to him that most revolutions commence when the proletariat revolts against hopeless economic, rather than civil, conditions. It cannot be reiterated too often that to create and perpetuate an orderly, intelligent, aware, and responsible Spanish citizenry was Azaña's greatest general political ambition, his most specific ambition being a reorganization of the army. That the improvement of workers' economic conditions was not his *primary* aim, is implicit in his recurring statement that "liberty does not make men happy; it simply makes them men."

If, in Azaña's opinion, an institution like the church opposed the kind of progress he thought essential to the training of this radically improved citizenry, whose first loyalty was to its state, then the church must go. Thus, as he says in the essay "Una constitución en busca de autor" (A Constitution in Search of an Author—shades of Pirandello!), his opposition to the church in Spain is not based on theological hatred; it is simply an attitude of reason. When this article first appeared in the January 12, 1924, issue of *España*, it ignited a polemic which enlivened future issues of that and other periodicals. As the reader might expect, Azaña was not loath to fire broadsides at the church from *Plumas y palabras*. In one essay, "Los curas oprimidos" (The Oppressed Priests), he explains why the clergy should cease complaining that it is oppressed; then in the next article he speaks out against the wealth of the church in Spain.

The two best essays are the first and the last, the last entitled simply "Madrid," originally serialized in *La pluma* and praised by several critics as the best essay ever written on Madrid. Azaña takes his reader on a verbal Cook's tour of the back streets, where we meet various interesting types, ride on Madrid's street cars, see its animals and vehicles, learn its history (or lack of history), praise or condemn its weather, and, incidentally, learn some of the habits of one of its dwellers, Manuel Azaña, who does not attend the theater or *tertulias* (so he says) or the bullfights or church functions, but who does take long walks during the day in the winter, or at night in the summer, to infuse his spirit with the sights, smells, and noises of the city.

The first essay, over one hundred pages in length and entitled simply "El *Idearium* de Ganivet," is a classic debunking of Ganivet's *Idearium español*. Very little known, this brilliant work by Azaña ought to be studied by every student of Spanish literature who would claim a knowledge of the so-called Generation of 1898, among whose avant-garde, criticized by Azaña, are counted Angel Ganivet, Joaquín Costa, and Miguel de Unamuno. It goes without saying that a writer's identification with a given school is usually by others' ascription, rather than by the individual writer's subscription (otherwise, for example, there have been no existentialists in Spain, and few in France!); but of all the literary schools or coteries of the nineteenth and twentieth centuries in Spain, the Generation of '98 as a body has emerged with the least attack from critics, scholars, and fellow writers, despite the fact that Azorín peddled copious dull prose as poetic writing, Valle Inclán stole whole sections intact from Casanova's *Memoirs,* Baroja wrote more hack novels than inspired ones, and Unamuno—well, he alone has been brought to task from several quarters: by scholars like Ronald Hilton, by creative writers like Ramón Sender, and by the church. Although some literary historians categorize Azaña himself as one of the '98-ists, perhaps because of his advocacy of a Europeanization of Spain, of housecleaning in the Spanish social structure and in the governmental superstructure, Azaña himself never spoke well of the '98-ists as a group. As he points out in another of the essays in *Plumas y palabras* entitled "¡Todavía el '98!" (Still the '98!), the '98-ists did no more than transform literary values; aside from this, they neither pinpointed nor solved the major difficulties of Spain: they tore down old edifices but rebuilt nothing. Specifically, Azaña regarded Ganivet as an immature pessimist, who, lacking in both technique and information, should have lived more before he philosophized.

Azaña dissects the *Idearium* by working from the general to the specific. Anyone who has studied Azaña's scholarly works, like the treatise on French military policy, and knows his fetish of fact and logic, might guess that straightaway Azaña will accuse Ganivet of

59

vagueness, sentimentalism, and an insufficiency of analysis, which leads to arbitrary conclusions. To put it more plainly, Ganivet is uninformed, has not read and observed enough to give his conclusions substance of argument. Among the specific points that Azaña rejects is the theory of *"senequismo"* (Seneca-ism), a stoic quality attributed to the Spanish people by Ganivet. Instead Azaña believes that historically the Spanish spirit has been infused with the will to found ("la voluntad de *fundar"*), exemplified in founders like Santa Teresa and Cortés. Nor will Azaña allow Ganivet's claim to have lived in a spiritually decadent epoch, wherein is conceded more importance to the railroad than to works of art. No enemy of material progress in the manner of Ganivet or Unamuno, who seemed to think all engineers were uncultured and who defined sociologists as the alchemists and astrologers of the twentieth century, Azaña insists that civilization does not have to choose between what is beautiful and what is useful, to the detriment of one or the other. Azaña also disagrees with Ganivet's childish point of view on the inevitable emancipation of women, which, since it is inevitable, Ganivet sees as a consequent debasement of men and society in general, as if it were a question of balancing a scales. When the career woman is no longer a rarity, but a commonplace, says Ganivet, "it will be necessary to ask Providence to send us a new invasion of male and female barbarians [*bárbaras,* a pun], because, carried to the extreme, barbarity is preferable to absurdity." Strong words, yet the weakest argument in his book. Ganivet is equally narrow in the amount of religious freedom he would allow, because of his belief that any constructive force of the national character is based upon the pillars of tradition. Naturally Azaña, critic of the church and its intolerance, was to take him to task here. In fact, Azaña's main course of rebuttal throughout is to maintain that solutions to the matters which Ganivet discusses are not so simple, as well as to demonstrate the difficulty of what are apparently the simplest problems in Spain. Azaña concludes, therefore, that the *Idearium español* is for the semi-cultured public and that its worth is "equal to the sum of its readers' ignorance."

Accordingly Unamuno becomes an antagonist of Azaña, for Unamuno praised the *Idearium* and was, besides, an intimate friend of Ganivet, with whom he exchanged many personal letters after their university days, and whose suicide Unamuno lamented publicly in his numerous articles and essays. Azaña was well aware that Unamuno not only admired Ganivet's works but tended to support some of Ganivet's theories, like the one about the Seneca complex of the Spanish people.

Sooner or later—it might as well be now—we ought to examine, however briefly, the relationship between these two men of diametrically opposed temperament, the one (Unamuno) an austere kind of grass-roots nationalist with a primitive instinct of religion, and the other an internationalist and a fastidious cosmopolitan with a rationalistic mind totally unawed by Unamuno's tragic sense of life. Unamuno and Azaña knew each other in the Ateneo, and later in the Cortes, as well as elsewhere. Among Unamuno's mass of correspondence—he saved everything—which his daughter Felisa and Professor García Blanco of the University of Salamanca have sorted and arranged in a neat file at the Casa Rectoral in Salamanca, there are eighteen unpublished letters from Manuel Azaña, two undated and the rest dated as follows: June 25, 1918; December 19, 1918; September 10, 1920; February 22, 1921; August 2, 1921; August 23, 1921; January 17, 1923; March 14, 1923; June 15, 1923; July 8, 1923; August 6, 1923; October 26, 1923; November 2, 1923; December 22, 1923; January 12, 1924; May 25, 1928. Incidentally the file also shows forty-two letters from Cipriano Rivas Cherif. All but one of the letters from Azaña

61

are handwritten; many of them request articles from Unamuno for *La pluma* and, later, *España*. For example, in the letter dated January 12, 1924, and written on stationery with the letterhead of the Ministerio de Gracia y Justicia, Dirección General de los Registros y del Notariado, where Azaña was employed, Azaña announces that in today's mail he is sending to Unamuno a check for seventy-five pesetas for an article, and also that Unamuno's article on "El socialismo político español" was killed by the censor.

The Azaña correspondence shows that before the advent of the Republic, his relations with Unamuno were politely cordial. But the dogmatic nature of each of those men made a clash inevitable. Everybody knew that Azaña's blade could be sharp, though he usually dulled the edge before he struck at Unamuno, whom he obviously respected as a worthy opponent. Right here in *Plumas y palabras*, for example, is an eight-page article about Unamuno entitled "The Lion, Don Quijote, and the Lion Keeper," in which Azaña reproaches Unamuno for not living up to his principles, although he wrote privately in one of the still-unpublished letters to Unamuno dated November 2, 1923: *"Lo del león y el leonero podemos transigirlo si usted quiere, reembarcándolo, con su jaula, para Africa"* ("We can settle that business about the lion and lion keeper, if you like, by reshipping it, together with the cage, to Africa"). Accompanied by Count Romanones, Unamuno had called on Alfonso XIII at the palace in 1922, an act of seeming capitulation which angered not only Azaña but the whole Ateneo. Unamuno undoubtedly knew that his visit to the palace would be criticized. At the last moment he tried to renege, though the day and hour had been set well in advance. Romanones finally found him and drove him to the palace. Unamuno was persuaded to leave his Basque beret in the car, but dressed in his accustomed Mennonite-like garb he marched in for the audience one hour late. Unamuno did most of the talking during that hour-and-a-half visit, which the King concluded when he had heard enough of Unamuno's ideas on politics and religion. Romanones witnessed the entire interview and affirmed that the leave-taking between king and scholar was cordial.

Now Azaña maintains that one is either for or against a system or institution, not personally for or against a given king. This is a most tenable position, given the fact that, by one of the paradoxes not uncommon in Spain, one of the members of the Ateneo with membership card number 7777, was no other than Alfonso de Borbón, his domicile listed as Palacio de Oriente and his profession stated officially as—King of Spain. In his essay on Unamuno, Azaña concludes that "the character of Unamuno is impregnated with quixotism. Perhaps the essence of quixotism is not the love of justice, but the eagerness to win eternal name and fame . . . he was going to meet the lion." On the other hand, in an essay on the Generation of '98, Azaña praises Unamuno for having been the only one of the '98-ists to face the basic issue: "not that of being a Spaniard or not, nor that of how one is to be a Spaniard, but that of being or not being a *man*." It is possible, nevertheless, that Unamuno and Azaña did not understand each other well even on this question, because Unamuno's Man is conceived largely in the existentialist image, with its resultant despair at the enormity of his responsibility to himself and to all other human beings, a luxury with which Azaña's more objective concrete Man—the citizen —cannot afford to overwhelm himself, lest he fail to respect the state.

We have already observed that Unamuno came into contact with Azaña in the Ateneo. Back in 1917, together with three other writers and at the invitation of the Italian government, they had also made a trip to the Italian-Austrian front during the First World War. Then from 1920-24 Unamuno was a frequent contributor to the two magazines edited by Azaña, until the February 16, 1924, issue of *España* announced Unamuno's exile and the dictator's decree which closed the Ateneo. Unamuno was exiled from 1924-30 by Primo de Rivera on account of what was really a trivial incident: the trial of a certain young lady in whose behalf the dictator had attempted to intervene, by means of a letter of recommendation to a magistrate, who not only refused to comply with the "recommendation," but who in effect made the letter public by including it in the court records of the case. Unamuno discussed the incident satirically in a letter which he wrote to a friend in Buenos Aires. When through the friend's indiscretion the letter was published in an Argentine newspaper, Primo de Rivera vented his wrath by exiling Unamuno to Fuerteventura in the Canary Islands in February of 1924, and by taking similar action against other intellectuals who defended Unamuno. Perhaps Primo de Rivera later regretted his hasty action, for it provided a natural *cause célèbre*, but at any rate Unamuno was not very closely guarded and on July 9, 1924, French friends rescued him and landed him in Le Havre. Unamuno lived in France six years. At first he was in Paris, where he wrote articles for the French radical newspaper *Quotidien*, which had organized his rescue. After he tired of Paris, he went to live in Hendaye, within sight of the Spanish Pyrenees. There he spent the remainder of his exile. When the dictatorship had finally fallen and Unamuno returned to Spain on February 9, 1930, he received a hero's welcome and gave at the Ateneo a speech which inflamed the already heated general agitation for a republican state.

On May 3, 1930, Azaña spoke at the Lyceum on "Cervantes y la invención del *Quijote*," which forms the lead essay in a collection to which Azaña was to give the name *La invención del Quijote y otros ensayos* and publish in 1934. In this essay Azaña disagrees with Unamuno's frequently expressed concept of Don Quijote as an independent character with greater dimensions than the spirit of his creator. Rejecting this Pirandellian point of view,[6] but without berating Unamuno, Azaña points out the autobiographical nature of the novel and the consequent fact that Don Quijote could not have existed without both the realistic and poetic substance with which Cervantes nurtured his creation. In his interpretation of the novel, Azaña is unwilling to allow any detachment of Don Quijote from his surroundings. What is more, since these surroundings are Spain, and can still be consulted in the types and landscapes of present-day Spain, they are of prime importance in understanding and appreciating the novel. The cross that Cervantes bore through self-identification with Don Quijote is what history, with time, has consolidated as the expression of Spain; and thus Don Quijote can still have a "route" because of the enormous wealth of national life from which he is inseparable.

Perhaps Unamuno made no refutation because Azaña's interpretation follows conventional lines of analysis of *Don Quijote* and therefore was hardly a new challenge to Unamuno's originality. Actually, so far as can be determined, Unamuno's only mention of Azaña in print was in the conservative Madrid daily *Ahora*, whose February 28, 1934, issue carried an article by Unamuno entitled "Acción y contemplación," dedicated to Don Manuel Azaña. In passing, it may be of interest that the highly esteemed actress Margarita Xirgu, who had performed in Azaña's *La corona* in 1932, played the title role of Unamuno's prose translation of Seneca's *Medea* at its première in June, 1933, at Mérida, in the Roman amphitheater, midst other natural surroundings appropriate to classical tragedy. The published portions of Azaña's memoirs indicate that he was in the audience that night along with many other government officials. But back in November

[6] For more information on this analogy, see my article "Unamuno and Pirandello Revisited," *Italica*, XXXIII, No. 1 (March, 1956), 40-51.

of 1932 Unamuno had attacked Azaña verbally when, in a speech at the Ateneo, he ranted against what he termed Azaña's dictatorial methods of government, which he said were worse than the processes of the Inquisition. That speech caused considerable uproar, although Azaña's reaction to it in his memoirs was mild. Two months later, however, in an entry in the memoirs dated January 18, 1933, Azaña spoke of an informal gathering of "the other day" in which Unamuno "among other stupid words, said that we were in civil war . . . ." Unamuno's words accurately foretold the armed revolt of the Left of October, 1934, an event which even Madariaga admits to be no less inexcusable than the Generals' uprising of July, 1936, that precipitated the Spanish Civil War.

Fourteen months after Unamuno returned from exile, the Republic was proclaimed. Unamuno was elected deputy to the constituent parliament and then appointed head of the Council of Public Education. To the floor of the Cortes he carried his passion for the heterodox and his public criticism of personalities. His speeches in the Cortes were vocal literary essays with the same sermon-like quality that characterized most of his written essays. At first the Cortes would listen to him politely and, since they were Spaniards, savor the occasions when that venerable scholar would convert their lawmaking body into an academy. But as the months went by, the superior air which Unamuno adopted on the floor of the Cortes began to rankle in some of the deputies. One day a deputy named Gassol challenged him with: "The tone of Mr. Unamuno, when he speaks of political matters, has a certain something which I confess irks me sorely." Actually Unamuno delighted in demonstrating his unfamiliarity with parliamentary procedure, and in a speech he even said once that legislation was certainly not his calling. The truth is that he never really showed an interest in any but the cultural aspects of the matters resolved in the Cortes. For instance, one of the few times he had anything vital to say was on the language question: the debate on the official status of Basque or Catalonian, as opposed to Castilian, stirred Unamuno to make a long speech interspersed freely with quotations of poetry. Later, when the Catalonian Statute of autonomy was being debated, obviously its only aspect that stimulated Unamuno to vocalize his opinions was the one concerning the official position of the Catalonian language at the University of Barcelona. Back when the voting for the President of the Republic had taken place in the Cortes, Unamuno received one vote, which rumor attributes to have been his own, although this may have been an unfair assumption. He did win another presidency, however, that of the Ateneo in 1933, an office which he held through 1934 and in which he had succeeded Ramón del Valle Inclán, who as president of the Ateneo had in turn succeeded Azaña in 1932. With regard to Unamuno's service to the state, by 1933 he had become wearied of what he would have termed the hollowness of politics in action, and he renounced the political adventure in order to return permanently to his beloved University of Salamanca, where in 1934 he was declared to be its rector for as long as he should live. This was to be but two years.

The political antagonism between Unamuno and Azaña manifested itself mainly during the years of the Republic; but, although it is undocumentable, it was widely echoed that Unamuno used to warn even in the 1920's that Azaña was a writer without readers capable of starting a revolution in order to be read. (Azaña's own version of his own predicament, uttered later to his brother-in-law, was: "I am a writer lost in politics.") Notwithstanding, at the very beginning of the Republic, before Azaña became Head of the Provisional Government, Unamuno spoke of Azaña in favorable terms; and even afterwards, Azaña returned the compliment in his great speech of May 27, 1932, on the floor of the Cortes. With the passage of time, Unamuno assumed a totally opposite attitude concerning both Azaña and the Republic itself. He began to write editorials for *Ahora* in which he ended by attacking even the Republican Constitution (as he had already attacked it in the Cortes) on June 5, 1936, the same Constitution that he himself had helped to formulate. Unable to accept the Popular Front and its presumed exaltation of labor, Unamuno looked to fascism with hopeful eyes. Now Azaña's open enemy, he declared himself in favor of the insurgents at the outbreak of the Civil War. When the Rebels took possession of Salamanca and set up a headquarters there early in the war, Unamuno could see at first hand their methods and aims, whereupon he then reversed his position again with the famous *"venceréis pero no convenceréis"* ("you will conquer but you will not convince") retort in ceremonies inaugurating the 1936 school year at the University of Salamanca. Removed from the rectorship of the university and confined to his house by order of the Nationalist officers, who were unwilling that a figure of his stature should defect, if he were so inclined and the chance presented itself, Unamuno died from a cerebral hemorrhage at home in the evening of the final day of 1936. In the last days, Unamuno's despair over the tragic national events was great. Yet perhaps Unamuno has received more than his due from posterity, and Azaña, less. Now, twenty-some years after the end of the Spanish Civil War, most Republicans-in-exile count Unamuno as one of their own side, while at the same time the figure of Azaña is tarnished in the minds of many because of his supposed unfavorable conduct at the end of the Civil War, and the maliciously propagandized circumstances of his death in 1940.

We have seen how in the late 1920's Manuel Azaña was finally achieving some recognition, both as a writer and as a leader of purposeful men, even though it seemed to him at times that the Pyreneean-like barriers of monarchy and dictatorship would forever prevent the winds of freedom from blowing across Spain. In 1928, while Unamuno was still in France, Azaña wrote to him on May 25 (one of the letters that Unamuno kept) the following statements: "No puedo vencer mi desconfianza en la revolución de las gentes . . . . Aquí se estaba incubando un huevo, que prometía ser de avestruz y me temo que sea de *gorriona*" ("I cannot conquer my distrust of the peoples' revolution . . . . Here an egg was being hatched, which bid fair to be that of an ostrich, and I am much afraid that it is only a *sparrow's*"). But the year 1930 found Azaña at the helm of two important organizations: the Republican Action party that he had helped found in 1927, and his spiritual hearth the Ateneo of Madrid, which had made him its president from 1930-32. Azaña's candidacy was proposed and supported behind the scenes by Valle Inclán and a politically inclined clique which overrode the objection of other members who thought Azaña "lacked personality." These two offices made Azaña doubly suspect to the police, who had more than ample reason to watch the Ateneo. That literary society had become a hotbed of republicanism— the alliance of republican parties even held its meetings there—as well as (said the rumors) a repository for small arms stored among its many books. Not for this, however, was Azaña called the "little colonel," nor even because of his interest in French and Spanish military affairs, but rather because of his physical appearance, his apparent intractability, and his self-assured demeanor that suggested Napoleon to the caricaturist. For many years Azaña had treasured his membership in the Ateneo above all his other activities; now he was its president in a propitious hour.

The surviving exiled Republicans and literati who were once members of the Ateneo would scarcely recognize their Ateneo Científico,

Literario y Artístico today. In Azaña's time the most important literary salon in Spain, it is now a submissive vehicle to the state's "directed culture," this mission facilitated by expanded floor space. Enlargement by the acquisition of adjoining property, however, has not altered the exterior of the original building, unimpressively sandwiched in a row of buildings at Calle del Prado 21, where it has always been only two blocks away, around the corner, from the Spanish Parliament. The street name and number have somehow remained the same since the present Ateneo was constructed in 1883 and opened in January of 1884, transferred there from outmoded quarters on Calle de la Montera, although the institution was founded originally on still another site in 1835, with the Duque de Rivas as its first president. The tread of generations of *ateneístas* has worn thin the steps of the marble staircase that still leads from the columned entrance up to the various salons, auditorium, and library; but not because of its physical antiquity is the Ateneo now only a shell whose interior life has dried up.

The place is usually deserted but for the several guards with nothing to do, or the few researchers who cogitate at the old-fashioned desks in the library. The directorship of that library, once entrusted to writers like Ramón Pérez de Ayala and Enrique Díez-Canedo, is now assumed by a priest. Today cheap contemporary furniture rests irreverently on the parquet floors of the *salón de conversación*, located off the main hallway wherein hang the portraits of renowned *ateneístas* of the past. Though Unamuno's portrait is there, notably lacking in the collection is a painting of Azaña or of any other Republican writer, statesman, or past president of the Ateneo politically prominent enough to arouse dangerous thoughts among the members. Many years have gone by since the Civil War, and yet the ruling regime seems more unsure of itself than ever, its affiliate branches of national culture being highly sensitive to any evocation of the days of "inorganic democracy," as the Republican era is deprecatingly termed.

One significant part of the Ateneo has been allowed to age with all its original stateliness: the quaint nineteenth-century lecture hall. Except for the addition of a bust of Franco strategically centered on the stage, apparently nothing has been touched in that 532-seat auditorium since the last century. Every faded ornament preserves an imperishable dignity; every worn seat recalls a famous occupant; and the tiny stage evokes sentimental reminiscence of all the noble ideas exchanged there, of the distinguished writers and statesmen like Manuel Azaña who have declaimed from its rostrum, and of the keen listeners who have risen to debate from either the members' seats or from the public gallery. More than twenty thousand men and women have belonged to the Ateneo since its founding in 1835 with 329 affiliates. Toward the end of the nineteenth century, the Ateneo of Madrid was one of the first intellectual societies to admit women: Emilia Pardo Bazán and Blanca de los Ríos were once members. In later times other women intellectuals, with or without membership, participated in the *tertulias* in the halls of the Ateneo. Women are still welcome, but with less exclusive qualifications. Of the old timers, men and women, nowadays only a few phantoms from the past remain on the active rolls of the Ateneo or, for a nostalgic moment, occasionally stroll into the once-great house that spawned the Republic in 1931. Only they can remember Manuel Azaña and the pre-1936 importance of the Ateneo in the cultural and political life of Spain.

On August 16, 1930, the leaders of the various antimonarchist political parties met privately at the *Unión Republicana* headquarters in the popular summer-resort city of San Sebastián. The Catalonians were represented, but not the Basque nationalists, even though the meeting took place in a Basque city. No Communist representation was invited, and none attended. The next day these delegates signed a pact of co-operative coalition toward the ultimate overthrow of the King. Thus, overnight, in San Sebastián the *Junta Revolucionaria* was formed and then converted into the Provisional Government of the future Republic, whose principal ministries were projected as follows: Niceto Alcalá Zamora, President of the Republic; Manuel Azaña, Minister of War; Marcelino Domingo, Minister of Agriculture; Alvaro de Albornoz, Minister of Justice; Miguel Maura, Minister of the Interior; Fernando de los Ríos, Minister of Education; Francisco Largo Caballero, Minister of Labor; Alejandro Lerroux, Minister of State; and Indalecio Prieto, Minister of Public Works. Changes and additions to this government were made later, although the cabinet remained largely the same.[7] Another meeting, separate from the first, took place at the end of August across the French border in Hendaye. This one was attended by Count Romanones, long an influential figure in Spanish national politics. The main result of the latter session was a verbal agreement that municipal and provincial elections should precede the election of a national parliament. Romanones continued to support a constitutional monarchy.

By autumn, revolutionary committees were springing up everywhere. After its initial conference in San Sebastián, the Central Revolutionary Committee held a series of meetings in Madrid. They decided that December 15, 1930, would be the day of general revolt on which the Republic would be proclaimed. These plans were thwarted, however, by some gun-jumpers in Jaca three days ahead of time, at dawn on December 12. By December 20, government troops

---

[7] When the Republic was declared on April 14, 1931, the Provisional Government was as follows: Alcalá Zamora, *idem*; Azaña, *idem*; Domingo, Minister of Education; Albornoz, Minister of Development *(Fomento)*; Maura, *idem*; los Ríos, Minister of Justice; Largo Caballero, *idem*; Lerroux, *idem*; Prieto, Minister of Finance *(Hacienda)*; Santiago Casares Quiroga, Minister of the Navy; Nicoláu d'Olwer, Minister of Economy *(Economía)*; and Diego Martínez Barrio, Minister of Communications.

had quashed the abortive revolt and its accompanying sympathy strikes, whose only salutary effect was one of propaganda for the Republican cause. On the other hand, as a result of the premature revolt, the plans of the Central Revolutionary Committee became known, and the revolutionary manifesto was captured before it could be implemented. Among the signers of this manifesto were all the members of the Provisional Government itself, plus Santiago Casares Quiroga, Luis Nicoláu d'Olwer, and others who played prominent roles in the Republic in the years to come. At the moment, however, all of them who could be found were jailed. Among those arrested were Alcalá Zamora, los Ríos, Maura, Largo Caballero, Eduardo Ortega y Gasset, Casares Quiroga, and Albornoz. Albornoz was defended by Victoria Kent; Alcalá Zamora and Maura were defended by Angel Ossorio, who in 1934 was to defend Manuel Azaña when he was unjustly accused of complicity in the Barcelona rebellion. Marcelino Domingo and Indalecio Prieto fled to Paris, while the police sought Azaña in Madrid that very night of December 12. Probably the fact that Azaña was still small game politically, by contrast with some of the politicos who were arrested, saved him from more concentrated effort for his apprehension.

On that night of December 12 Azaña had tickets for the Teatro Calderón, where a Russian opera company was performing. He risked attendance despite the early-morning events at Jaca and the redoubling of security measures occasioned by the Queen's presence in the theater. Azaña and Doña Dolores were watching the performance when Don Cipriano arrived late and alone, having first taken his wife home from the reception to which he and she had been invited at the home of the First Secretary of the U.S. embassy. The occurrences of that evening are substantially the ones reported in the book *Horas del cautiverio* (Madrid, n. d.), by Eduardo M. del Portillo and

Carlos Primelles, except that Sra. de Azaña remained in her seat the whole time and Azaña did not escape first to the house of Sindulfo de la Fuente or hide in only four locations. The account in the book goes as follows: When Azaña suspected that he was being watched, he pretended not to notice, and during the second intermission he and Sra. de Azaña and Don Cipriano all went out to the lobby where he smoked a cigarette. Instead of remaining in the lobby, Azaña feigned a distracted air and went off to the stage door, apparently with the purpose of greeting some performer. From there, he slipped out into the night while Doña Dolores and her brother returned to their seats. Having made his escape, Azaña went first to the house of an intimate friend, Sindulfo de la Fuente, the first of four places where he elected to hide.

The rest of the story as reported by Portillo and Primelles is untrue. Unfortunately even so sensible a book as Henry Buckley's *Life and Death of the Spanish Republic* (London, 1940), among others, carries a similar version. The inaccurate reporting does, however, demonstrate the effectiveness of Azaña's friends' plan to leak false leads to the police in order better to protect him. The false account says that Azaña decided to leave Madrid, and undisguised (some versions say he traveled in disguise) he went to the North railroad station where he bought several newspapers and a ticket to Burgos. The train left without incident although he was still sought by the police. In Burgos he was met by an auto, which whisked him off to San Sebastián. The following night he crossed into France on foot, unnoticed, beyond the border guards' shack and near the town of Viriato. Once in France, Azaña took a train to Pau, where he installed himself until the Berenguer cabinet crisis. Since he then expected political events, he decided to return to Madrid. Accordingly he went back to the border and openly purchased a train ticket to Madrid. Once again in Madrid, he even went out hunting not far from the city and frequently attended clandestine meetings at night in Madrid.

Apparently all of this is pure fantasy to the last detail. Here is what really happened, as related to me by Sra. de Azaña and Cipriano Rivas Cherif: Azaña spent the first night at the house of a friend, the Mexican writer, Martín Luis Guzmán, on Calle de Velázquez. Though offered asylum by the Mexican embassy the next day, the fugitive declined and went to the house of another friend (name forgotten) just before the police searched Guzmán's residence. Azaña's third refuge was a small hotel or *residencia* owned by the sister of still another unnamed friend. There Azaña spent Christmas Eve by posing as a professor from Valladolid on Christmas vacation; his assumed name, Mariano Alcañiz, matched the initials on his suitcase, although the success of this unoriginal ruse bespeaks the relative disinterest of both the police and the lodgers of the hotel. Next Azaña went to the house of his father-in-law on Calle de Columela. There Doña Dolores could visit her husband without arousing suspicions, and the servants were trustworthy. Azaña lived in the bedroom of his recently deceased mother-in-law (the mother died while Cipriano Rivas Cherif was in Argentina), a room sealed off by the father for ostensibly sentimental reasons readily accepted as plausible by friends and relatives. After Azaña had spent three months in that room, one day he revealed himself to Amós Salvador, who had come to the house on an urgent political errand. Immediately after this visit Azaña thought it best to change quarters again. He went then to the house of Sindulfo de la Fuente and stayed there until it seemed safe to return to the Rivas Cherif home, where this time he remained only briefly. The tedium of confinement had begun to annoy him and to persuade him that he might take the chance of hiding in his own home with its familiar books and other comforts, especially since he conjectured that no one would expect to find him in his own apartment. So there he went and there he stayed until the proclamation of the Republic on April 14, 1931. And what had he done during all the solitary hours between December and April? He had worked on the novel *Fresdeval*, which was still unfinished when he died in 1940, but which will be included as a posthumous work among his complete works when they are published. Rivas Cherif tells how on that beautiful spring day he and Martín Luis Guzmán went to tell Azaña that the Republican flag had been raised over the Post Office building in Madrid, and that Azaña's jovial reaction had been: "Another month and I would have finished the novel!" Azaña had already gone out openly earlier that day, however, to see Miguel Maura (member of the Provisional Government) at his hotel, for Azaña had guessed that the time had finally come to banish precaution.

Political events had moved swiftly while Azaña was in hiding, December 12, 1930 to April 14, 1931. When Primo de Rivera's successor, General Dámaso Berenguer, announced that elections to the Cortes would be held under the old (1876) Constitution, he was met with a wave of protest and resigned on February 14, 1931. The King attempted to come to terms with the revolutionists; he even invited their participation in his new government under Count Romanones. When the invitation was declined, because the Revolutionary Committee would accept nothing less than a constituent parliament, the King placed Admiral Aznar at the head of a government dedicated to holding three elections. First would come the municipal elections, next those for provincial office, and finally a national vote for representatives to the Cortes. In March of 1931 the arrested members of the Revolutionary Committee were tried and freed. The municipal elections were held on April 12. Results were close. The antimonarchist parties probably elected slightly fewer councilors than their monarchist opponents, but of greater significance was the fact that practically every large city had voted antimonarchist. The city dweller was freer to vote for a change than his country cousin, because the monarchist big landowners could threaten the economic life of many a village and thus control its vote. Two days later, the newly elected municipal councils of numerous large cities (including Barcelona, Valencia, and Seville) declared a Republic. Since their action went unopposed by the Director of the Civil Guard, none other than the same General José Sanjurjo who later was to lead a revolt against the Republic, the King and his family were persuaded to recognize a *fait accompli* and leave the country. In a nation noted for its political violence, the most radical change of the century had come about without bloodshed, and even before the holding of the provincial and national parliamentary elections. What remained to be seen, however, was whether this transformation owed more to widespread republican conviction than simply to the weakness of the old regime.

Here are the details of the changeover in Madrid. On the evening of April 13, soapbox orators harangued crowds in the main streets of Madrid without incident. The King must go, they said. Indeed the King was up late that night receiving reports and watching to see what developed. The next morning, Tuesday, April 14, the streets of Madrid were calm again, but toward mid-afternoon it was announced on the radio that the Republic had been proclaimed in Barcelona. Shortly thereafter, the Republican tricolor was raised on several buildings in Madrid, including the Palacio de Comunicaciones at about 4:00 P.M., as the Guardia Civil looked on but did not intervene. Shouts of *Viva la República* could be heard in the streets while streams of enthusiasts began to flow into the Puerta del Sol. So far, it was only an effervescence; no hostile acts had occurred.

Later that afternoon of the 14th, the King met with certain ministers of his cabinet, including his Minister of State, Count Romanones. Toward midday the King had sent Romanones to ascertain the terms of the Revolutionary Committee by means of an interview with Niceto Alcalá Zamora. The latter, as head of the Committee, was soon to become the Provisional President of the Republic. The third man present at that meeting was Dr. Gregorio Marañón, at whose home they met, as a face-saving gesture (neutral territory) for Romanones. Meanwhile most of the Committee waited at the residence of Miguel Maura, to which Azaña had gone. Speaking for the Committee, Alcalá Zamora, ex-Minister-of-the-King-turned-republican, gave the King and his ministers until sunset that day to hand over the government to the Republican Committee. In return for this peaceful transfer of authority, the Committee would guarantee the King's safe departure from Spain. Later, on June 3, 4, and 5, 1931, the daily *El sol* published Romanones' own accounts of the last hours of the monarchy, data which also appeared in a privately circulated book written by Romanones. Though their interpretation differs, the facts are essentially equivalent to those recorded by Berenguer in his book (*De la dictadura a la República,* Madrid, 1946), which then piqued Romanones to respond with another book of his own entitled . . . *Y sucedió así* (Madrid, 1947), whose first edition sold out in a hurry. According to Berenguer, it was Romanones who had convinced the King on April 14 that all was lost, and that the King had better plan to leave immediately in order to prevent large-scale public disorder and bloodshed. According to Romanones, only at the King's behest did he perform the onerous function of King's messenger to Alcalá Zamora, who had once been Romanones' own secretary. Romanones claims that the King himself made the decision early that morning of the 14th to leave the country. However the King reached his conclusion, his departure probably prevented civil war, for the new government had already installed itself before the King released his brief farewell message to the nation. Manuel Azaña and the other ministers had gone to the Ministerio de la Gobernación (on the Puerta del Sol, and now the Dirección General de Seguridad), where he and the rest of the Provisional Government made an appearance on the balcony from which Alcalá Zamora then gave the speech that proclaimed the Republic.

Accompanied by the deposed Minister of the Navy and several aides, King Alfonso XIII also took Prince Alfonso with him and left Madrid by 9:00 P.M. that evening in a convoy of three autos. Their destination was Cartagena. By dawn they had sailed from Spain in a cruiser named, ironically, "Príncipe Alfonso," which took them to Marseilles without incident. From Marseilles the King went to Paris and, less than a month later, to London. Abandoned by the aristocrats and protected by *ad hoc* people's militia, the Queen and her other children followed the King to France by land, after the government had organized a safe departure for them. Ultimately the King's peregrinations led him to Italy, where he died February 28, 1941, in Rome, after having formally abdicated the throne on February 13, 1941, in favor of his third son, Don Juan. A marble coffin now awaits Alfonso XIII in the Escorial, where some day he may be buried with the other kings of Spain.

By evening on April 14, the popular enthusiasm in the Puerta del Sol had risen to a deafening roar. No traffic could move. Bunches of Spaniards were hanging like grapes from lampposts, from stranded trolleys, from any vehicle or object which offered prominence. It was astonishing where all the Republican flags had come from—almost as astonishing as where the Republic itself had come from.

Ever since the Pact of San Sebastián, Manuel Azaña was to be provisional Minister of War. The apocryphal story is told that he marched into the offices of the War Ministry that night of April 14 and announced to its occupants that they had a choice of two courses of action, either to make way for him or to throw him off the balcony, but that in the latter case the consequences might be most grave. Actually Azaña did go to the Ministerio de la Guerra toward midnight in the company of Comandante (later General) Juan Hernández Sarabia, who was to become Azaña's chief administrative aide in the years to come, but the transfer of authority was effected pacifically. Thus the president of Madrid's principal literary society took charge of the Spanish army, a fact which caused not inconsiderable smiles among the *tertulias* of café life about town. The mirth subsided, however, when the conversationists saw the efficient War Minister in action; and soon great things came to be expected of this scholar who brought not only honor, integrity, and efficiency to the office, but also a sound knowledge of comparative military policy and—of importance to his underlings—the practical perspective derived from his own previous employment in the civil service.

Was his character altered when the reserved and introspective Azaña suddenly became a high functionary? Not in the slightest. Though he could have established himself at the Palacio de Buenavista, traditional residence of War Ministers, and finally did so later when he became also Prime Minister, for the present he and his wife continued their simple life in the top-floor flat with its glass balcony at Calle de Hermosilla 24 *duplicado* (now number 36), only instead of trudging home alone laden with papers and books as he had done for so many years, the recent fugitive now arrived with an escort, which caused a sensation among the unsuspecting neighbors. In all, both before and after his marriage, Manuel Azaña maintained that apartment for eighteen years, until he moved to Calle de Serrano 38 at the end of 1933. Though he never forgot to pay the rent on time (250 pesetas a month in 1931) nor to greet the concierge and the other tenants courteously, he never indulged in small talk with any of them. He had always lived to himself and received few visitors: occasionally a friend or literary acquaintance, or on a Sunday his various nieces and nephews whom he loved very much and who, with the disarming candor of most children, had known the secret of demolishing the aloofness of their learned uncle. Now, however, the phone was ringing all the time, a mountain of mail arrived each day, and a line of people was always waiting to see him. Though he had lost his privacy the new War Minister remained his accustomed tranquil, almost indifferent, self.

Manuel Azaña had arrived with the Republic. It should have been advantageous to come on the scene suddenly as he did. He had few, if any, established enmities or enemies. He had no party promises to fulfill, nor anybody to please. The nation seemed to ask of Azaña and the Republic only: "Show me the way." But a painfully sinuous road lay ahead. The sober task of building a democracy is not the same thing as the signing of a pact on a sunny day in San Sebastián. Making a revolution is not the same thing as knowing what to do with it once it is made.

III   The Republic, 1931-1934. Rise and Fall of Azaña.

THE MOMENTUM of popular enthusiasm carried through April, May, June, 1931—days of organization, consolidation, stabilization, and political campaigning. On June 28, Republican Spain elected a Constituent Cortes, whose sessions commenced on July 14 in Madrid.

This new Parliament was a rare assemblage of types and talents, the deputies notably lacking in the titles of nobility that had characterized many previous parliaments under the monarchy. The Socialists, with 116 deputies, were the largest single political party represented. Minority groups were numerous, among them Azaña's Republican Action party with 30 deputies. The venerable Socialist Julián Besteiro was elected president of the Cortes, which counted among its illustrious but politically inexperienced members (one for each 50,000 of population) not less than 50 university professors, 41 physicians, 123 lawyers, 30 editors, 16 engineers, 8 priests, and a handful of well-known creative writers like Unamuno (representing Salamanca), Pérez de Ayala (Oviedo), Ortega y Gasset (León), and Madariaga (La Coruña—Valle Inclán had also stood for election in La Coruña but was defeated), as well as the son, Sigfrido, of Blasco Ibáñez. Had he not died in 1928, probably Blasco Ibáñez himself would have figured prominently in the Republican government. The July 21, 1931, edition of *El sol* lists also, among others, 18 businessmen, 4 notaries, 6 pharmacists, 6 public officials, 2 veterinarians, 6 printers, 1 jeweler, 1 chauffeur, 1 tailor, 1 baker, 3 miners, and 27 laborers. Imagine such a Congress in Washington: 50 college professors on the one hand and 27 laborers on the other. These were the men—there were also two women, both lawyers, Clara Campoamor and Victoria Kent, the latter now an exile and editor of the magazine *Ibérica* in New York—who were bent upon extirpating what they considered to be the traditional institutions of oppression in Spain: the aristocracy or big landowners, the military, and the church. In their zeal to break cleanly with the past, the leaders of the Republican Constituent Assembly and the majority of its deputies fomented a spirit of drastic reform which produced on December 9, 1931, after almost five months of bitter debate and considerable opposition, a decidedly Leftish Constitution, one perhaps excessively liberal, progressive, and democratic for a nation unused to shouldering the collective social responsibilities essential to the perpetuation of such a Constitution. Manuel Azaña, who had been elected deputy from the provincial capital of Valencia, was among the avant-garde of those who insisted upon the most sweeping reforms.

Parts of this Constitution have been compared to both the Mexican one of 1917 (Querétaro) and that of the German Weimar Republic of 1919, but the truth is that the deputies examined and discussed nearly all modern constitutions, and thus maybe unknowingly utilized parts of many constitutions. One of the democratizing features of the Spanish Republic's Constitution was its stipulation of a unicameral parliament. The provision for a senate (to have been elected by representative boards from agriculture, industry, universities, and other professional groups) was eliminated after the first draft as unacceptable to, among others, the Socialists. Surely it was an impractical Constitution in its failure to reconcile and cement differences of opinion, to wit, Articles 3 and 26 which not only separated church and state, but in effect alienated them irrevocably. In many ways it was an idealistic Constitution, as evidenced by Article 6, authored by Salvador de Madariaga, which says that "Spain renounces war as an instrument of national policy." While Article 6 thus renounces war, Articles 113 and 114 contain budget provisions in case of war; and Article 76 delegates the Presidential duty of declaring war—a defensive war, naturally, although this, unstated, is one of the many contradictions in the 1931 Constitution.

The first sentence of the first Article may seem particularly visionary: "Spain is a democratic Republic of workers (*trabajadores*) of every class (*de toda clase*)," etc. A concession to the Socialists, this definition (whose first draft had read simply "Spain is a democratic Republic") would appear to intend the democratization of the Republic, a happy land where everyone does his part for the common good, for as Article 46 says: "Work, in its diverse forms, is a social obligation . . . . " The wording of that introductory definition was ill chosen, even if the idle stockholder or land proprietor in the capitalist Republic became in this way a worker, because *worker* and *class* were in the 1930's, even as they are today, loaded words associated with Marxist doctrine. The enemies of the Republic always said that Article 1 was communistic, though the Republic did not come in on Communist wings. Surely the inference was entirely a wrong one, but the Republic exposed its aims to misinterpretation in the very first Article of its Constitution; and this Article gained wide publicity.

What is not generally understood, however, is that the "Republic of workers" was not so much an aspiration to an unrealizable Utopia as it was a wish to encourage a productive society wherein a man is urged to earn his keep, esteem his citizenship, bear his just obligations to the state, and thus contribute his share toward the functioning of that Republic. If this was the ambition of the Constituent Cortes, then its "anticlerical" legislation should not be so termed; and what may at first sight seem to be aimed at extirpating the church was only a movement to make the church bear the temporal as well as spiritual burden, to require the church to pay its own way like any other private institution within the Republic. One day a deputy named Eduardo Barriobero (executed by the Civil War victors in 1936) rose to his feet to propose an amendment to the Article dealing with citizenship; he proposed that monks should lose their citizenship; his amendment was defeated by only a scant margin of votes. Revengeful anticlericalism? No, but so interpreted in the press, domestic and foreign. The reasoning behind the amendment was simply analogous to what Azaña had indicated in the *Garden of the Monks:* that the monk, selfish in his own pursuits, is a kind of anti-citizen who contributes nothing to the state. Quite apart from whatever sect directs and sustains the monk's passivity in national life, the fact that he is not a "worker" condemns him, and not the fact that he is Catholic.

The third item of Article 1 also merits attention: "The Republic constitutes an integral State *(Estado integral)*, compatible with the autonomy of the Municipalities and the Regions." Again in Article 8, mention is made of an "integrated" *(integrado)* state. Obviously it was desired to avoid saying either "unitary state" or "federal state," since the first would have alienated the Catalonians and perhaps the Basques, both of whom were counting on eventual autonomy for their respective regions, and the second would have indicated only a hypothetical condition which did not yet exist. The Constitution created, therefore, a *potentially* federal Republic, as evidenced by Articles 11 and 12, which define the conditions under which any region may, for historical, cultural, and economic reasons, present its statute for a type of autonomy roughly equivalent to that of a state in the U.S.A. Article 13 was supposed to be the safeguard that prohibited federation of autonomous regions, but the very fact of provision for regional autonomy would seem to have made the Republic a federal state (even though Article 19 might tend to deny this), with all the dangers thereto appertaining. The Catalonian tendency to separatism had long been a thorny issue in Spain, and the provision for regional statutes of autonomy was one of the agreements in the Pact of San Sebastián. After the Constitution became effective, the Catalonians duly presented their statute for approval. Despite powerful opposition from the large bloc of the Cortes who feared separatism, Catalonia finally won its autonomy mainly through the efforts of its principal proponent—Manuel Azaña.

If the fundamental cause of the U.S. Civil War was the question of state versus national authority, if states' rights can still be a burning issue in the democratized U.S.A., a federal type of government is even harder to manage in Spain, where an inherent deficiency in co-operative values easily develops into explosive extremism. Witness the previous attempt to decentralize the government in Spain: the federal Constitution of 1873. Just as in 1931, the Catalonians began to act unilaterally even before the Constitution became effective. The Constitution of 1873 divided Spain into fifteen states, each with its own military force and financial autonomy in the matter of raising and spending funds. Certain cities in southern Spain began to force loans from their wealthiest citizens and even to issue their own currency. As nearly always, whenever Spain takes a liberal turn, violence was directed against the church and the army. As moderate freedom had to become immoderate, and that immoderate freedom was converted into anarchy, the national government soon found itself to be without authority or credit, and almost bankrupt. Then came the usual string of prime ministers with brief office: Pi y Margall, Salmerón, Castelar.

For order to be restored, Valencia had to be bombarded; Cartagena not only resisted the government troops, but joined Murcia in an attack on Alicante—and Murcia declared war on Germany! The army took command and disbanded the Parliament. A small-scale civil war ensued. The general outlines of the breakdown of central authority of that First Republic were to be re-enacted in the rise and fall of the Second Republic of 1931-36, only this time the drama was played on a larger stage and at a time when the spectator nations saw fit not to watch the performance, but to participate in the act, each to its own ends. Basically it was by the lack of conservatism or caution in handling certain historical Spanish problems that the Spanish Constitutions of both 1873 and 1931 seemed to invite their respective conflicts.

Many Spaniards criticized the Constitution of 1931; and the first President of the Republic, Niceto Alcalá Zamora, was one of them, though he did not publish his book (*Los defectos de la Constitución de 1931*, Madrid, 1936) until after the Cortes had deposed him from the Presidency. Although the Constituent Assembly of 1931 may have attempted to affirm much that it could not in reality deliver, it did develop on paper a very "modern" Constitution (albeit a prolix one), notable for its social guarantees and for its delineation of Spain's full international obligations as an aspirant partner in the world community of nations. To this end, Spain was committed to subscribe to, and participate in, the League of Nations; and Article 7 of the Constitution, an Article approved almost without discussion, pledged respect for international law. In the matter of civil guarantees, the Constitution was largely a socialized document assuring fair treatment to the "workers of every class." The second paragraph of Article 46 says that "the Republic will assure every worker the conditions necessary for a worthy (*digna*) existence"; the next paragraph speaks of laws to regulate conditions of employment, like minimum pay, work hours, sickness, insurance, and so forth. Social benefits, group guarantees, and civil liberties of all kinds were well covered, including newly won civil rights for women. Women could now not only vote, at the established voting age of twenty-three for both sexes, but they gained other previously nonexistent civil rights as well, including the right to divorce, with due cause. Although the debate was not nearly so violent as the wrangling on the famous Article 26, which dissolved certain religious orders, the question of women's suffrage (Article 36) produced one day on the floor of the Cortes a memorable exchange of views between Clara Campoamor and Victoria Kent, who held opposing opinions expressed in consecutive speeches. Renouncing an ideal, Miss Kent proposed that the female right to vote be postponed, and with good reasons. The essence of these reasons, in which Azaña concurred, was that Spanish women were not yet sufficiently won to the Republic. "Today," she concluded, "it is dangerous to concede the vote to women." Then Miss Campoamor spoke. The male Cortes enjoyed the contest. Women's vote won, 161-121, whereupon a deputy shouted: *"¡Viva la República de las mujeres!"* The comic aspect aside, it became evident too late that Victoria Kent was right.

Among other items of note in this historic Constitution, the state attempted to sustain and promote public education, declared its non-recognition of titles of nobility, and stipulated (Article 58) that the Cortes was to meet for at least three months every February 1 and for at least two months each October 1. The President of the Republic was to be elected by the Cortes for a term of six years. In sum, the 1931 Constitution manifested the intent that Spain should be brought quickly into the twentieth century. In return for its many individual guarantees, the Constitution demanded above all that Spaniards be good citizens—and here one sees the guiding hand of Manuel Azaña. In many lands this Constitution might have been viewed as a mild one, but in Spain it meant a sharp rupture with the past. As Azaña later observed, the most basic elements of progressive democratic government, taken for granted elsewhere, have to be defended as radical theory in Spain.

In order finally to achieve its single fundamental document of national organization, the Constituent Cortes worked as hard as any legislative body had ever done in Spain. They were a dedicated body who met at all hours of the day and night to debate scrupulously the tiniest of details in the Articles of the Constitution. Even after the Constitution had been voted, any event of public disorder was debated immediately in the Cortes and resolved posthaste. (Once there was a luncheon given for the Minister of War and Prime Minister, Manuel Azaña, at the Carabanchel military encampment in the suburbs of Madrid. In postprandial speeches, Generals Caballero, Villegas, and then Goded spoke in a vein interpreted by Lt. Col. Mangada as inimical to the Republic. Mangada, whom Azaña in his memoirs qualifies as "crazy, completely mad," lost his temper, tore off his jacket and stamped on it. By 3:30 P.M., definitive action had been taken: Goded was no longer Chief of Staff, the other generals likewise were relieved of command, and Mangada was in the military prison. At 4:30 Azaña was reporting the incident to the Cortes. After his brief speech, the matter was closed. During the Monarchy, "street events" regularly closed the Cortes; during the Republic, such happenings tended to keep the Cortes in session extra hours until the occurrence was fully aired in public, as further evidenced by the case of General Sanjurjo's rebellion in 1932.) What a potpourri of amusing anecdotes, literary quotations (frequently in the original language, whatever that might be), historical references, and impetuous verbal volleys took place in that assemblage! How often the deputies shouted *"Viva la República"!* On the whole, their comportment was as good as that of any Cortes under the Monarchy, but they would not have been Spaniards if the academic and philosophic tone of their debate did not often make an athenaeum of their Parliament. Those were the days of optimism, ephemeral as it was.

Even at the start of the Republic, however, both the Left and the Right wings seemed to outnumber the Center, in the Cortes and among the population at large. From the very moment that the Constitution was ratified, on December 9, 1931, reactionaries began a violent campaign against its reforms and against men like Manuel Azaña, who, as he assumed the office of Prime Minister, found it his duty to protect the Constitution. Here, in the early months of 1932, was the real beginning of the alignments for the Spanish Civil War of 1936. Attacked by the Right, moderates like Azaña were forced gradually to support and be supported by elements farther Left than their tastes inclined them. Thinking to protect its own interests, neutral or uncommitted capital was thus persuaded to turn to the Right. By 1933 the already multifarious political parties were splitting into even smaller units. The result was excessive ministerial change and the return of improvisation to government. By 1936 the displacement had become nearly complete, with scarcely any power remaining in the Center to reconcile the Right with the Revolutionists. In essence, the only real forces in Spain were social ones: feudal-type domination on the one hand and working-class supremacy on the other, both of them masquerading under the names of political parties. This phenomenon was particularly apparent among the Left groups, where the trade union was in itself a political party, or identified itself with one. Azaña's early method of containing these extremes was to adopt a strong attitude of bluff, which much of the foreign press mistakenly interpreted as dictatorial. Azaña was a patriot by nature, but the times demanded that he be a militant patriot. One of his first threats was that Spaniards must either respect the Republic or fear it. When the Right finally became convinced that there was nothing to fear, Azaña was finished, and with him the Republic.

In retrospect, it is possible to delineate the four major stages of the Republic between its inception in 1931 and its exhaustion in 1939. The first Constitutional government, from December of 1931 to September of 1933, was that of Azaña and the reformers. This was also the best government of the Republic, the biennium of the intellectual revolutionaries, like Azaña, whose personal leadership, the result of persistent conviction and convincing oratory, rammed through the Cortes the progressive legislation that the reactionary successors of the Right were to nullify when they controlled the government during its second stage, from December of 1933 to February of 1936. That second stage has come to be called the *Bienio Negro* or Black Biennium. Each of these governments had to deal with considerable opposition and civilian disorder; in fact, each had to quash an organized local uprising. The brief third stage of the Republic came in February of 1936, with the victory of the Popular Front and Azaña's return to a position of leadership. This period lasted only until July of 1936, when the generals revolted. The initial failure of their coup forced a total chaos of civil war upon the nation until the Republic was finally exhausted in the spring of 1939. That rebellion, met by revolution, was the fourth and final stage of the Second Spanish Republic. In none of these stages could the various Republican groups achieve sufficient cohesion among themselves—not even in war.

With regard to Azaña himself, his innate and sometimes naïve straightforwardness made him intolerant of the more devious and subtle procedures of other deputies with less probity than he; in short, his chief political drawback was his inability to reach a *modus vivendi* with crafty professional politicians like Alcalá Zamora (whom the

Cortes elected President of the Republic, even though he had resigned the Provisional Presidency), Lerroux, and Largo Caballero, all of whom he disliked personally. Except in Azaña's speeches, which were to him a kind of aesthetic experience, he simply could not be diplomatic: he was a bulldozer. The best way to follow his headlong course through the peacetime years of the Republic is to study his speeches, most of which he himself gathered in three collections, published by Espasa-Calpe, with these titles:

1. *Una política* (1930-32), Bilbao, Madrid, and Barcelona, 1932. This includes forty-five speeches, most of them in the Cortes, from February, 1930, to September, 1932.

2. *En el poder y en la oposición* (1932-34), in two volumes, Bilbao, Madrid, and Barcelona, 1934.

3. *Discursos en campo abierto*, Bilbao, Madrid, and Barcelona, 1936. This contains speeches of 1935.

Collectively these volumes of oratory not only reveal Azaña at his apogee of power, but they tell the story of the vital years of the Republic as well. It is not an exaggeration to say that Azaña *was* the Republic.

As a parliamentarian Azaña had no equal. He was not the only great orator in the Cortes, but his style was quite the opposite from the florid one of Alcalá Zamora. Azaña dazzled his opponents with hard-hitting words of dry reason. The irrefutable logic, the rich and precise vocabulary, the originality and profundity of thought, the depth of historical perspective, the syntactical precision of his long and perfectly balanced sentences—all of these characteristics of Azaña's writing now became channeled into oratory. He manipulated paradoxes, invented metaphors, and made profitable use of illustrative parody. Lacking only in the ability to be brief—in spite of his gift for synthesis—Azaña did have the essential quality of all great orators, which is lucidity.

In his oratory, Azaña's underlying aim was invariably didactic and dialectic. He took it upon himself to educate Spain to democratic life. He was constantly orienting his parliamentary audience to its duties. Ever mindful of the Constitution, he was the perpetual pedagogue and lawgiver on what a republic is and how a parliament should function. He tended always to the academic. Even in his simplest statements to the Cortes, Azaña scarcely ever uttered any judgment without commenting on the suitability or legality of that judgment, as in his speech of August 17, 1933, when he said, "The radical party, utilizing its perfect right, and moreover an opportune one, fixes its political position with respect to the Government."

He wrote down his speeches to the last word, yet he argued extemporaneously with astonishing ease. Always master of himself, he defended his positions with total aplomb when he was interrupted, which was frequently, for at times there seemed to be few gentlemen in the Cortes. Although Azaña was given to sudden anger in private conversation, he practically never lost his temper in the Cortes, where measured words were often abandoned by the deputies. By mid-1933 he did, however, begin replying to personal attacks instead of sloughing them off, but even the incessant taunts could scarcely provoke him from the self-imposed decorum dictated by a pride in his concept of civilized public debate. Neither did he lack appropriate theatrics; he merely insisted on the same good taste that characterized the artist in him.

Azaña usually began a speech by appealing to reason and ended the speech by seeking a response from the emotions. His physical mode of delivery was predictable too. Every Azaña speech was a solemn occasion. A taut expression of sarcasm and disdain in his voice and person became characteristic. Aware that he was generally thought to be cold and unemotional by nature, he even alluded to this reputation in a speech that he gave at a Republican banquet in Valencia on April 4, 1932. The next month during his great speech of May 27, 1932, in the Cortes, he reacted again: " . . . I, who pass for a hard, intransigent sectarian man . . . ," and he reiterated in the Cortes on June 14, 1932, for the third month in a row: "I, with my habitual coldness . . . . " More than a year later, on August 17, 1933, Azaña was still trying to convince the Cortes that "although it may be said otherwise, I am vulnerable to emotion." He usually expressed his disdain by means of a mimicking or mocking facial gesture. When he wanted to stress a point that he was making, he would extend both hands, elbows bent in a V, palms upward, fingers separated, and all with the suggestion of a lifting movement. If there was anything notable about the voice itself, other than its habitual clarity, it was that the pitch was a little higher than the pachydermous head and corpulent torso might suggest.

Recall that Azaña was nearsighted. When his eyes were not lost behind the thick lenses of his glasses, a condition that contributed to his normally expressionless physiognomy, those seemingly compassionless and scornful orbs appeared to threaten and even pierce the object of his glance. When the Cortes was in session and Azaña was not speaking, he would take off his glasses to read some document or reference and hold the printed material close up. Then he would commence his nervous habit of putting on and removing the glasses frequently. To put them on, he habitually pushed them up over the center of his nose. Then he might light a cigarette. He had his own way of smoking, which included a propensity for allowing the ash to grow so that, if it did not fall on his well-tailored but usually wrinkled suit of British wool, as sometimes happened, he would flip off the ash with a slow and very precise series of taps of the straightened index finger upon the top of the unsmoked portion of the cigarette. When it became his turn to speak, he would extinguish the cigarette and rise with a haughty air of confidence and self-possession.

Sparing of humor, Azaña never entertained his audience; he hypnotized it, enchained it, pierced its varied prejudices with incisive arrows of logic loosened from an intellect that even his bitterest adversaries respected. Although sometimes the profundity of his arguments made them too lengthy, Azaña's only consistent oratorical peccadillo was perhaps an excessive fondness for the first person singular. (This penchant for talking about himself is also apparent in his writings, and it is not un-Spanish.) Still Azaña spoke so well that his adversaries found it hard to oppose him—not that their position often was not equally as tenable as his, but they could not match his persuasiveness, born of a sincerity of conviction, with sufficient brilliance to neutralize the magnetism of his arguments. For Manuel Azaña, nearly every speech was a triumph. In spite of the jealousies and hates which his success had aroused in a few of the most illustrious deputies of the Cortes, especially in Alcalá Zamora and Lerroux, who were also orators of note, Azaña gradually became so much the oratorical master of the Cortes that his energies were misinterpreted by some as a sign of personal ambition dangerous to the Republic. One day a deputy of the opposition rose and spoke of the shadow of Mussolini in the Cortes. The Spanish opposition press always vilified Azaña mercilessly—such was politics in the Spanish Republic—but one would hardly expect to read irresponsible reporting in a distinguished newspaper like the *New York Times*. This is just what happened with respect to Azaña.

Reference is to the Sunday, April 2, 1933, edition of the *New York Times*. Page 7 of Section 8 has an article bearing this headline: AZAÑA A COOL DICTATOR OVER TROUBLED SPAIN. Written in Madrid, the dispatch was signed by Frank L. Kluckhohn and was possibly a result of his personal enmity toward Azaña, though the *Times'* readers of that day could only assume that they were reading, as usual, all the news that's fit to print. The gist of Kluckhohn's dispatch was that Azaña, whom he calls one of the "new dictatorial rulers of Europe," is a Marxist schemer who "has made Spain a blue-denim land," albeit with always a "token of constitutional procedure." This simply was not true, yet the article gave the impression that an Azaña dictatorship was an accomplished fact. Totally unfair to Azaña, lines like these helped to form public opinion in the U.S.A. with respect to the Spanish situation.

Of all the leaders of the Republic, Azaña was the one who remained the most uncompromisingly legalistic and constitutional. If he did have any excess, it was an excess of faith in the Constitution of the Second Spanish Republic, a document which was his bible. Dictatorship? With his prestige, Azaña had plenty of opportunity for absolute rule in a land not unused to dictators, but he rejected all attempts to project him into unconstitutional power. At the October 3, 1933, session of the Cortes, when he was accused of personality-cult politics by his archenemy Alejandro Lerroux, Azaña replied to his accuser: "But if I had been ambitious, do you think I would have spent so many years in a library writing books which are not important to anybody, not even to me myself?" Then he inquired of Lerroux whether he thinks he, Lerroux, would now be seated on that bench if in the last two and a half years Azaña had been anything less than a man of probity. What Azaña should have asked is whether it seems likely that a man bent on dictatorship would submit his "dictatorial" program to debate and countenance accusations of his person. "I have had in my hands, gentlemen of Parliament," continued Azaña, "a power as few have had in this country in modern times . . . . " With the powers invested in the Prime Minister under the famous Law for the Defense of the Republic, this was entirely true. What is not generally known, however, is the entry in Azaña's own memoirs[1] of January 15, 1933, in which he gives this pathetic account: "Three deputies of different parties have spoken to me today of dictatorship, as the only possible remedy for the anarchistic uprisings, if they continue. This is the national propensity, the after-effects of the past, and what is coming from the outside. Is it that Spain cannot live in democracy and under law? No one wants to obey unless it is by force. Friends and enemies of the Republic and their enemies of both extreme bands are doing everything necessary to propagate the idea that 'one cannot go on this way,' and thoughts are directed to a dictatorship. The Republic is today in pincers." Here is another entry, July 7, 1933, from his memoirs: "Galarza [Angel Galarza, lawyer, journalist, deputy to the Cortes] was there too, who, as on other occasions, was telling me that I ought to become the dictator and put an end to all this."

These confidences, written in 1933, demonstrate that affairs had become critical even that early. Still Azaña refused to resort to dictatorial powers, either then or in 1936, when a departure from strict constitutionality might have prevented or delayed the Civil War. In the first of the two previous quotations, Azaña said essentially what he was to say again later in his book *La velada en Benicarló*. It is lamentable that the man could not find some way, short of dictatorship, to stop the strikes, burnings, killings, and general atmosphere of proletarian agitation. Some of his statements in the Cortes would seem to indicate an indifference to it all, but the truth is that he simply chose to remain strictly constitutional.

If Azaña's enemies accused him of dictatorship while his friends urged him to it, both reactions are traceable to his leadership through oratory. To understand this paradox, maybe it should be pointed out

[1] Reference is intended to page 250 of the stolen portion of Azaña's memoirs, published in Franco Spain in 1939 as *Memorias íntimas de Azaña*, edited by Joaquín Arrarás. See Chapter VI for more data on the stolen diary.

that the spoken word is vital in Spain; and the importance of the spoken word is disproportionate to that of actual deeds. This fact, which Kluckhohn did not grasp, was the great fault of the Republican Cortes, whose deputies were so often given to inordinate admiration or criticism of one another's speeches. We in the U.S.A. would scarcely think of classifying the respective competence of our congressmen by a yardstick of their oratorical attributes, and many of our Presidents have been notoriously poor public speakers, yet we have a stable government. Azaña's star rose, however, with his parliamentary and extra-parliamentary oratory, and as time went by, he became increasingly vain about his public performances. As a writer he had been generally unappreciated; as an orator he was a colossal success. In the prologue to Volume I of his 1932-34 speeches (*En el poder y en la oposición*), Azaña appeared to be convinced that "one speech is worth more to the reputation of a man than a dozen books." Again and again he recorded in his memoirs, somewhat immodestly, the extent of his persuasiveness. Here are some of the entries at random:

> I have inspired calm, security and serenity in Parliament. I have pleased them and they applauded a great deal.
>
> I improvised a speech which Parliament received with delirious acclamation (*aclamaciones delirantes*).
>
> They applauded very much . . . .
>
> . . . a resounding success. The majority, standing, shouted their enthusiasm.
>
> . . . I gave a speech which caused a strong impression.

Of a speech which was transmitted throughout Spain and to Spanish America, he wrote:

> The diffusion of the speech has been extraordinary . . . . At the

President's residence, piles of extremely impressive telegrams are being received today.

. . . I gave a very lively speech that was found pleasing.

As Azaña himself knew (because he said it), every speech is a kind of total collaboration, inseparable from the unreproducible circumstances of the moment, the audience, the sometimes ephemeral nature of the topic, and other conditions. Let us picture, nevertheless, Azaña making his speeches, and in this way trace the course of his leadership through the first years of the Republic. Only the most important addresses will be listed, or the ones which sometimes led into far-reaching political aspects of the Second Spanish Republic.

Speech of February 11, 1930, at a Republican Banquet

"Liberty does not make men happy; it simply makes them men." In this pre-Republic speech, Azaña utters for the first time publicly the maxim he was to use repeatedly to good advantage and which explains aphoristically his concept of a republic. A republic does not give; it exacts. Human dignity is achieved only through freedom of choice, whose essential condition is personal integrity. Fulfillment of responsibility to self, therefore, is what makes a citizen in the democratic state.

Speech of July 17, 1931, at a Banquet Given by Republican Action for Its Candidates to the Cortes

" . . . if the Spanish Republic goes under, ours will be the blame. If we do not know how to govern, the blame will be ours."

Speech of September 14, 1931, at the National Congress of Republican Action

Azaña rejoices that the Republic has its enemies—a sign of health (compare Unamuno's assertion that a parliament is fecund only when it is fired with contention)—but anyone who fails to respect the Republic will find that "If someone knocks over a chair, I will knock over the table."

"Spain has entered the Republican orbit forever . . . . Notice must be given that a monarchy in Spain is physically impossible, and that another attempt at dictatorship would only precipitate a social cataclysm." Prophetic?

Speech of September 29, 1931, in the Cortes

Scorning the Russian concept of military discipline, Azaña would abolish the death penalty in the armed forces' tribunals. Recall that Azaña was, by preference, Minister of War, a portfolio which he retained along with the Premiership.

Speech of October 13, 1931, in the Cortes

Although he had spoken in the Cortes before, this speech marks Azaña's real debut as a great parliamentary orator. Some say it was the best speech ever heard in the Cortes. This was the memorable afternoon when Azaña argued in favor of the famous Article 26 of the Constitution, which separated church from state and dissolved the Jesuits. Everyone in the Cortes that day knew a great orator had been born, and outside in the corridors after the session Azaña was surrounded by deputies who wished to congratulate him.

Azaña put the complex matter simply: *"España ha dejado de ser católica"* (Spain has ceased to be Catholic). This single sentence, tied for eternity to the name Azaña, more than anything else he ever wrote or said, was his personal declaration of war, rancor from the garden of monks finally crystallized into national policy. The ultimate approval of the Article by a vote of 178 to 59 took place with the Basque delegation and other prominent deputies absent in protest and the provisional President of the Republic threatening to resign. Despite its comfortable majority, this vote created the first major schism within the new Cortes, and Alcalá Zamora did in fact resign.

As in the case of the legal pronouncements on racial desegregation in the U.S.A., the principle involved is less debatable than the method of its application and the timetable for its enforcement. Azaña's aim was admissible: the independence of the state and its first claim upon the allegiance of its citizens. The Spanish Republic should not find itself in an inferior position in its dealings with the Vatican or any other state. The Republic should enjoy national esteem in the world community, especially with respect to Spanish America. In the twentieth century, the question of separation of church and state is so elementary that most nascent parliaments do not even need to discuss it. It may even be reasonable to imagine, as did Azaña, that Catholicism owes more to Spain than Spain owes to Catholicism. Intelligent, enlightened thinking would separate church and state in Spain, and Azaña always did what was intelligent. But sometimes intelligence can exceed practicality. Maybe it was unwise at this juncture for the newborn Republic, not yet on its feet, to court the wrath of the Spanish church, a power unto itself.

The unfortunate phrasing of "Spain has ceased to be Catholic," isolated from the rest of the text, distorted Azaña's intended meaning. In the first place, he did not mean that Catholicism was to be outlawed in Spain. His very next lines speak of "personal conscience." He meant that the state was no longer to be officially identified with any religion, no longer to be dictated to by any *collective* religious conscience. Secondly, these words were intended to be as much a summary as a prediction, and should not have surprised anyone: Azaña simply synthesized the innumerable comments on the religious issue that had

102

already been exchanged on the floor of the Cortes. Few people read the speech or heard the phrase in context, least of all those who would have admitted privately that Spanish Catholicism of 1931 no longer inspired the masses of the Spanish people, who then and now affirm their Catholicism more than they practice it.

Speech of October 20, 1931, in the Cortes

This is the speech that secured the passage, on the next day, of the highly controversial *Ley de Defensa de la República* (Law for the Defense of the Republic). This law, whether justified or not, showed that the Republic was already weak, notwithstanding Azaña's affirmation that the Republic was not in danger, that he wanted the law as a standby measure. In effect, this law temporarily nullified Constitutional guarantees whenever the government (in the person of the Prime Minister) chose to invoke it to counter those types of aggression against the Republic which the law defined. Both its strength and its weakness lay in its definition of what constituted an aggressive act. The *Ley de Defensa*, used frequently and sometimes indiscreetly, became a frightful weapon for silencing newspapers, breaking up meetings, and hauling malcontents off to jail. Such was the dilemma of the Republic: freedom including freedom to subvert the government and perhaps topple the Republic, or Constitutional freedom annullable at any given moment by arbitrary and dictatorial administrative fiat? The *Ley de Defensa* was a harsh law, but the campaigns against Azaña and the government in general were unbelievably scurrilous. The law was passed, against opposition from the Right, but there were to be many more speeches in which Azaña had to defend its operation and application.

Speech of December 2, 1931, in the Cortes

This speech on military policy is one of Azaña's best and most convincing declamations. The study of military matters had been one of his principal activities, and as Minister of War Azaña was initiating momentous reforms in the organization of the army. Convinced that no real military policy had existed in Spain since the end of the eighteenth century, he had ruminated for many years on the theories which he now possessed the authority to put into practice. Naturally the reforms did not go unopposed.

We have already speculated, in Chapter I, that the origin of Azaña's interest in military affairs was aesthetic, that basically his military interests were motivated by a desire to curb the disorderly and unharmonious effects of the military upon Spanish public and intellectual life. Fundamentally he detested coercion or violence in any form. To put the army in its proper perspective in the new society was merely to comply with the spirit of the Republic's Constitution, which allowed a standing army only for purposes of national defense. Azaña's adversaries, however, accused him of malice. They said that he had harbored a grudge against the army because of an incident in his youth. A story gained currency, and persists today, that Manuel Azaña was expelled as a cadet from the Toledo Alcázar (military academy) on account of "unnatural practices." Even recently, I have heard this tale from the lips of several Spaniards old enough to have lived through the Republic—Spaniards both inside and outside Spain—and I have seen more than one reference to it in print (e.g., see S. F. A. Coles's *Franco of Spain*, p. 134, published in 1956); but until someone can prove to the contrary, there is no concrete evidence that would indicate Azaña's having enrolled in any military academy at any time in his life, Kluckhohn's *New York Times* article ("he studied in the military academy") notwithstanding.

As a result of traditional featherbedding, plus the effect of surplus personnel from the then-recent colonial wars in Spanish Morocco, the army was unrealistically top-heavy with officers. There was one officer for every six men. Azaña met the problem headlong with his typical bulldozing methods. The Minister of War suddenly found himself accused of persecution by some of the very same generals, including Franco, who were to lead the rebellion in 1936. Able to sway groups, even multitudes, with his oratory, Azaña was undiplomatic in some of his personal relationships, particularly when the vested interests of others conflicted with execution of the principles in which he believed. He was somewhat lacking in what the Spaniards call *don de gentes*, or winning ways. In no way was his political non-professionalism more evident than in the rash imposition of his own convictions, honest as they were, without regard for personalities, circumstances, or conse-quences. The army needed reform; that was obvious. Azaña insisted on a clean sweep all at once, the same course he had followed in the question of state dominated by church. In both cases, what he did was as risky as the way in which he did it.

The most significant of Azaña's numerous military reforms was the unprecedented *Ley de Retiros* (Deactivation Law), whereby more than twenty-one thousand officers were given the choice of pledging their loyalty to the Republic or of resigning. The fact that about half (Azaña said ten thousand) chose to resign was not due exclusively to their insecurity under the still-unannounced military policy pertaining to the organization of commands and units. Neither was it due to any widespread fear of general reprisal for the suppressive role of this same army during the years of dictatorship, because a considerable number of the officer corps had adopted a liberal bent by 1931, a condition evidenced by the fact that the army had not interfered with the decla-ration of the Republic, as it might have done. Rather, many officers were tempted to retire and disappear from the scene because Azaña's generosity allowed them to do so *on full pay,* and with retention of their uniforms and titles, even their arms. Despite this inducement, if the Minister of War had been able to organize and equip his divisions and to announce assignments first, perhaps more trusted officers would have remained, knowing what the future held and receiving proper recognition for their loyalty. Thus, perhaps the total result, which saw the army reduced from sixteen divisions to eight and the personnel budget lowered correspondingly, might have been more qualitative than quantitative. Instead of ridding the army of enemies of the Republic, the decree allowed many anti-Republicans to conspire all the better in comfortable retirement, while enough irreconcilables of questionable enthusiasm for the Republic—martinets like Francisco Franco, Emilio Mola, and Manuel Goded, who would have remained under any circumstances—not only stayed on active duty and signed the oath which they were to break in 1936, but even received key commands. One wonders why Azaña did not proceed more cautiously and perhaps select his own corps of officers, especially the highest ones, instead of resolving the matter bureaucratically and trusting to luck. Here, right here, was formed the nucleus of the hostile army that revolted in the summer of 1936 under the leadership of its officers, only a handful of whom remained loyal to the government or, for other reasons, refused to revolt.

The majority of the *Guardia Civil* (the national police force) also declared for Franco in 1936. Always feared, particularly in the rural areas, the Civil Guard had been retained practically without reorganization from the days of the monarchy and dictatorship. This was Azaña's second error. The brutality and ignorance of those men who wore the three-cornered hat had no place in a modern republic. A more elite security corps, the *Guardias de Asalto* or Assault Guards, was formed later; still the *Guardia Civil* remained in all its arrogant glory. Little by little, one begins to compare the fate of the Spanish Republic with that of the German Weimar Republic. Surely the German example had not taught the Spanish Republicans much. While the Spanish Republic was following the same precipitate course, the Weimar Republic was in the final stages of foundering, not so much because of Hitler himself, but because of the weaknesses in political structure that made his rise possible, including the conciliatory retention of most of the public servants, in and out of uniform, unweaned from the authoritarian *ancien régime*.

Azaña's failure to establish a loyal Republican army did not become gravely evident until it was too late. Most observers could see that at least he was striving for a positive program of military change, salutary, it was hoped, for the nation as well as the army. But the War Minister's transformations were mostly repressive in nature, and in Spain it is axiomatic that an army does not long remain politically uncommitted or neutral, especially when it is the same army from a previous regime of privilege. Prior to the Azaña reforms, an army officer enjoyed numerous special advantages in matters of legal position, tax rate, travel on common carriers, and other fringe benefits which he took for granted as part of the privilege of his caste. Azaña's aim in eliminating or reducing those privileges was to make the army officer like any other man in that "democratic Republic of workers."

Defending the old order, General Emilio Mola Vidal wrote a book that he published in 1934 after the Right wing had gained control of the government. This is the same General Mola whose four columns converged on Madrid in the autumn of 1936 and whose fifth column (as he invented the term) was inside the city ready to fight from within. Entitled *El pasado, Azaña y el porvenir* (The Past, Azaña, and the Future), the book was republished in 1940 as part of Mola's *Obras completas*. Spokesman of an army accustomed to intervention in the civil and political life of the nation, Mola, on page 29 of the 1934 edition, maintains that "militarism, where it exists, constitutes in itself a society which develops a civilization, that is, a morality. The end product of this morality is the exaltation of the fatherland by means of a simple system: war. This system may not be righteous and it may not even be in accord with contemporary philosophical theories; but there is not the least doubt that it is the system of natural law: the right of might, practiced by mankind since the early tribal era up to the present epoch of nations and empires, in which democratic doctrines are now in decline." Mola is speaking, but it could have been Hitler. The General goes on to prove that (unfortunately, he says) there is no militarism in Spain because there is no national mission or ambition. *Ergo* Azaña's treatment of the army was unjustified! After attacking Azaña's anti-militarism (pp. 158-59), on a later page (275) Mola affirms that war is a "natural phenomenon" and an ineradicable "biological necessity." Article 6 of the Constitution is therefore "above the laws of the Universe [with a capital *U*]."

These are the early manifestations of Spanish fascism, the Falange having been founded in October, 1933, with such pseudo-Nietzschean ideas of extreme nationalism imported from Italy and Germany. In Spain, where writers can become ministers of state, generals of the army can become writers. Such was Mola, national police chief under the Monarchy, and destined to head the clandestine *Unión Militar Española* (Spanish Military Union), founded in 1934. If Azaña clipped the wings of the officer class, the U.M.E. in alliance with the Fascists helped it to fly again. Besides the support and tutelage of the Fascists, the U.M.E. counted on the collaboration of numerous retired officers who, having retained their uniforms, could still march in parades, attend official functions, and provoke incidents that tended to implicate loyal elements of the army.

There is no doubt that Azaña improved the efficiency and technical organization of the army. It is said that both the discipline of the troops and the modernization of equipment were noticeably improved when the new Minister of War reviewed his first big parade under the Republic. But politically the army remained less a threat to aggressor nations than to its own government, and in October of 1934 those same Spanish public servants in uniform were to arrest unjustly and hold prisoner their ex-Minister of War.

Speech of December 17, 1931, in the Cortes

"I have always maintained that unanimity is a fastidious thing, and that a government without opposition cannot last: because the greatest cause of corruption and disintegration of a majority is precisely the lack of opposition."

Azaña remained imperturbable before a quarreling parliament and restive nation so long as the Constitution and law were respected. His often-reiterated "It does not interest me" (no me interesa) can easily be interpreted as unconcern or egotism, but the utterance is more likely a calculated pose of aloofness to instill respect for the law and to encourage free play of democratic processes. "No me interesa" means "I don't like it, and I disagree with it, but I don't interfere with it, because it is legal."

Speech of January 21, 1932, in the Cortes

Incidents of public disorder engendered this speech. Aside from Azaña's condemnation of their destructive violence, his "no me interesa" attitude is apparent: "It does not frighten me that there are strikes, and in the case of a legal and peaceful strike I cross my arms, as long as order remains undisturbed, because it is a lawfully recognized right."

" . . . the law is inexorable and impassive."

" . . . extreme respect for the Republic and for its institutions."

Azaña invokes the words *lícito, legítimo, ley, disciplina,* and *Constitución* with the frequency and force of hammer blows in his speeches, just as he had done with very nearly the same political and legal vocabulary in *La corona.*

Speech of February 12, 1932, in the Cortes

This is a lively harangue with numerous angry interruptions by the deputies. It concerns the suspension of newspapers under invocation of the *Ley de Defensa.* In defense of the action taken, Azaña affirms that "everybody can say what he likes, as long as he does not attack the Republic in its acts defined by law."

Speech of March 9, 1932, in the Cortes

More on the same topic.

"It is inexact to say that the *Ley de Defensa de la República* has been applied discriminatorily to the press." Accused of being excessively legalistic and rigid, Azaña replies: "This is the criterion with which we govern, gentlemen of parliament: a strict defense of the political concept of general freedom, and a repression, of a degree suitable to the need, always responsible to and in accordance with the exigencies of the situation, every time that someone or something infringes upon the guarantees of freedom of the nation as a whole."

"*No nos interesa.*"

Speech of March 10, 1932, in the Cortes

On the budget of the armed forces.

" . . . without military aviation we are absolutely defenseless, because the other nations, with whom Spain could be in conflict, have powerful military aviation . . . . "

" . . . Spain is a peaceful country . . . we have said so in the Constitution . . . but nobody is master of his own peace . . . . "

Speech of March 28, 1932, to the Republican Action Party

In this talk, entitled "The Republic as a Form of National Life," Azaña applies a paradox of traditionalism both to himself and to the Republic. "Some would be surprised," he says, "if I stated categorically that I am the most traditionalist Spaniard in the Peninsula." And of the Republic he asserts that "despite appearances, the present Republic is the form most deeply rooted in Spanish tradition."

"We are democrats, and because we are, we have a secure policy: the law. The law! . . . one governs with the law, with Parliament, and a democracy disciplines itself by means of the law . . . . "

Speech of March 29, 1932, in the Cortes

Speaking on a policy for the Spanish protectorate in Morocco, which somewhere in his memoirs he rightly recognized to be the Achilles' heel of the Republic, Azaña summarizes what has been accomplished so far in the rehabilitation of Morocco. Graft and sinecures have been reduced, along with the budget and the size of the foreign legion. His plan is to send only volunteer soldiers to Morocco and to colonize the territory by offering homestead lands. He would clean up and build up Morocco, civilize it with schools and sanitation.

Speech of April 4, 1932, at a Republican Banquet in Valencia

" . . . the Republic has come forever, forevermore. And I should tell you moreover . . . that no danger threatens the Republic, none, of any kind possible."

" . . . *no me interesa.*"

111

Again he offers a reminder that the Republic does not make men happy; what it makes them is, simply, men.

Speech of May 27, 1932, in the Cortes

Here is the first of Azaña's famous series of speeches championing the Catalonian Statute for regional autonomy, a three-hour oration that runs sixty-five printed pages until he reaches the last words of the brilliant final synthesis. More than a speech, it is a historical treatise on the long-standing Catalonian problem, especially insofar as the problem is related to its counterpart of stubborn Castilian centralism. Solve it now, is his message. He shows how the question is analogous to the one of Spanish colonialism. "We ended a war in Cuba with the promise of autonomy. It was not fulfilled. A Spanish Parliament rejected the autonomous reform that Don Antonio Maura brought for Cuba, and it precipitated another war. We had the opportunity to compromise and we refused; we preferred to face a war with the United States; and the few men who told the truth then to the Spanish people, among them a venerable statesman and a young writer who at that time was beginning his career and who is sitting here, Don Miguel de Unamuno, were reprehended as bad Spaniards, traitors, and filibusters."

At the time that Azaña was speaking, the Cortes was empowered by the Constitution to grant regional autonomy to any region which both qualified for it and wanted it. Certain obstacles, like the question of education and its linguistic ramifications (Catalonian versus the Castilian language), had to be cleared by amendments before the Statute was finally approved by a vote of 314 to 24 on September 9, 1932. Azaña had rammed another bill through the Cortes, though the vote itself did not reflect the intensity of the battle, from which Azaña

112

emerged as the most vigorous of all the proponents of Catalonian autonomy.

The new hero of Catalonia, Azaña himself, journeyed to Barcelona a few weeks later to present the Statute formally and to receive the homage of an immense crowd, to whom he addressed on September 26, 1932, a short but passionate speech from the balcony of the Generalidad (Catalonian Parliament) on the Plaza de la República. "A people to whom justice is done," he said, "remains marvelously in bondage to the just deed." After so many decades, the hopes of the Catalonians seemed finally to be realized. But the Catalonians did not "remain marvelously in bondage to the just deed"; so jealous of their freedom, they did not learn how to keep their house in order.

Speech of June 22, 1932, at the Republican Action Center in Madrid

When has there ever been a revolution which permits such a heap of liberties that at times they appear to be libertinism? Azaña replies with familiar words: "That's the way we Spanish Republicans are . . . . the Republic is immortal. . . . the Republic has come to Spain forever."

"He who does not have a sporting spirit cannot govern . . . . "

Speech of June 28, 1932, in the Cortes

This is about the military incident at Carabanchel (see above, page 90) involving a public verbal clash of loyalties among high-ranking army officers. Azaña describes what took place. Ever conciliatory in his attitude toward rebellious officers, he reaffirms the loyalty of the army: "For the army I have nothing but praise; I can only extol their moral and spiritual situation. The army, in its great majority, is proper, is loyal to the institutions, fulfills its professional duty. . . . the army is composed of good Spanish citizens . . . . "

Speech of July 19, 1932, in the Cortes

As his memoirs reveal, Azaña was not really so naïve about the loyalty of the army as his speeches during 1932-36 would suggest. What he did was always to adopt in public an attitude of confidence in the institutions of the Republic, in order to prevent the spread of discontent and mistrust.

The fears of a military dictatorship were vocalized on the floor of the Cortes as early as 1932. In the present speech, Azaña attempts to neutralize some of Lerroux's apprehensions. This kind of talk, says Azaña, succeeds only in weakening military morale and in alarming the nation unduly. "There is talk about a military dictatorship as a possible reaction to a supposed dictatorship of the proletariat and of the Socialist party . . . . " Ostensibly Azaña is not at all alarmed. His unflagging constitutionality would allow all things within the limits of the Constitution, including its protection of what he knew to be anti-Constitutional elements and causes. "Repeatedly I have said that nothing is more abhorrent in a parliament than unanimity . . . . "

Speech of August 10, 1932, in the Cortes

Here is Azaña's account of General Sanjurjo's attempted military rebellion in Seville. The uprising is suppressed; there is no reason for alarm.

Sanjurjo's conspiracy had included an attempt to assassinate Azaña. Azaña had learned of the plot but, characteristically, maintained his aplomb. When Sanjurjo made his move in Seville, monarchists

114

attacked the Central Post Office and the Ministry of War in Madrid. With gunfire visible and audible on all sides, Azaña could be seen at his balcony in the Ministry, where he tranquilly puffed on cigarettes until the rioters were disarmed. Sentenced to death, Sanjurjo was reprieved by Azaña and sent to jail. Later pardoned, Sanjurjo helped to plot the revolt of July, 1936.

Speech of August 11, 1932, in the Cortes

More on Sanjurjo's abortive rebellion. As in the speech of the previous day, Azaña rationalizes that this event has been "most profitable" for the Republic because, since it failed, it proves the "strong moral health of Republican institutions." He continues: "I hold the conviction that in view of what occurred, with the lesson received and with the measures that the Government and Parliament are going to adopt, events like these will never happen again."

Speech of August 18, 1932, in the Cortes

Prime Minister Azaña was less worried, at least publicly, about the army than about the Jesuits and the great landowners. The speech of August 18, 1932, is the first of his series of speeches on the expropriation of property from conspirators against the Republic. He would deprive of their economic means all those who have declared themselves against the Republic. It is not, he says, a problem that should be dropped in the lap of some judge; rather, it is one of which the Constitution will allow solution by legislation of the Cortes. Patient and outwardly optimistic about the army, Azaña takes a different position—either we finish them or they will finish us—as he returns to what is fundamentally the religious question.

Speech of September 7, 1932, in the Cortes

Subject: the seizure of the assets of the Company of Jesus, who had been defensively manipulating their financial empire ever since the Constitution became effective. By now, Azaña's attitude toward the power of the church and its composite elements is well known, but here he unveils for the first time his innermost motives for bridling the activities of the church. Azaña's words are revealing, for they transcend the simple ideal of citizenship in the church-separated state. When Azaña refuses to admit any difference between his action as a man of letters and his sentiments as a writer, he addresses the following remark to Ossorio, with whom he had more than one verbal bout in the Cortes: "It is an error, Mr. Ossorio, because one cannot establish in the spirit of a man such a division and compartmentization; that crisis of religious conscience and Spanish conscience, which you have had the elegant courtesy to read, is the origin of all the vigor of my political action . . . and my trip through the garden [*El jardín de los frailes*], which furthermore you honor by mentioning here, is how I have acquired the unbreakable resolution that, *so far as it is within my power, no Spaniard will come to find himself in a situation analogous to the one in which I found myself* [italics mine]." Even though the deprivation of the church's traditional position in education was a question of principle within Azaña's concept of citizenship, even though it was simply a matter of applying the Constitution, which decreed the dissolution of the Jesuits, we know now the depth of Azaña's resentment.

Perhaps it is time to mention a little-known circumstance in the personal life of Manuel Azaña. A few of the apologists for the Franco regime have maintained that the Second Spanish Republic was one big Masonic plot, that Freemasonry controlled the revolutionary aspects of the Republic through its affiliates highly placed in the groups and parties of the Left, that Freemasonry cemented the Popular Front electoral bloc of 1936, and that Freemasonry was governing the country on the day when the Spanish Civil War began—all of which is vast exaggeration. One of these apologists is Eduardo Comín Colomer, among whose books is one entitled *Historia secreta de la Segunda República* (in two volumes, Madrid, 1954-55), which is a kind of "Who Was Who" in Spanish Freemasonry during the Republic. On page 42 of Volume I, it is claimed that on March 5, 1932, Manuel Azaña was initiated into Masonry and the "Matritense" Masonic Lodge, located at Calle del Príncipe 12, in Madrid. It is further affirmed (I, 208) that owing to Azaña's eminent position in government at that time, his secret initiation presented a new opportunity for a long-standing project of Spanish Freemasonry: Iberian union, a form of conspiracy against Portugal.

Freemasonry in Spain never has amounted to much, because, for one reason, as Gironella observed in his note to the American translation of his *The Cypresses Believe in God,* "certain constants of the Spanish temperament operate under any circumstances. A Spanish Freemason is not an international Freemason. A Spanish Communist is not even an orthodox Communist. In every instance what is characteristic is a tendency toward the instinctive, toward the individualistic, and toward the anarchic." Even in a land where Freemasonry might be considered a quasi-revolutionary activity, equivalent to clandestine anti-Catholicism, and a role quite different from its devolvement in the U.S.A. into a kind of social organization, it is difficult to believe that the proud individualist, scoffer, skeptic, and intellectual, Azaña, had capitulated to secret signs, grips, and rites, even though one such as he might have subscribed to the Masonic code of tolerance, freedom, and obedience to civil authority.

Recently when the opportunity presented itself, I asked several prominent Republicans-in-exile whether they knew anything about Azaña's having been a Mason. The reply was that, though they did not know, they doubted it very much. Later I learned on good authority that it is true, Azaña did become a Mason, although I cannot verify the date or place of initiation given by Comín Colomer. When I put the same question to Azaña's widow in Mexico City, her answer was no. Her reply seemed genuine enough; she really did not know. It is, nevertheless, a fact that Azaña was initiated but, because of inactivity, did not attain any grades beyond the initial one. He joined probably at the urging of his friends; and a man like him, particularly at the age of fifty-two (if Comín Colomer's date of initiation is correct), was not going to find his already well-defined ideology altered or reformed by the rites of Masonry.

Those in Spain who accuse Azaña of being a Mason, as though it were a criminal charge (which it is now in Spain), forget one important fact: no atheist can be made a Mason. To this extent, the Francoist writers have crossed their purposes with inconsistency when they call the leaders of the Republic both godless and Masonic.

Speech of September 9, 1932, in the Cortes

Having concluded his arguments with respect to the Jesuit empire in Spain, in this speech Azaña sets his sights on agricultural reform that would expropriate lands from the aristocracy.

Azaña's concept of the whole "revolution," as he calls it, is that it is a "work of reconstruction of Spanish society." The old must be torn down before the new can be built. "Is it possible to adopt a reform measure, one of basic reformation of the economic order, without a number of people or a social class being hurt, even though it may not be our prime intention to hurt them, and another social class being favored by the reform or profiting from it?" Such is Azaña's reply to Ossorio's charge of persecution of a social class. "So someone suffers in the fray! What am I going to do about it, sir! We too have suffered [here a prolonged ovation interrupts Azaña's words] when we were governed tyrannically; and, the laborer as well as the intellectual and the professional man, we have been censured and abused in our legal rights and in our personal lives, and I have yet to hear a voice be raised in defense of our dignity as Spaniards and our freedom as men; I have not heard one, and I deplore the fact that now the voices which are heard here are to defend the lands of a duke or of a marquis." This appeal for support brought down the house with a standing ovation from a majority of the deputies.

Speech of September 30, 1932, in Santander

Four days after the triumphant address of September 26, 1932, in Barcelona (see page 113), when Azaña formally delivered the Catalonian Statute of Autonomy, he journeyed over to Santander to speak on what the Spanish embassy in Mexico entitled *Presente y futuro de la República Española* (Present and Future of the Spanish Republic) when the following December it published the speech in monograph form for distribution in Mexico. At that time the Republic's ambassador to Mexico, Julio Alvarez del Vayo, was a supporter of Azaña. Alvarez del Vayo wanted to tell Mexicans about the Azaña government and to publicize the Republic's accomplishments as well as its plans for the future. Though Alvarez del Vayo and Azaña later disagreed on the conduct of Republican affairs during the Civil War, the former always openly admired Azaña's intellectual qualities, and says so in his post-Civil War books.

Speaking candidly on the army, Azaña declares that "Spain is not prepared to defend herself from foreign aggression." He summarizes the work of the Cortes on military reform, the Catalonian Statute, the Agrarian Law, the religious question, the budget, public education, public works, etc.; and he speaks of the political parties. He tells how he and his party, although aligned with the Socialists, are not Socialists in the revolutionary sense of the word; rather that he and they stand for "the most elementary things of social justice, which no republican can nor should refuse to vote for and establish."

When Azaña's enemies caricatured him as cold, solitary, unapproachable, a constantly disgusted misanthrope, their reaction is partially traceable to one of his favorite remarks, "I don't have any friends," whose meaning can be misinterpreted out of context—like "Spain has ceased to be Catholic." In this speech Azaña explains himself well: "The Republican Action party never will be a party of friends, and much less a party of Mr. Azaña's friends. . . . The Head of the Government [i. e., Azaña himself], in politics, does not have friends nor does he want them. . . . Nobody can hope for anything from me personally, neither within the party nor out of it, absolutely nothing . . . . " That was true: Azaña was incorruptible; but he did allow himself, perhaps unknowingly, to be surrounded with sycophants.

"No me interesa."

Speech of November 14, 1932, in Valladolid

"And this dryness and this coldness of Castilians, which so much resemble mine, this dryness and coldness of the Castilians on the surface, are political virtues. I attribute them to another political virtue, to a civic virtue: decorum."

Speech of November 14, 1932, to Military Personnel of the Valladolid Garrison

This is really a group of three speeches, the first one addressed to the officers. None of the speeches on this day brought forth the accustomed clamorous applause. It was a rather solemn occasion.

With words unmistakably directed to the high-ranking officers, Azaña admonishes the uniformed men that they have two roles to perform: the role of Spanish citizen as well as that of professional soldier. After he has reminded the officers pointedly that the military is no longer "a privileged class above the rest of the citizens," he contrasts this concept with the one of the past, when on occasions of national crisis the army had seen fit to act on its own authority and to intervene in affairs of state. "This is what you as military men must avoid." Clearly it is an admonition. But then Azaña removes the sting from the expression "privileged class" by applying the expression antithetically: "privileged class" in that their duty and responsibility are greater than those of Spanish civilians. This military duty, he affirms, is silent obedience to the legitimate national will, and the sole function of the military is to defend Spain from foreign attack upon her independence and liberty. The Republic, he concludes, is counting on the loyalty of its military officers. It is a curious speech: warm on the surface, but with its cold core. Plainly it is an exhortation to the higher ranks, who could surely interpret his words properly, not to do what they actually did in 1936—rebel.

That day Azaña spoke also to the noncommissioned officers. With less-calculated words, he pointed out to the men the new ways open to personal advancement through merit, while at the same time he invoked citizenship, discipline, and service to the Republic.

Speeches of February 2, 3, 23, 24, and March 2, 3, 7, 16, in the Cortes

Early in 1933 there had been anarchist riots in the east and southeast—strikes, land seizure, minor insurrections of every kind which culminated on January 11, 1933, in a violent incident at the town of Casas Viejas in the province of Cádiz, where Assault Guards joined Civil Guards in a pitched battle against anarcho-syndicalists. A number of lives had been lost on both sides, and the Azaña government was accused of brutality in having ordered an execution of anarchist prisoners. Though Azaña denied the charges vehemently, the wide publicity given to the episode plunged his cabinet into a state of disrepute of which Lerroux and the Right wing made great capital. In a speech to the Cortes on February 2, Azaña expounded his government's position in the matter of public disorder. Then the next day, in reply to accusations of Lerroux, Azaña defined and redefined obsessively his own concept of constitutionality and reaffirmed that he personally was neither authoritarian nor ambitious of power. The incessant and mostly unjust attacks upon Azaña and his party piqued his indignation more than usual. On February 23, and still again on February 24 midst angry remarks from the floor, Azaña continued to asseverate to the Cortes that he had not—as he had been accused—withheld information on the Casas Viejas incident. In additional speeches of March 2, 3, 7, and 16, to the Cortes, Azaña was still debating the Casas Viejas affair, from which his government never regained its former prestige. In his speech of March 2 Azaña said: "I do not have the slightest pretention to any kind of political grandeur; I am not even a statesman, nor have I ever said that I am, nor do I aspire to be one . . . . "

Speech of April 9, 1933, in the Bull Ring of Bilbao

"Don't believe in phantoms," says Azaña, assuring his audience that there is absolutely nothing to worry about from outside the Republican camp. But even if there were trouble, he is sure that the Spanish people would not let themselves be subjugated again.

Speech of April 26, 1933, in the Cortes

Azaña states positively that he is neither a Marxist nor a Socialist. He tries always to maintain his equanimity, he claims, because "it is the only defense that a man of government has: not to lose his good humor."

Speech of October 2, 1933, in the Cortes

Azaña is out as Prime Minister, having resigned in September. Lerroux has formed a new government, which appears before the Cortes on this day. Every bench is taken. Azaña is sitting in the center, among the deputies of his Republican Action party for the first time. Lerroux and his new government enter. Mildly polite applause greets them as they seat themselves at the *banco azul.* Lerroux reads a speech in which he promises to restore law and order. When the speech is over, Indalecio Prieto rises to challenge the new government. Then Azaña speaks, for the first time as a plain deputy. In words taut with emotion, Azaña announces his intention to play politics as soon as he has liquidated his responsibilities as outgoing Prime Minister. He swears he has kept his promise never to engage in politics during the more than two years that he has presided over the government. Reminiscing, Azaña reveals that his underlying motivation as Head of the Government has been "the ineffable pleasure of creating things," whose dynamics he likens to the work of an artist or

123

artisan. It is a moving speech, one of Azaña's best. Lerroux withholds his counterfire until the next day.

Speech of October 3, 1933, in the Cortes

Lerroux has made a speech of personal attack on Azaña, a fusillade under which a lesser man than Azaña might either have squirmed with embarrassment or seethed with rage. Instead, Azaña sat imperturbably and afterward rose to defend himself with vigorous, but measured, words. Azaña had hoped for better treatment, he says, on the occasion of the last session of the Constituent Parliament. Here is the essence of Azaña's reply to the malicious attack: "But do you think you annoy me? No, nobody annoys me, Mr. Lerroux, for two reasons: in the first place, because at bottom I have the asceticism of my race; for many, many years I have ceased to worry about all the things of life, and, since I have experienced almost all of them, they leave me absolutely indifferent; in the second place, because I have a devilish pride, and nobody annoys a proud man."

The Lerroux government was short-lived. The Cortes was dissolved, and new elections were set for November 19.

Speech of October 16, 1933, to the Republican Action Party, in Madrid

"When I presided over the government, an observation was often made concerning me. It was said that when I was Prime Minister I resorted too much, I conceded too much, to intelligence, to knowledge, to the comprehension of things." This may be true, he admits, but he is proud of it.

Azaña speaks of the twofold aspect of the world crisis: the economic crisis and the crisis of the individual in relation to his state. As he takes up the theme of Spain's relationship to other European nations, one anticipates hearing some concrete proposal, but he loses himself in familiar platitudes on civilization, human life, liberty, civic obligation, moral transformation, the sporting spirit of politics, the Spanish people, and universal civilization. On the danger of a revolt within the Spanish Republic, Azaña reasons: "The Republic can go under in only three ways, which are already enough [laughter]: either by an act of force through violent seizure of the means of power, or by a soft and stealthy takeover of institutions infiltrated with a distorted republican spirit, or by an electoral defeat. Of the first way, there is no fear at all . . . . "

On October 29, 1933, scarcely two weeks after Azaña had assured his party that there was no danger of a revolt within Spain, the Falange was founded in Madrid by José Antonio Primo de Rivera, son of the deceased dictator of the twenties. Fascism, which had imposed itself on Italy and Germany, had finally come to Spain. Only seven months previously, the German Weimar Republic had perished with the voting of the "Enabling Act" on March 24, 1933, a date which, for practical purposes, marked the "legal" beginning of Hitler's dictatorial power to organize his Third Reich.

What is fascism and why did it inevitably come to Spain? Although the fanatical nationalism known as fascism bore its own type of chaos, it had gained its various footholds in Europe as the supposed solution to another kind of chaos in which unemployment and the power of organized labor were challenging the authority of the state and the respect for law. Put simply, and the observation is unoriginal, fascism is the last stand of capitalism. As such, fascism is the enemy of the proletariat, whether or not the rebellious working class has embraced communism as its political vehicle of opposition to the bourgeoisie and the aristocracy. It did not matter, therefore, that in 1933 the apparent political strength of communism in Spain was practically nil. What did matter was that the guarantees of the Republic had allowed the pendulum of power to swing to the Left, after centuries of oppression from the extreme Right. The demands of the workers began to exceed good sense; incessant major strikes paralyzed the Spanish economy and by 1936 had put the Republic in mortal danger. Though initially unsuccessful, more because of the determination of the proletariat than because of governmental countermeasures, the military uprising of 1936 was to be the coup de grâce for the suffering Republic.

Proletarian extremism, protected by the constitutionality and folded arms of super-democrats like Azaña, and even encouraged by less moderate leaders than he, had created conditions whereby free enterprise was scarcely possible. Here are a few examples taken from the personal observations of the well-known writer Pío Baroja, who a few years later was to declare for Franco:[2]

> Eight or ten years ago there were in Madrid some twenty publishing houses; of these more than fifteen were small businesses, and only three or four were large ones. Because of the demands made by the workers, with the backing of the Government, for higher wages, shorter working hours, and the hiring of extra printers, all but two or three of the publishing houses have had to shut down. As a result authors, editors, and printers have been left destitute. The logical procedure would be to reckon an industry's capacity first, and then make demands accordingly.
>
> In the construction field the demands of the National Confederation of Workers were comical: a forty hour week; a minimum wage of 16 pesetas ($2.18) a day for peon and mason; if the worker's wife became ill, or bore a child, the employer had to shoulder the expenses; if the worker happened to be young and was drafted into the army, the employer had to continue to pay him half his wages; rheumatism and

[2] The excerpts are taken from an article published by Baroja in *La Nación*, the Buenos Aires daily, and republished as "The Mistakes of the Spanish Republic" in *The Living Age*, January, 1937, pp. 422-27.

126

similar ailments were to be considered as occupational diseases for which the employer was to pay compensation. Besides all this, the employer was compelled to pay for the upkeep of asylums, schools and hospitals. They might as well have added that he was required to serve the worker his chocolate in bed, do his washing, and amuse the comrades' children!

The Popular Front sent workers to the farms and compelled the owners to pay them whether or not there was work for them to do. Many of the owners, seeing that they could not stand the strain, abandoned their land; then they were fined.

An attempt was made to establish Socialist doctrines in the villages, but without success. To the village where I spend the summer, Vera de Bidasoa, came a Socialist delegate from Pamplona, imposing restrictions. The shops were to be open only eight hours a day, and to close on Sundays. This regulation showed how ignorant the politicians were of the habits of the shopkeepers in these towns. The village shopkeeper's shop is also a part of his house. He eats and lives in his small establishment. To close his shop is to close his home. Furthermore, the people who live in the country districts are in the habit of going to the villages very early in the morning, and their shyness and distrustfulness make them dislike carrying on their business transactions in the presence of others; nor do they care to have witnesses when they exchange their dozen eggs or piece of lamb for wine, coffee, or sugar. The firmly established ways of the peasants cannot be changed by a decree or an order. Again, Sunday is the peasants' favorite day for shopping and bartering, and the only good day for the shopkeepers. I do not know if the delegate from Pamplona did or did not believe that his orders were going to be obeyed. At any rate, the shopkeepers of Vera de Bidasoa and of the nearby villages clung to their old-time customs.

Democratic socialism, like any other form of democratic political theory, is workable only if there is intelligent direction, voluntary restraint among the governed, and realistic goals. But in the 1930's the extremists among the Spanish Republicans preached a partly

Utopian, partly anarchistic, partly dictatorial but, above all, unattainable socialism for Spain. Take the case of Joaquín Maurín, for example, who in 1935 published a book[3] in which he called for an Iberian Union of Socialist Republics; speedy nationalization of everything—land, railroads, ships, industry, mines, banks; abolition of all debts; municipalization of transportation and warehouses; state monopoly of foreign trade; six-hour work day (while at the same time quadrupling production!); arming of all workers (including professional people); in short, an armed dictatorship of a theoretically democratic but largely anarchistic proletariat.

The success of any democratic process requires, most of all, patience; but the Spanish worker of the 1930's was aflame with impatience. So varied and individualized are Spaniards' concepts of freedom and patriotism, so resistant are Spaniards to collective, long-range political goals, that one could scarcely expect them to create a workable socialist state without first disciplining themselves to the moderate reforms of a popular government. Because too few men of the ilk of Manuel Azaña could put country above party, union, religion, profession, or economic position, democracy brought a new type of disorder to Spain while it tried to stamp out the old. The early Azaña government, instead of attempting to teach discipline, should perhaps have enforced it by means of Constitutional amendment, which, unlike the *Ley de Defensa*, might have reinforced the Constitution instead of abrogating its authority with discretionary powers that pleased nobody. The very fact that fascism gained a foothold points to a deterioration of the democratic process. The paradox is, however, that until the founding of the Falange, the Comintern and large segments of the "oppressed"

[3] *Hacia la segunda revolución* (Barcelona, n.d. [prologue signed April 14, 1935]). The same Joaquín Maurín gave the main address, "The Third Spanish Republic," to the Republicans in exile in New York on April 14, 1962, thirty-first anniversary of the advent of the Second Spanish Republic.

masses considered Azaña to be their enemy and referred to him as a Fascist: even on the floor of the Cortes he was practically accused of being a Fascist dictator. It cannot be emphasized too often that Azaña was always on middle ground, but that with the rise of fascism and the increasing opposition from the Right, he was forced either to shift to the Left or fade from the picture.

The rise of fascism in Spain was predicted by Leon Trotsky, the heretic from Moscow who wrote a series of amazingly prophetic pamphlets on the "revolution" in Spain. In one of these tracts (*The Spanish Revolution in Danger*), signed April 24, 1931, with the Republic only ten days old, Trotsky wrote that "the defeat of the Spanish revolution . . . will lead almost automatically to the establishment in Spain of *genuine* Fascism on the style of Mussolini." But there are some important differences between fascism as it developed in Spain and the fascism of Italy and Germany. First of all, we have already noted how Spaniards tend to replace the international characteristics of any institution with Spanish ones. Secondly, Spanish fascism, unlike the German and Italian prototypes, allied itself initially with the church (or vice versa), whose spiritual unity it recognized to be an essential factor in producing the strong nationalistic sentiment that was its goal in Spain. For the Spanish Fascists the church was a means to an end, and not an end in itself, as it could be said to have been for the Spanish traditionalists. Thirdly, Spanish fascism had no attainable worlds to conquer outside of Spain (with the possible exception of Gibraltar), which more than anything else explains the durability of Spanish fascism. Fourthly, Spanish fascism not only lacked a passionate leader as practical as Mussolini, or as fanatical as Hitler, but its writers like Giménez Caballero invented such nonsense ("Spain, the land chosen by God"; "the Spaniard was born to rule and not be a subject"; "the 'universal kingdom' of Spain"; "Don Juan, the saint of Spain who leads her 'mystically' "; "bullfighting, the rite of sacrifice and blood to purify our caste") that men like Azaña found it hard to take them seriously and perhaps thus underestimated the possibility of a Fascist revolt.

Speech of January 7, 1934, at the Bull Ring in Barcelona

Azaña is now playing politics, giving fighting speeches throughout the land. Now he is free to attack his enemies and to criticize the opposition government. He even claims to be a new man. He has already decided, it appears, to move more toward the Left. But there are some ideals he can never modify: "They have always reproached my policy of relying too heavily on reason, on the serenity of judgment. Yes; and I am not disposed to change my ways."

Speech of April 3, 1934, in Madrid, to the Constitutional Session of the Republican Left Party

In the national elections at the end of 1933, the parties of the Left lost decisively their majority in the Cortes. Azaña's archenemy Lerroux emerged as the new power and on December 16, 1933, headed a government which was to last until March 28, 1934. Azaña's own Republican Action party itself had lost twenty-five of its thirty seats in the Cortes. The Right wing, now in command, seemed determined to tear down the house that Azaña had built. Accordingly some of the Left-wing parties agreed to find a means to new strength through unity. It was decided to amalgamate Azaña's Republican Action group with the parties of Marcelino Domingo and Santiago Casares Quiroga to form a stronger fourth party.

Azaña had just been named president of this newly formed Republican Left (*Izquierda Republicana*) party, a party less to the Left than its name would indicate. Although he maintains he did not seek the post, this is his speech of acceptance and appreciation. "Today is born a new republican party, composed of three parties which have been dissolved and whose followers will surely be with us. We are born because general republican opinion has wished it thus." The new Azaña speaks with an air of false modesty. His partisan speeches do not ring so true as did his nonpolitical ones in the Cortes. But times have changed. With the Republic casting about in treacherous waters, pretense was a form of valor.

Speech of April 16, 1934, in Madrid, to the Young Republicans

Speaking to youth, Azaña declares that the future of the Republic depends upon young men who know how to do things well and who will not be discouraged easily by failures. Take his own case: the Republic is three years old and yet he must start anew. But he has learned something: that inflexibility of personal conviction in politics does not pay, because "public justification is necessary in politics, and I was unable to transmit either my own prescience or my own conviction to the millions of citizens who support the Republic . . . . One must be resigned!" Here, as he had done before, Azaña invokes the sporting spirit in politics: if the opposition gets one goal, we'll get five.

The sporting spirit is of course a democratic political ideal, but little more than lip service is paid to political fair play even in the most traditionally democratic countries. Yet Azaña, even the new Azaña, never let go of that ideal which he called the sporting spirit. His dedication to it left him ever vulnerable to the machinations of unscrupulous opponents; there was nothing sportsmanlike about the revolt of the army in 1936.

Speech of April 21, 1934, in Bilbao

This speech, entitled *Grandezas y miserias de la política* (The Grandeur and Misery of Politics), is one of Azaña's best known, deservedly so. The scholarly and philosophical discussion of democracy as a concept of government, together with an illuminating commentary on the nature and origin of revolutions, makes this speech a classic Azaña raises the question—in the most significant part of the speech—whether a person eminent in one of the arts can serve actively and successfully in the political life of his country. He concludes that politics, like art or love, is not a profession, but instead a faculty. Eloquence is helpful, but there have been a lot of eloquent fools. "Of a man who does not feel a thrill face to face with a beautiful woman, we can say without calumny that he does not have the erotic faculty; and of a man who does not feel emotion when he is faced with a political matter, however well he may speak, we can say that he does not have the political faculty. Political emotion is the sign of the vocation, and the vocation is the sign of the aptitude. . . . At the bottom of all great political emotion there is always a little bit of quixotism . . . . " This political emotion must include a historical sense as well as a sensitivity to people, opinions, and things of the moment—to realities. What must the politician avoid most? Loss of his ingenuousness and his spontaneity through exaggeration of either the qualities or defects which the masses attribute to him. What is Spain's greatest ill? According to Azaña, it is lack of moral vigor: weakness of civic spirit.

Burdened with the collective Spanish conscience that he had imposed upon himself, disheartened by the electoral defeat of late 1933, exhausted from his previous duties as Head of the Government and present responsibilities as head of the new Republican Left party, pressed constantly to deliver speeches, Manuel Azaña needed a respite. Having learned to appreciate the benefits, real or imagined, of thermal baths, he spent much of the summer of 1934 in Catalonia, in and around the spa of Sant Hilari (San Hilario) in Gerona. He returned there again in the summer of 1935, after a tumultuous year between summers.

Trouble had been fomenting in Catalonia ever since the national electoral victory of the Right wing at the end of 1933. All of Spain, in fact, was smoldering with the same fundamental conflict between labor and management, between peasants and landlords, a struggle intensified by the electoral reversal from Left-wing domination. General strikes and worker violence were met with governmental repression and brutal police methods. At the same time, the politicians were quarreling among themselves. In the Basque provinces, which still envied Catalonia its Statute of Autonomy, municipal legislation sometimes conflicted with national laws, and heads of local government were imprisoned or they resigned in protest against the Cortes' failure to act on the Basque Statute. Because the national agrarian laws were left unenforced, the Catalonian Parliament passed its own agricultural law, declared illegal by the national Tribunal of Constitutional Guarantees. Then the Basque and Catalonian deputies strode out of the Cortes, and Luis Companys promulgated the law anyhow, despite the trusteeship of Republican authority in Catalonia inherent in his office as President of the Catalonian government. Separatist sentiment was burning everywhere. In Catalonia, Companys fanned the flame with passionate speeches, while Largo Caballero preached proletarian revolution to his Socialist workers. Although Manuel Azaña, the voice of moderation, disapproved of any organized rebellion that might lead to an overthrow of the government, and privately counseled the leaders of the Left against such activities, he declared publicly that the Left-wing Catalonians were the only remaining republican force in Spain. According to law, the national Cortes met on October 1, 1934. The cabinet promptly fell, an event which in the popular mind presaged a possible Fascist sabotage of the Republic. The large cities suffered another general strike, which turned out to be the first phase of the Left's own armed rebellion that led to two months of martial law in Spain. Even one who is so anti-Franco as Salvador de Madariaga claims that the rebellion of 1934 stripped the Left of every shred of moral authority to condemn the military revolt of 1936.[4] Maybe he is right, but in 1934 the law ultimately prevailed whereas, without means of enforcement, it did not and could not prevail in 1936.

In Madrid the conflagration was promptly extinguished and Largo Caballero was jailed. In Asturias, largely in the city of Oviedo, a short-lived but full-scale civil war ensued. The Spanish army was sent to crush thousands of miners, who used their ample quantities of small arms and huge stores of dynamite to blow up the University when defeat became imminent. The workers, who had set up a local prole-tarian dictatorship, committed as many atrocities as did their con-querors. It was a nasty situation, more than a thousand killed and another several thousand casualties, the kind of violence that Azaña abhorred. In Catalonia, Companys had proclaimed a *de facto* Cata-lonian state as part of a Spanish Federal Republic. At the same time he publicly invited anti-Fascist leaders to establish in Barcelona a pro-visional national government. This invitation led to the unjust impli-cation of Azaña in that abortive Barcelona separatist rebellion, which

---

[4] Salvador de Madariaga, *Spain: A Modern History* (New York, 1958; latest revision), p. 435. Alejandro Lerroux, also writing in exile, made the same observation on page 321 of his book *La pequeña historia. España 1930-36* (Buenos Aires, 1945).

saw Companys jailed on October 7 and the Catalonian Statute suspended. Even the old rival Lerroux knew that, come what may, Azaña was no separatist.

On September 26, 1934, Jaime Carner Roméu, a rich and honest Catalonian who had been Finance Minister in Azaña's government, died of cancer in Barcelona. An industrialist himself, Carner had been an opponent of the famous and infamous millionaire Juan March.[5] Together with Indalecio Prieto and Fernando de los Ríos, Azaña went to Barcelona by train to attend Carner's funeral and was still in Barcelona when the fighting commenced on October 6. Without evidence, or even a specific charge, the police arrested Azaña at the home of a friend. As a maximum-security measure, ridiculous in itself, Azaña was kept incommunicado on one and another warship in the Barcelona harbor. Early in the evening of October 9 his "detention" was first announced over the radio in Spain. Azaña's wife Dolores and her brother Cipriano Rivas Cherif took a train to Barcelona. Scarcely had they installed themselves at a hotel when the police came to search Sra. de Azaña's room and baggage. (Azaña later asserted that he and his family had been under surveillance ever since his resignation from the Premiership.) Although Sra. de Azaña arrived on October 12, she was told she could not see her husband until November 2. When his "detention" became prolonged, however, she was allowed to visit him on the ship every morning.

Azaña wrote a book in which he recorded all his anxiety of those days in Barcelona. It is entitled *Mi rebelión en Barcelona* and was

---

[5] Juan March, one of the richest men in the world and backer of General Franco, died in Madrid on March 10, 1962, in his early eighties. Jailed for illegal business procedures during the Republic, he helped sabotage the Republic and outlived almost all his Republican antagonists.

published by Espasa-Calpe in 1935.[6] Its frontispiece consists of a document "To Public Opinion" which affirms Azaña's integrity, condemns his persecution, and bears an impressive list of signers who have protested his arrest, none of whom were his political coreligionists. This document, signed in November of 1934 by men like Azorín, Américo Castro, Federico García Lorca, Juan Ramón Jiménez, Eduardo Marquina, Gregorio Marañón, Ramón del Valle Inclán, and Alejandro Casona, was prohibited from publication in any newspaper of Madrid. Azaña dedicated his book to Angel Ossorio y Gallardo, who had served as Azaña's lawyer in the case until it was finally dismissed. Ossorio y Gallardo had been a member of the Constituent Cortes and had headed the committee which edited the first draft of the Republican Constitution. Basically a conservative, a real gentleman, and a veteran of lost causes, Ossorio declared for the Republic when the Civil War broke out in 1936. He exercised several important ambassadorships during that war and remained in Buenos Aires at the end. Always a prolific writer on legal topics, and the best source of data on the Azaña case, Ossorio y Gallardo in exile continued to earn a living with his pen.

In November of 1942 the J.R.E. or *Juventud Republicana Española*,

[6] This was not his only book during the 1931-36 years. He published collections of his speeches (see above page 93), the second edition of his Staël-Holstein translation (see Appendix) in 1931, the translation of another George Borrow work (see Appendix) in 1932, also in November of 1932 a study on "El teatro de Galdós" in *L'Ere Nouvelle* of Paris, and in 1934 a book of four essays under the title *La invención del Quijote y otros ensayos* (Madrid: Espasa-Calpe). The title essay, "The Invention of *Don Quijote*," has already been noted on pages 64-65. The second essay, "Tres generaciones del Ateneo" (Three Generations of the Ateneo), Azaña had originally read as a lecture when he was president of the Ateneo back on November 20, 1930. If he could have known then what lay ahead in December of 1935 when the Ateneo was to celebrate its one hundredth anniversary! The third essay, "Valera," is biographical, like his other studies of Valera. The fourth essay is a short study of Valle Inclán entitled "El secreto de Valle Inclán" (The Secret of Valle Inclán), which had appeared previously in *La pluma*. None of the other three essays had been printed in *La pluma*, *España*, or anywhere else.

Why and how did Azaña continue to publish books midst the travail of his official functions during the Republic? Balzac once wrote: "The power of reflection in the midst of the complications of life is the unmistakable sign of a strong will."

a Republic youth organization in exile, published in Mexico City a seventy-six page pamphlet entitled *Azaña: Una vida al servicio de España*, a work of homage to Azaña by a number of notable exiled Republicans. One of the contributors was Ossorio, who wrote succinctly but significantly on the Barcelona affair and the effect that it left on Azaña:

> Among the infinite dirty dealings and infamies of the Government of Sr. Lerroux [in his book Lerroux disclaims responsibility for Azaña's detention] and the CEDA [Confederación Española de Derechas Autónomas, a Catholic Right-wing political organization headed by José María Gil Robles, and thought to have collaborated with the Fascists], there is none which surpasses that extraordinary outrage. [Azaña] is imprisoned on a boat without its being known by whose order, he is thrown before a Military Judge and a Civil Court Judge and the House Supplicatory Commission, all of whom do the most foolish and absurd things to hold prisoner a man whom they cannot find any way to accuse of anything; that imprisonment is prolonged about three months without anybody's indicting the prisoner, even though in Spain nobody can be held without indictment more than 72 hours; the prisoner is a member of the Cortes whose apprehension the Constitution prohibits except in a case of *flagrante delicto* [a fact which Lerroux claims to have pointed out to the Judge], a Constitution whose desuetude is mocked by the President of the Cortes; the Head of the Supreme Court resorts to the most repugnant maneuvers so that the case will go on and on and on and so that the people can be deceived into attributing nefarious political crimes to Don Manuel; the Cortes, which never grants letters rogatory to prosecute any deputy, not even for common-law crimes, grants this one, "because it is not a juridical question but a political one and it is advisable to clear it up"; with wicked intention the Prime Minister supplies newspapermen with the most opprobrious and calumnious information; the Government takes to the Cortes a bill to render the Supreme Court ineffectual in order to expel the judges who do not lend themselves to the consummation of injustice; and at the end of

three months' imprisonment and another three months' proceedings to execute the formalities requested, the Supreme Court rejects the prosecution of Azaña and issues a stay of proceedings. So in a country where—as I have just said—no one can be held without arraignment, an ex-Prime Minister of the Provisional Government of the Republic has been jailed for three months without any charge being brought against him, and accused slanderously for six months, by a Government none of whose courts has been able to prove the slightest trace of a crime. This happened during the Republic. One ought not be too surprised at what has happened since.

Azaña honored me by making me his defense lawyer. In this capacity I went to visit him one day on the destroyer "Barcaiztegui" ["Sánchez Barcaiztegui"], the last ship that served as a jail for him. My daughter went with me to the harbor. The ship was anchored at four meters from the dock. Don Manuel, wearing a beret, appeared aft. As soon as he saw us he turned to my daughter and in the best countenance imaginable said:

"Josephine, take a good look because it is the last time you will see me without paying. As soon as they take me to the Madrid jail I am going to charge five pesetas per ticket."

I boarded the ship and closeted myself with my prisoner in a small wardroom that was part of his quarters. I was with him more than three hours while we crammed ourselves with candy, because each of us had a terrible sweet tooth. What was that man's state of mind? What was under his skin? Grief? Wrath? Fear? No. Disgust. An absorbing, overbearing, unconquerable disgust. That spectacle of treason, ingratitude, abasement, and collective meanness, that moral poverty of Republican officials, that indecorous attitude of a Parliament, indecorous not because it refused to defend him but because it would not defend itself, the barefaced lies from the top echelon of Government (that he had written an anarchistic and destructive manifesto, that he had given an inflammatory speech from a balcony, that

Upper left: Azaña in custody on the ship, Barcelona, 1934. Center: Victorious arrival of Nationalist troops at Puigcerdá on the French border, 1939. Lower left: Loyalist refugees from Catalonia entering France at Le Perthus, 1939.

he had fled through a sewer! etc., etc.), that vacillation of Justice, which in the final analysis was the only thing that saved him but which also displayed lamentable weakness . . . all of it, everything which occurred at that time was something more than unjust and vexatious: it was nauseating.

The essentials of the case are thus synthesized.[7] Here are some of the external details, again in translation from Ossorio's account:

He is led from his lodging to police headquarters, to the Judge Advocate, to the Major General, to the steamship "Ciudad de Cádiz," tumbling along between two civil guards with rifles, bayonets fixed.

On his arrival at the Major General's office he is not allowed to go to any room, rather he is left to sit in the patio between his two guards.

For the officer of the Civil Guard, the prisoner is no longer Don Manuel Azaña: he is "the escortee."

The clumsy haggling about quartering him on the "Ciudad de Cádiz" is endless.

His wife goes to Barcelona, asks permission to see him, and is put in turn for a visit two weeks later.

During Azaña's incarceration his only brother, Don Gregorio, presiding officer of the regional high court in Zaragoza, dies exasperated by the disgusting events.[8] Don Manuel tells me with a bitter smile:

"Will you believe me that the Prime Minister has not sent me his condolences? Neither a message, nor a telegram from his secretary, nothing, absolutely nothing. I who have just governed the nation as provisional Prime Minister do not exist any longer in either an official or private capacity . . . . "

That man, whom I had seen courageous and smiling on the tenth of August of 1932 when Sanjurjo's sublevation put his life in imminent danger, now appeared before me as exhausted, beaten, his faith gone, his illusions lost.

[7] For more information, see the copies of letters in the Appendix.

[8] Gregorio Azaña died of a heart attack on November 24 and was buried in the family plot in Alcalá de Henares, his body taken there from Zaragoza.

And this was true. In the spring of 1935 the case was dismissed, though Azaña had been released from custody on December 28; but imagine the impact of the entire affair upon an individual so proud, even by Spanish standards, as Manuel Azaña. From then till the end of his life in 1940, he was a disillusioned man who had aged noticeably. One day he confided pessimistically to Cipriano Rivas Cherif, "The Republic is finished," an opinion later confirmed by the Civil War. The six months' outrage had shattered his faith in Spanish Republicanism. It had also left him with a retaliatory rancor, although the book in which he summarized laboriously everything that had happened to him in Barcelona, the terribly tedious *Mi rebelión en Barcelona*, was a work surprisingly more self-vindicative than vindictive. With nothing proved against him, the attitude of self-justification was hardly characteristic of—as he had been labeled so often—an aspirant dictator.

Azaña's persecutors had miscalculated. They did break him physically and wound his pride irremediably; for the man who has been to prison, even though he is released later as innocent, always bears a stigma, like the innocent victim of rape. But the Fascists, Monarchists, and other schemers among the Right wing had wanted to silence Azaña by isolation, thus to reduce their political opposition. Instead they only succeeded in bringing his name into public focus again. Even though Azaña may have felt that the Republic was finished, he stuck by it as a parent clings to his dying child, or a captain to his sinking ship. Love or duty, whatever it was, his self-identification with the fate of the Republic re-established Azaña's popularity in 1935 and carried him the following year to the very Presidency of the Republic.

IV

The Republic, 1935-1936. The Road Back.
Apotheosis of Azaña.

"IT WAS inevitable that Azaña's popularity and authority should grow in proportion to his unjust persecution."[1] Diego Martínez Barrio wrote this in 1943, with the Republic and Civil War behind him, when there was time for reflection. He wrote it with perfect candor of conviction. A Spaniard himself, and high official of the Republic, Martínez Barrio did not feel constrained to explain, to reinforce, or to restrict in any way the generalization implicit in this statement, one in which non-Spanish peoples might see a *non sequitur*. Something inherently Spanish emerges from this logic, something paradoxical that helps to explain also the electoral victory of the Popular Front alliance.

In Spain and the Spanish countries, there is hardly any surer key to "popularity and authority" than the touchstone of a jail sentence, particularly an unjust one, though the political climate and reportorial bias can often make it difficult to distinguish the just from the unjust. Until 1934 Azaña had managed to stay out of jail. Most of the prominent conspirators of the Pact of San Sebastián were imprisoned after

[1] Diego Martínez Barrio, *Orígenes del Frente Popular español* (Buenos Aires, 1943), pp. 25-26.

the Jaca uprising in 1930. Their martyrdom therefore exceeded his, and neither they nor the Republican masses ever really forgot that. Even the Right-wing press of then, and now, uses words to the effect that "he wasn't even in jail" to belittle Azaña's role in the formation of the Republic. In 1934 Azaña finally became a martyr. Since Companys and Largo Caballero also accompanied him behind bars, their prestige rose too, although they may have been guilty and he was not.

Can there be in such matters as the prestige-generating incarceration some psychological transfer from Catholicism, whose most revered saints are martyrs? Do not Spaniards react as Catholics to such concepts as life, death (fate, in the sense of doom), marriage, glory, sin, *"dejar nombre,"* even when they are anarchists or atheists? Every people has its own collective psyche, even when, as in the comparatively young U.S.A., a national ethos has emerged from a blend of heterogeneous traits. Every total atmosphere is formed by an aggregate of persistent small things. At an early age a person becomes representative of a given ethos when he learns to accept the validity and inevitability of these small things without justifying them. I once stayed in a Spanish town where the seemingly incessant clanging of church bells—just one of the myriad Catholic externals in a Catholic country—woke me up too early every morning and frazzled my nerves periodically throughout the day. Why? Because I was unused to ubiquitous church bells; theirs was not one of the accustomed sounds of my day-to-day life. Yet one can be sure that the sound itself disturbed no anarchist or atheist of that town, nor would he object to a bell ringers' union, while at the same time he might be shouting, "Down with the church!" Just as there exist conditioned national patterns of reaction to the composite of sensory stimuli among a people, also certain generally predictable and equally national conceptual patterns must develop from the composite of spiritual and intellectual stimuli. What is glory, what is heroism, what is pride, what constitutes an insult, what constitutes manliness, what constitutes success? These concepts vary in definition from people to people, and also from religion to religion when a given religion dominates the spiritual life of a people. Catholicism defines glory, for instance, by the example of its martyrs, beginning with Christ (an anarchist who succeeded, said Malraux in *Man's Hope*); and Spaniards swim in a river of Catholic ideals which channels the reactions of the individual, whether or not he practices the rites of that religion or even formally subscribes to it. One of these reactions, then, is the respect due martyrdom, and it is not any wonder that Manuel Azaña emerged from prison strong in prestige if weak in spirit.

As soon as he was released, Azaña plunged back into politics, after first having defended himself against new attacks in a speech to the Cortes on March 20, 1935. Having analyzed the reasons for their defeat by the Right in the 1933 elections, the Center and Left-of-Center parties were beginning to see that their best chance to regain control of the government in any future elections would be through the establishment of a pre-election coalition: a unified program and slate of candidates that would avoid dissipation of strength among the numerous small parties. To this end, the representatives of three parties signed a document in Madrid on April 12, 1935. The pact set forth seven principles of a united program while concomitantly it allowed each party to remain a separate entity. The signers of this document were Azaña for Republican Left, Sánchez Román for the National Republican party (*Partido Nacional Republicano*), and Martínez Barrio for Republican Union (*Unión Republicana*). After these groups began work on their joint program in the summer of 1935, with great speeches by Azaña, other parties joined them to form what became known later as the *Frente Popular* (Popular Front), whose formal pact among nearly all Left parties (including Socialist and Communist) was signed on January 15, 1936, just eight days after President Alcalá Zamora had authorized new elections to the Cortes. It was arranged that a single slate would go into office if the Popular Front were victorious, but that whoever went into office was duty-bound to carry out the aim of the entire Front. Even the Anarchists gave their moral support and in some cases their votes.

If a voting Anarchist appears to be a contradiction in terms, it is even stranger to tell that during the Civil War certain Anarchists held regional political offices as well as military commands. The Anarchists claimed that their presence in government was only an emergency arrangement, because they refused to be identified as a political party. Followers of Mikhail Bakunin, who differed violently with Marx on the question of individualism, as opposed to collectivism, in their otherwise similar social doctrine, were in Spain a unique breed of uncontrollables who typified the Spanish tendency to cast international institutions in a national mold. Spanish individualism probably gave Bakuninism its foothold in Spain when the movement failed to attract followers elsewhere. Having rejected compulsory law and government, the Anarchist made his social doctrine almost a kind of religion in its reliance upon the integrity and innate goodness of the individual in his dealings with the large or small community of other human beings. In terms of political theory, anarchism is communism without a central government endowed with absolute powers. In practice, the Bakunin variety of Anarchist was a revolutionary, expert in the art of destruction. In Spain the Anarchists specialized in arson, with a predilection for the burning of churches. During the early part of the Civil War, many loosely defined Anarchists formed undisciplined bands of marauders, an embarrassment to the Republic, of the type who indiscriminately burned and destroyed the city of Irún before its fall. If anarchism, like communism, is tenable in some of its theories, anarchism in practice was—as Russian communism still is—a nightmare of intolerance toward the opposing individual's political opinions.

Aware that in a Popular Front program he would have to compromise more than he had ever done before, and consort with elements whose revolutionary tendencies exceeded his own by far, Azaña apparently recognized that the time had come for Machiavellian politics. He knew that the Popular Front was a Russian concept, but the task of the moment was to salvage the Republic, even if Republicans had to ally themselves with Communists to survive. Azaña knew also that if the Popular Front did succeed in winning, the election would be close and the nation harder than ever to govern. But chances had to be taken.

Azaña made three eloquent speeches in 1935. Together with a fourth speech, they form a book which the Espasa-Calpe firm published in 1936 under the title *Discursos en campo abierto* (Speeches Out in the Open). Though all these speeches appeared in newspapers and probably Azaña would have had them published in book form anyhow, since that was his custom, this time he had a special reason for their publication as a unit: the book came out as soon as practicable after the formalization of the Popular Front in January, and before the elections. The first speech, the one before the Cortes, was not physically *"en campo abierto"*; but according to Azaña's own estimate, the other three were delivered before a combined total of seven hundred thousand people, the third one having been addressed to the largest open-air audience ever gathered in Spain. On May 26, 1935, Azaña spoke at the Campo de Mestalla in Valencia. In the text of this speech he referred to the assemblage as "one hundred thousand Republicans." It was a fighting speech in which he attacked the existing government with every weapon in his verbal arsenal. Then on June 14 he spoke before another huge crowd at the Campo de Lasesarre in Baracaldo, a suburb of Bilbao up in the hills which surround the Basque capital. He leveled the same broadsides at the government but had very little that was concrete or positive to offer beyond an invocation of the usual platitudes of regeneration, social justice, Republic, freedom, democracy, and so forth.

Before Azaña made his next speech, he took his wife to Paris, Holland, and Belgium for a late-summer vacation of about a month. Autumn found him back in Madrid preparing for what must be considered the zenith of his popularity, his speech of October 20, 1935, at the Campo de Comillas, Madrid. It was fitting that Manuel Azaña's greatest day should have come on the outskirts of Madrid, the city which had been the focal point of his productive literary and political life.

Campo de Comillas was a barren hillside at Carabanchel, a working-class suburb on the southern bank of the Manzanares river, a vantage point which gives the same panorama of Madrid that Goya painted. The space had been walled in to make a kind of meeting ground for the people who flocked there from all over Spain on that bleak Sunday morning. They came by car, truck, train, bus, horse, donkey; and tens of thousands came on foot. Although admission was by tickets, whose prices ranged from one to five pesetas, the gathering was so huge that it seemed to spill over the whole barren terrain, and thousands of the spectators could scarcely see the speaker. Loudspeakers had been set up but did not work well. Unable to see or hear, many of that great assemblage could hope only to share the tide of mass emotion generated that day.

The occasion is even more fantastic when the other circumstances are known. Henry Buckley was there that day and commented (*Life and Death of the Spanish Republic*, p. 182) in the following manner:

> The meeting had not been widely advertised. It was frowned on by the authorities and in some cases the Civil Guard turned back convoys of trucks carrying spectators. All vehicles bringing people from afar were stopped some miles outside Madrid, thus causing endless confusion and forcing weary men and women to trudge a long distance after a tiring ride . . . . No one was forced to go to that meeting. Presence there, in fact, was much more likely to bring the displeasure of employer or landlord. How many of the great figures of Europe to-day could bring together spontaneously, without the slightest party organisation or preparation, a mass of 200,000 people in order to hear a speech lasting less than two hours and not accompanied by the most simple form of parade or demonstration which could appeal to the spectator of pomp and show?[2]

Had these people come only to hear Azaña or had they come in a spirit of protest? There had been, at the time, a financial scandal implicating Rightists in the government. As a result, an increase in unrest was anticipated from the Left, who feared that the embarrassed Right would resort to a *golpe de estado*. Each side was alert to an explosion. The Comillas assemblage was a pacific show of force by the Left, a demonstration of mass solidarity that could hardly have failed to impress anyone. Not a single noteworthy incident occurred that day despite the jostling of the crowds by cavalry, summoned by the government, and the presence of truck-mounted machine guns at strategic places. The Popular Front's guards controlled their own rabble rousers

---

[2] Azaña himself estimated the crowd at four hundred thousand. Rivas Cherif told me he thought it was closer to one-half million. Antonio Ramos Oliveira claims one-half million; Claude Bowers says one-quarter million; Frank Jellinek vacillates between one-quarter million and four hundred thousand; Constancia de la Mora says over four hundred thousand. The London *Times* of October 22, 1935, which covered the speech (the *New York Times* did not), said two hundred thousand.

as well as the opposition's *agents provocateurs,* who were undoubtedly present.

That day Azaña was a symbol to the masses, their last hope for leadership in a disintegrating democracy. Pipe fitters and stone masons, and the seven men who had walked all the way from Asturias, had not come to bear witness to the intellectual prowess of Manuel Azaña, maybe not even to assimilate his words, for Azaña was never earthy; instead they had come to hear a program, a plan, and to rally round a leader. The speech that they heard, or maybe did not hear, was on the whole a sensible one, dedicated to the restoration of ethics in government, yet one which dealt more specifically with the past than with the future, and one replete with the usual democratic slogans. Azaña spoke on international policy, budget, education, social legislation, jurisprudence, agrarian reform, taxes, etc., but in nearly every case his message was: all we need to do is apply and follow the laws voted three years ago, make functional the institutions already created. He had no new schemes to offer, no original or drastic proposals to cement Right with Left. Still consistent in his role of torch-bearer of the ideal republic, he counseled a return to 1931. Perhaps it was an attempt to convince himself, by convincing others, that a return to 1931 was possible, for the ex-prisoner probably knew his glorious Republic was moribund. As in the case of Azaña's two previous open-air performances of 1935, the occasion was more impressive than the speech, which was perhaps neither so brilliant as some maintain nor so uninspiring as others affirm. Let us, however, hear out Buckley (p. 184), who formed his impression as he sat midst the mass of humanity that Sunday morning:

> He talked to these workers and peasants about international relations, about gold reserves and monetary complications, and all in an uninspiring, matter-of-fact voice. It would have been an excellent address

148

for a Rotary Club luncheon. I think he was terrified of the crowd, afraid of what it might do if he warmed its passions. He was afraid that he was not big enough to dominate this crowd. And he was right. He had nothing to offer it. His life diet had been nineteenth-century Liberalism. According to this, one fostered civil liberties and then sat back to watch the nation flourish in bracing airs of freedom . . . . If Azaña had been a bigger man he might have set to work to form a party, to build up a machine which would work and which would have answered the heart-breaking plea of the people of Spain. But he was a cultured, intelligent product of his environment. With his intelligence and ideas he could have attained the rank of statesman with no difficulty in either contemporary Britain or France. But it was not enough. He was not big enough to adjust himself.

The underlying theme of Azaña's speech that day was a personal condemnation of Lerroux and his whole government of the last two years, the Black Biennium. The long-standing antagonism between Azaña and Lerroux was well known, ever since the days when Azaña was Prime Minister and had been provoked by Lerroux's personal attacks in the Cortes. Then when their governmental positions were reversed, it was probably Lerroux who, despite his denials, was at the bottom of Azaña's alleged implication in the Barcelona affair. More than anybody else, Lerroux was still the pebble in Azaña's boot. Two such men could never agree: Lerroux, the pettifogging professional politician, and Azaña, the punctilious intellectual who learned too late not to expect sportsmanship from his political adversaries. Azaña was now demanding that the Republic be liberated from bad enchanters like Lerroux, whose government had already fallen in May of 1935, but who at first succeeded himself and later occupied the post of Minister of State in the subsequent Joaquín Chapaprieta government. As a result of the financial scandal, in which Lerroux's nephew was implicated, Lerroux resigned from the Ministry of State only ten days after Azaña's Campo de Comillas speech.

Here are some of the most significant points and quotations from the Campo de Comillas speech, along with some other observations: (1) "Here we continue the campaign that the Republican Left party initiated, whose antecedents are known to you, and which culminates— but does not terminate—in this public function." By his leadership of Republican Left, Azaña thus claims credit for the establishment of what developed into the Popular Front. He had, in fact, been urging a unification of Left and Center parties since October of 1933. (2) Deploring the menacing presence of the cavalry and the machine guns mounted on trucks at intersections ("as if we were going to go from here to storm the Ministries and seize the Government by violence"), Azaña inteprets the hugeness of the gathering as an indication of electoral strength, and the reason more people have not come to make it one-half million is only that no more bodies could possibly fit into the area. (3) It is no longer a question of differing policy or politics. "The fact is that the Government, in all its branches, is functioning systematically and deliberately against republicans . . . . The fact is that in Spain, a country still camouflaged under republican colors, the name and condition of republican has come to be a pretext for prison, for exile, for beatings, for every kind of personal ruin . . . . " (4) Denouncing the government for its total ignorance of the international situation, Azaña maintains that international politics should not be a changing party matter, because international policy is determined by invariable factors of geography, economics, and other constant realities. "The international policy of a country is inherited from regime to regime . . . . " Spain's international ends of peace and preservation of territorial integrity and independence are best achieved through the League of Nations, not only best achieved in this manner, but necessarily achieved so, because "Spain is a weak country, without the resources to convert itself into a great power." He knows the weakness of the League of Nations, but its failure would be a "universal misfortune," and for Spain to contribute to such a failure would be suicide. Yet Spain's position in Geneva is still a question mark, Azaña insists; moreover, nobody has asked the Spanish people what that position should be. (5) The Cortes tends to abuse its power. Even he himself, in the Cortes, had to defend the prerogatives of the President of the Republic. The present Cortes, motivated only by destruction and vengeance, has "paralyzed, destroyed, and abandoned" the agrarian reform and has wasted money scandalously. (6) Azaña promises to balance the budget. Intricate budgetary matters, beyond the interest or understanding of his huge audience, are the longest single topic of the speech. (7) Deviating from his old slogan, that the Republic is for all Spaniards, that there must be "humanity, tolerance, and understanding," Azaña proceeds to make one of his very few contradictory and openly revolutionary remarks. He asserts that the Republic "must destroy absolutely the privileges of the moneyed classes who now subjugate the people." (8) "All Europe today is a battlefield between democracy and its enemies, and Spain is not an exception. You must choose between democracy, with all its shortcomings, with all its faults, with all its mistakes or errors, and tyranny with all its horrors. There is no choice. Ours is made. In Spain one hears frivolous and vain talk of dictatorship. We find it repugnant not only by doctrine, but by experience and through good sense . . . . Dictatorship is a consequence or political manifestation of intolerance; its propellant is fanaticism; and its means of action, physical violence. Dictatorship leads to war . . . it stupifies peoples and drives them mad."

Judged as oratory, Azaña's concluding paragraph is masterful. After having invoked silence for meditation upon the martyrs of the Republic, he works a verbal crescendo worthy, in musical terms, of a Rossini: "The silence of the people declares their grief and indignation; but the voice of the people can blast awesomely like the trumpets of Judgment. Let my words not glide over faint hearts, and may they pierce yours like darts of fire! People, for Spain and for the Republic, united!!" A frenzied ovation met these last words; the huge crowd was on its feet. Thousands upon thousands of clenched fists were raised, but Manuel Azaña did not return the salute.[3] This was an unforeseen critical moment of truth. The proud intellectual could not bend to popular revolutionary symbolism. This moment told more of Azaña than any of his words that day; it showed the paternal had not been converted into the fraternal, that in his innermost heart he was not a revolutionary. Azaña craved a Popular Front victory, but at the same time the thought of such a victory must have terrified him.

On February 16, 1936, Spaniards went to the polls. Azaña's own Republican Left party won 82 seats in the Cortes; the Socialists won 89; the Communists exactly 14. In larger terms, the Popular Front total was 258 deputies; the Center parties won 62; the parties of the Right had 152. The electoral system, however, did not reflect the closeness of the total popular vote. The actual number of votes polled gave only a narrow victory to the Popular Front, which had looked upon the election with more hope than confidence. But there is no doubt that the Right lost, despite its control of the election machinery

[3] The Popular Front salute, clenched fist symbolic of unity and strength, is said to have been invented by a German Social Democrat named Edgar André, who was executed by the Nazis in 1936. It may have been seen earlier in Spain, but the first report of its use dates from September, 1935 (see Buckley, op. cit., p. 179). During the Civil War, this salute became a widely accepted form of greeting among the many Republican components. For additional reference to Edgar André, whose name is missing from most of the standard encyclopedias, see Gustav Regler's novel The Great Crusade (New York and Toronto, 1940), p. 53, and André Malraux's novel Man's Hope (New York, 1938), p. 331. One of the early battalions of the International Brigades was named the Edgar André Battalion; it fought in the November-December, 1936, battles at Madrid.

and its confidence in victory. Although the Socialists had won more seats than Republican Left, a close alignment of the Catalonian Esquerra party with Republican Left put Azaña at the head of 103 deputies and gave him control of the largest bloc among the Left parties.

At the very moment that Manuel Azaña had reached the zenith of his power and popularity, the new situation already began to deteriorate. As soon as it was obvious that the Popular Front was to control the government, two simultaneous movements commenced: the defeated Right started its surreptitious and now earnest move toward ultimate military rebellion, while the Left renewed its internecine struggle for power (the several kinds of Socialists were especially intolerant of one another). Azaña became Prime Minister again and formed his government on February 19, immediately after the resignation of the government of Manuel Portela on the same day. All of Azaña's new Cabinet were democrats and moderates. It did not include any Socialists or Communists; far from being communistic or anarchical, it was perhaps too much on the conservative side. The next day, February 20, Azaña made a national radio broadcast to appeal for unity and moderation. This was to no avail. Despite Azaña's personal pleas to Largo Caballero for restraint, that extremist among Socialists renewed his revolutionary propaganda with speeches designed to incite the workers. The en masse amnesty of political prisoners brought a new wave of strikes, church burnings, agrarian unrest, assassinations, and every kind of revolutionary violence—worse than ever before.

In the Cortes itself, decomposition began with a stormy session on April 4. Azaña presented himself at this first meeting of the new Cortes and gave a speech intended both to reconcile the warring factions and to give assurance to the Right wing that he planned no reform measures beyond those stated in the election program of the Popular Front. The only thing he insisted upon was, as always, enforcement of the Constitution, especially such Articles as the one on agrarian reform which had fallen into desuetude during the last two years. It was a good speech, as everyone had come to expect of Azaña, but it quieted tempers only briefly. The core of the problem was how to control the extremists of both opposing bands if the government carried out its promise to enforce a Constitution that had become too harsh for the Right and too mild for the Left.

What had happened to the Popular Front? Why had the atmosphere become electrically revolutionary? Franco backers have always claimed that the Spanish Popular Front was a smoke screen for the Communists, an unholy alliance plotted by Moscow. Azaña himself rejected this assertion as false when he told the correspondent Lawrence Fernsworth of his firm stand against any pacting with the official Communist party, small as it was, with strings tied to the Kremlin.[4] Surely Moscow looked on the Popular Front favorably, and a handful of Communists had indeed been elected to the Cortes, but communism did not achieve party strength in Spain until after the Civil War had begun. In the early days of the war, the Communists mobilized themselves more quickly and efficiently than any other Loyalist group; and, with visible military aid arriving from Russia, they attracted partisans out of practical, rather than purely ideological, considerations.

The old revolutionary Leon Trotsky had a theory which discounted the long-range workability of any Popular Front. In a simply stated but keenly incisive article of December 17, 1937,[5] he showed how the interests of the proletariat and bourgeoisie, even though they might

[4] Lawrence Fernsworth, *Spain's Struggle for Freedom* (Boston, 1957), p. 177.
[5] Reference is to the latest revised translation, which appeared in pamphlet form in August, 1956 (Colombo, Ceylon) under the title *The Lessons of Spain—the Last Warning*.

be the same in solving certain practical problems in common, are so different in political coalition because their ends are so different. Spanish bourgeois elements were split, politically, between Left and Right. The bourgeois can be a Popular Fronter so long as private ownership and means of production are not threatened; that is, to the extent that the revolution be a democratic one, as Azaña wished. Basically a democratic bourgeois and, as Trotsky dubbed him, a "knight of right and freedom," Azaña now found himself in the forefront of a largely proletarian movement, whose undemocratic impulse was becoming no less difficult for him to check than the one from the Right. When Azaña could in good conscience move no farther Left, when the undemocratic constrictions were becoming most painful, a means of graceful exit presented itself—the neutral office of Presidency of the Republic.

As President of the Republic, Niceto Alcalá Zamora had the prerogative to dissolve the Cortes not more than twice during his Presidential tenure. With the elections of February, he had exercised this right for the second time. According to the Constitution, the new Cortes could vote an impeachment of the President of the Republic if in its collective opinion his second call for elections had not been clearly necessary. This is precisely what the new Cortes did, unheedful that the new majority in the Cortes did reflect a change in national opinion and the consequent fact of rightful dissolution of the previous Cortes. The instigator of the movement for deposition was Indalecio Prieto, a moderate Socialist and close friend of Azaña. He could have presented to Azaña a number of compelling arguments why the latter should allow himself to be elected President. Some of these reasons might have been that (1) with Prieto as Prime Minister and Azaña as President, the two of them would be able to see eye to eye and work together better than the outgoing President had done with any Prime Minister in the past, and maybe in this way (both were solid democrats) the Republic might be salvaged; (2) the Republic needed the stability of a President who, by dint of his personality, could control the state and would thus remain the full six years of his term; (3) unlike Alcalá Zamora, who was a zealous Catholic, Azaña held no reservations about any Article of the Constitution, which had proclaimed a lay republic; and (4) even though the assumption of the Presidency would neutralize Azaña politically, if he did not take the post himself it could go conceivably to one of the extremists.

The infusion of the Presidency with a vigorous personality was a more realistic motive for a change in President than the argument which said that the change might bring durability to the office, because the simple act of replacement under conditions of questionable justification rendered the office unstable, regardless of who replaced whom. Recall that one of the reasons for the failure of the ephemeral First Republic of 1873-74 was its string of four Presidents in a short space of time. Admittedly, however, a strong and uncompromising personality was needed to bring dignity to the Presidency of the Second Republic and infuse the office with some extra measure of authority, justly exercised, within its rather narrow confines established by the Constitution.

Taught by experience, and hypersensitive to the endowment of any given individual with powers conducive to dictatorial authority, the framers of the Constitution had perhaps limited too sharply the areas of executive jurisdiction of its President. The very fact that the President of the Republic was not elected by direct plebiscite precluded his claim to any popular assignation. Although the machinery was somewhat complex, in effect the Cortes elected the President. Inasmuch as he owed his office to the authority of the Cortes, he could be reminded of his obligation and even inferiority to that body, the deposition of Alcalá Zamora being a case in point. Yet it was reasoned that a republic needed a President, at least for ceremonial functions ("to personify the nation," as the Constitution read), even if the authors of the Constitution had decided that their republic did not need a senate. The powers conferred upon the President by the Constitution were mostly small ones, with the exception of his right to name governments and to dissolve the Cortes for re-election; in fact, the Constitution was equally specific in its delineation of his limitations as it was in the representation of his authority. One Article and one section, however, 76 d, armed the President with a convenient latitude of action in any situation of emergency by empowering him "to order the urgent measures which the defense of the integrity or the security of the nation demands, rendering immediate account to the Cortes." Here was where a strong President could make his authority felt, if he could count on the obedience of his legally constituted subordinates. But the question of legal effectiveness was the perpetually uncertain factor in the Republic.

On April 7, 1936, Azaña saw Alcalá Zamora deposed by the Cortes. Despite his dislike of the cunning Alcalá Zamora (the antipathy was mutual, although until 1936 their relationship had been at least formally cordial), Azaña may have intuited that it was both unwise and unjust to remove him. Whether out of pity, modesty, decorum, or lack of conviction, the Prime Minister took no active part in the movement against his President, yet he said nothing in the man's defense while Prieto's steam roller did its work. Diego Martínez Barrio became the President pro tem. One week later Martínez Barrio and the still Prime Minister Azaña reviewed together the parade celebrating the fifth anniversary of the Republic, a parade not without incidents interpreted by some as another abortive plot to assassinate Azaña. The campaign of defamation of Azaña had recommenced as soon as his name was proposed for the permanent Presidency. This time he acquired a new caricature in the press. Because the author of *La corona* was being catapulted to a position where he would personify the state, *Claridad* (organ of the Socialist wing headed by Largo Caballero) began to publish pictorial sketches of Azaña wearing a crown.

Quite apart from the impressive emolument, the perquisites of the Presidency were not unattractive to a cultured and cultivated gentleman like Azaña, who, at first, nobody thought would accept the Presidency. His personal popularity with the people may have convinced him that he could do more good from the Presidency, that he could effectively strengthen the office and thus the Republic as well; but anyone who has studied the personality of this man knows there are more private, yet equally compelling, reasons for him to have accepted the honor. Proud and somewhat vain as he was, ageing and maybe tiring, Azaña could take secret pleasure in the prospect of Spain's highest office. Here he could be both comfortable and grand, maybe have some leisure to read and write, and take a certain pleasure in the pomp and ceremony inherent to the office. He would miss the party politics, yes, but then he always denied being a professional politician; and here was a chance to retire honorably from active combat in order to become the peacemaker.

Whatever his motive Azaña accepted the Presidency. The formal and rather complicated balloting took place on May 10, 1936. Of the 911 electoral votes, Azaña received 754; all but five of the rest were blank ballots. From that day until virtually the end of the Civil War, Manuel Azaña was the President of the Second Spanish Republic. Spain gained a man worthy of her highest Republican office; at the same time she not only lost the best possible Prime Minister, even under the worsening circumstances, but found herself with a notably inept one in his place. Although Azaña had wanted Indalecio Prieto to be Prime Minister and had offered him the post, the vagaries of politics (specifically the opposition of Largo Caballero) conferred the office upon Santiago Casares Quiroga, who, though he too was a friend of Azaña, was not the man for the times.

Shortly after his election, Azaña established a temporary residence in the Casa del Príncipe in the hunting park of El Pardo, since the President's rooms in the National Palace were undergoing repairs. One of his first official functions was the formal reception of foreign diplomats at the National Palace. The U.S. ambassador to Spain at the time, Claude G. Bowers, attended this function. In his book *My Mission to Spain*[6] (page 230), Bowers described the event, and an affront by the Italian ambassador:

> There was more form and smartness than had been seen since the fall of the monarchy, and some of my colleagues, who had been scornful of the ultrasimplicity of Alcalá Zamora, were equally resentful of Azaña's departure from it. Officers in brilliant uniforms lined the stairway. We went through the old guard room into a magnificent apartment, and thence on through the porcelain room where Washington Irving presented his credentials to the child Queen Isabella, in the presence of her nurse, to the room where we were to be received. In an adjoining room a military band played the national anthem, and Azaña appeared, followed by his ministers and the Military Household, headed by General Masquelet. These grouped themselves behind the President. Azaña was pale, as usual. The doyen read an address, Azaña replied, and then passed down the line shaking hands with the heads of missions, smiling graciously. Thus did he approach the Italian ambassador.
>
> In execrable taste, in contemptuous disregard of the proprieties, and with true Fascist impudence, the Ambassador of Mussolini, at that

very hour deep in the conspiracy soon to flare in the military and Fascist rebellion, appeared in a spirit of insult in a black shirt and in boots. And when Azaña approached, ready with an outstretched hand, the Italian Fascist drew back and gave the Fascist salute. It was the sort of insult that had been rebuked at the King's levee at the Court of St. James. Azaña disregarded the deliberate insult and passed on, smiling.

In June, Bowers saw Azaña again and wrote (page 234):

In early June I gave my annual presidential dinner for Azaña. A few days before, a witty countess, who hated the Republic, knowing my daughter Patricia would be the hostess in the absence of her mother, undertook to advise her how to "please the President." She was to say, "How charming Spain was ten years ago"—which was in the days of the Dictator.

That night, Azaña drove in from the Pardo hunting lodge in high good humor, discussing plans to extend the beautiful gardens of the lodge and to establish the summer capital in Santander. Patricia found him an easy table companion and quite as charming as Spain had been "ten years ago"; and after dinner he was interested in the panels in the Goya room and in Zuloaga's portrait of the Duchess of Arion. He spent the evening in the ballroom talking entertainingly. Señora Azaña, a small woman with a very attractive face, with expressive blue eyes, and a soft, pleasant voice, was much younger than her husband. Her brother, Rivas Cherif, the dramatist and writer, had been Azaña's close friend from their early youth in the monks' school in the Escorial. [This is in error; Rivas Cherif and Azaña did not meet until 1914, when Azaña was thirty-four years old.]

There was nothing that night to indicate that in five weeks Spain would be engaged in a sanguinary war with guests of the evening on both sides of the barricade.

Portrait of Azaña with Presidential sash, by José María López Mezquita, now in the possession of the Hispanic Society of America, New York City. Courtesy of the Hispanic Society of America.

Five weeks passed. The army was still restless, as it had been ever since the man whom most of the officers considered to be their enemy, the man they condemned for the 1931-33 military reforms, had returned to power and was President. And in the Cortes, on June 16, 1936, the Right-wing leader José María Gil Robles made a speech "in which he indicted the government for its leniency with regard to the prevailing violence and crime: 160 churches totally destroyed and 251 set on fire or otherwise attacked; 269 persons murdered and 1,287 injured; 69 political premises destroyed; 113 general strikes and 228 partial strikes, as well as many cases of other forms of violence" (Madariaga, *Spain: A Modern History*, p. 459).[7] The Monarchist deputy José Calvo Sotelo spoke next, also with vehemence. Before dawn on July 13 Calvo Sotelo was led from his house, murdered, and deposited in a cemetery—all of this the work of Assault Guards in reprisal for the assassination of one of their lieutenants the previous day. Historians like to say that this event triggered the rebellion, but the rebellion had already been planned and would have come in any case. Although the dead lieutenant Castillo's whole company of Assault Guards was imprisoned, it was too late for evasive action. What each side wanted now was blood.

[7] It is ironical that the same Gil Robles was exiled by Franco on June 10, 1962, for participating in a conference of the European Movement Congress (for the evolution of a federated United States of Europe) a few days earlier in Munich. No Communists or Fascists are invited to the meetings of this worthy organization; all the participants are democrats of one kind or another. Before Gil Robles went to Munich, he had sent to Franco and to the Minister of the Interior a draft of certain resolutions to be proposed at the meetings, one of whose purposes was to examine basic conditions for Spain's eventual inclusion in the European Common Market. The thirty-eight delegates of the exiles met separately with Salvador de Madariaga while Gil Robles chaired the eighty-man delegation from Spain. The two groups met later in plenary session and showed a unanimity and solidarity which Madariaga describes as the real termination of the Spanish Civil War. When Gil Robles and the principal Spanish delegates returned to Madrid, their airplanes were met by Franco police who gave them the choice of exile abroad or deportation to the Canary Island of Fuerteventura (like Unamuno). Gil Robles chose exile.

On the eve of the insurrection, which originated in Spanish Morocco on July 17, a handful of moderate laborites and intellectuals seemed to be the only non-belligerent republicans left in Spain. Azaña had found the total situation to be as uncontrollable from the Presidency as it had been from the Premiership. Nonetheless he remained bound to the apparently unenforceable Constitution. Unable to impose order by legal measures, unwilling to enforce it by extra-legal ones, despondent of his inability to radiate stability from the Presidency, thwarted at every turn, Azaña appeared to have succumbed to circumstances and to the pre-Civil War comforts of the Presidency. Almost without exception both the Republican and Francoist chroniclers of the period assert that Manuel Azaña built himself a shell and withdrew into it, snail-like, shortly after the Spanish Civil War had become irremediably launched. This was not wholly true. No one was more sensitive to the tragedy than he, and no one worked harder behind the scenes to achieve a truce than he, for in his estimation no victor could emerge from such a war.

THE SPANISH CIVIL WAR has engendered thousands of books and pamphlets in many languages, but not one detailed military and political history that can yet be called definitive.[1] Mostly impassioned books of undocumented accusation, they are still being written today, one as contradictory of the other as they were several decades ago. If it is hard to reconstruct the day-by-day battle scene, the over-all picture of those three years is even more elusive. Many of the larger truths of the war spring from the paradoxical Spanish character, and this Spanish character is as enigmatic to the other Romance peoples as it is to the German and English-speaking peoples. Much is explained, however, by the varying regional nature of the war and the heterogeneous composition of each side.

Civil wars tend to pit political extremes one against the other, with the result that great masses of nonpolitical individuals are caught in

[1] A personal opinion is that Madariaga's *Spain* (1958 revision) comes closest along with Hugh Thomas' *The Spanish Civil War* (1961), which was a surprising best-seller in the U.S.A. for months. See the Bibliography for commentary on the Thomas history. Several detailed and rather complete military histories with abundant battle-maps and illustrative material have been published in Spain, but they are unobjective, inaccurate, and lack indexes.

the middle and forced to go along with one band of extremists or the other. After the Spanish Civil War had begun, nonpolitical Spaniards learned very quickly that neutrality was no less dangerous than self-commitment. Unlike the U.S. Civil War, which found opinion divided largely between two geographical regions, with very few exceptions all Spanish regions harbored all opinions in varying degrees of strength; and, except in the case of the predominantly Leftish industrial centers, the delineations of Republican and Rebel Spain were the result first of spontaneous group initiative and, only later, of successful military operations. The initial war map was not two semicircles, but a polka-dot moon.

This was an unusual war, for the Spanish are an unusual people. Azaña himself noted in *La velada en Benicarló* and elsewhere the Spanish tendency to destruction, born of the same mass unruliness which precipitated the military rebellion of 1936. At bottom it is the Spaniard's egoism, euphemistically termed his "individualism," which is responsible for the inconsistency of performance in most aspects of Spanish life (including the arts), and which seems to rebel against the co-operative standards in civil affairs so characteristic of the British and American examples of a free society. Anarchism has flourished in Hispanic societies because the Spaniard tends to reject authority exterior to his own. On April 21, 1934, in one of his best speeches ("Grandezas y miserias de la política"), Azaña had pointed out that "the greatest ill of Spain is its need of moral vigor," that in Spain what is most notably evident is not a lack of intelligence or education, but "the moral weakness of public spirit." More than anything else, Azaña had wanted to create a Spain of responsible citizens, to instill the concept of loyal opposition. Whether or not the rebellion was justified, the outbreak of the war proved the failure of his mission. He neither prevented the uprising nor could he stifle it. If the

Republic did ultimately win, the credit would not be his. Therefore, regardless of which side won, or whether the two extremes succeeded in mutual extermination, Azaña was a finished man in Spanish public life.

Although Azaña underestimated the strength and scope of the Spanish Fascist movement, he always knew that the military and civilian Right wing might rebel, even if he would never admit this in public. He preferred to dispel fear by denying the possibility of a revolt. We have seen how he repeatedly gave public assurance of Republican strength as he continued on the path of strict legality. As early as July 5, 1933, Ossorio y Gallardo had asked on the floor of the Cortes: "What if the majority should win even though it be inimical to the Republic?" In a speech of reply to the same Cortes the next day, Azaña discounted such a possibility while at the same time he admitted its legality. But Azaña then went on to chide the deputies who had been "overly worried, for some months now, by those phantoms of fascism, dictatorship, Caesar-ism, and imposition of minority opinion . . . ." "It is high time," he continued, "for Sr. Ossorio y Gallardo to calm down and be convinced that Spanish liberal feeling and Spanish democratic institutions are sufficiently rooted in legality and in the hearts of Republicans so that none of those dangers is to be feared." He was wrong, yes, but his words of assurance were for public consumption. In the February 17, 1933, entry of his memoirs, Azaña had written: "The only thing that breathes fear in me is what can happen to the army the day that I depart from this house. They will return to their old ways, one group and another, politicians and generals, and goodbye Republic." In the summer of 1934, the journalist Lawrence Fernsworth (then correspondent for the *Times* of London) had an interview with Azaña. Fernsworth posed this question: "What would happen if the Rightists managed to entrench themselves firmly and went ahead with their announced intentions?" Azaña's reply was: "There will be a civil war—and that would be most grave." Two years later, when the war did come, on July 18, 1936 (July 17 in Morocco), from the start Azaña lacked conviction in a Republican victory, a fact readily attested by his private secretary[2] and other intimates, and a fact that Azaña himself did not deny when he was interviewed by Fernsworth again in 1939 at the end of the war.

Yet the events of July 18, 1936, should not have been a great surprise. Weeks before that day, the Madrid press and other newspapers echoed rumors of a plot against the Republic. There were stories about the subversive activities of General Emilio Mola, who was the military commander in Navarra. Pamplona (Mola's headquarters), the rest of Navarra, and also parts of Castile had been secretly stockpiling arms, by contraband trade over the Pyrenees, months before the date of the declared rebellion. Fortunately for the Right, it had been arming itself throughout Spain better than had the revolutionaries. From Portugal, ex-General Sanjurjo not only played a principal role in the plot but was its leader-designate: he and Mola, both of whom were soon to die in airplane crashes, were the real masterminds behind the rebellion. The island commands of two other distrusted generals, Francisco Franco in the Canary Islands and Manuel Goded in Majorca, had supposedly relegated this pair to the sidelines, but in effect merely allowed them to conspire removed from the eyes of the government. Four months before the rebellion, on or about March 22, 1936, Azaña received Colonel Jesús Pérez Salas, a thoroughly upright and nonpolitical officer, who wanted to discuss

[2] Juan José Domenchina (1898-1960) was Azaña's official private secretary from October, 1931, to February, 1935, and from January, 1938, until the end of February, 1939. A man of letters in his own right, primarily a poet, Domenchina had been a contributor to Azaña's review *La pluma,* and also to *España.* He continued to publish books of poetry in exile in Spanish America.

the possibility and danger of a military uprising. At that time, Azaña told the Colonel that measures were not being taken against the officers for the very reason that such action would certainly ignite a still-uncertain revolt. Even as early as April, 1936, the "mad colonel" Julio Mangada (see page 90), later to fight on the Republican side, published a documented pamphlet which publicly exposed the Generals' plot, all to no avail. Another public warning was sounded by Indalecio Prieto, who was to serve as the wartime Republic's Minister of Defense from May, 1937, to April, 1938. Prieto's words of insight, buried in a speech at the Teatro Cervantes in Cuenca, May 1, 1936, were so keen that they ought to be recorded here. After he had commented upon the widespread spirit of military rebellion against the Republican regime, he stated: "General Franco, because of his youth, because of his talents, because of his network of friendships in the army, is the man who, at the proper moment, can lead . . . a movement of this kind."

The string of Prime Ministers appointed by Azaña during the spring and summer of 1936 represented an attempt, first, to avoid and then, after July 18, to extinguish the rebellion by conciliation. Apparently nothing could be done. The armies were marching; the people were in the streets demanding arms. No one would listen to reason, that no party or ideology was worth a civil war. Though some think the Rebels might have been willing at first to work out an agreement with the Republican government, because the insurgent generals delayed nearly a week in forming a government of their own, once the unions and other political and worker groups had taken matters into their own hands and formed their own militias, seemingly responsible to no one, and sometimes fighting one another, the Republican government was powerless to offer the insurgents any meaningful compromise, even though it tried. The people's reaction to the military uprising was not merely one of self-defense; the rebellion had bred revolution. Though there were no revolutionaries in the Republican government at the start of the Generals' revolt, the workers' immediate and violent opposition to the rebellion through their semi-armed political and syndical organizations proved that the lower classes were perhaps closer to a proletarian revolution than either Azaña or Franco had suspected. In one sense, however, despite slogans like the one adopted by the CNT-FAI,[3] "War and Revolution," the Civil War tended to control the same revolution which it had ignited, because the common self-defense against aggression united people of very different political ideologies to postpone social reform until after the essential task of winning the war. Still, it was a question of fascism on the one hand and a proletarian revolution on the other.

This dilemma marked the beginning of Azaña's captivity. He had wanted to resign at the very beginning, and almost did resign after the massacre of political prisoners in the Cárcel Modelo (Model Prison) of Madrid in August of 1936. On this occasion it was Angel Ossorio who dissuaded him from renouncing the Presidency. On other critical occasions both during and after the summer of 1936, on the one hand it was Indalecio Prieto and the sincere moderates who importuned Azaña to consider himself and his office as the necessary personification of the Republic abroad, while on the other hand it was those who received from Moscow their orders that the façade of a democratic Spain had to be maintained. Knowingly or unknowingly, Azaña thus became the essential tool of both factions. Brave with the

---

[3] CNT: *Confederación Nacional del Trabajo* (National Federation of Labor); FAI: *Federación de Anarquistas Ibéricos* (Iberian Anarchist Federation).

Battle fronts of the Spanish Civil War. By mid-February, 1939, all of Catalonia was lost to the Republic, though the Central Zone remained more or less stationary until the end of the war in the final days of March, 1939.

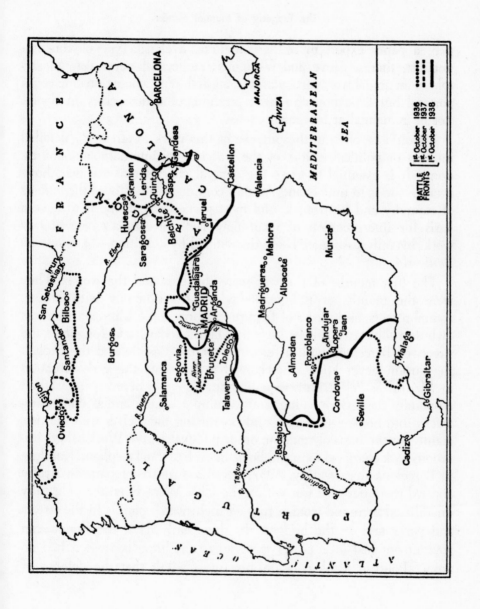

pen, a paper expert in military matters, a classic type of constitutionalist, that sensitive and fastidious intellectual never wanted any role in an actual war, particularly in a Civil War whose outcome could portend but little hope for his aspirations of a democracy in Spain. Yet he remained at his post.

It would be alien to the purpose of this work to attempt a detailed military or political history of the war and its international ramifications. It is essential to grasp the general character of the war, however, if one is to understand Azaña's conduct during those three years of captivity and heartbreak, and most particularly if one is to have a basis for interpretation of what may well be Azaña's best literary work, his only passionate book, uncramped by erudition—*La velada en Benicarló*.

The first months of the war were the best and the worst. They were the months of the people who, armed mainly with knives, common tools, and pieces of furniture, stormed the Montaña Barracks (whose rubble can still be seen in Madrid today) and fought in the streets of Barcelona with a ferocity that the Bastille and the French Revolution never knew. Someone has described the early situation in Madrid as "electrically equalitarian." People of every social and economic class were going and coming, seeking arms, converting trucks into homemade tanks, and organizing themselves into militias, mainly on the basis of trade union or political party. Workers' organizations took charge of most public utilities, like the Telephone Building in Barcelona that in May, 1937, became a source of partisan rivalry and led to a brief civil war within the Civil War. Even the politically unaffiliated men and women formed night-watch patrols in the streets and parks and on the bridges. In these early days, the Republican government had little power to organize anything, because it had no army. Political ideology aside, one must admit that the defense of

Madrid by the people of Madrid was one of the greatest spontaneous acts of "the people" in recorded European history. Lawlessness and indiscipline, however, saw thousands of innocent people and non-Falangists murdered at the moment of their capture or sentenced to be shot by the self-appointed tribunals of the militias. As bad as this may seem, the homicidal tendency may have been even worse on the other side, where the unjustified killings often occurred under official sanction, rather than in contravention of government orders. (Almost every Center-party or Left-wing Republican deputy who happened to be in territory seized initially by the Rebels, was executed.) To no avail did Azaña make an appeal, on July 22, that the indiscriminate executions cease. Even by the end of August, when it was apparent that an unsuccessful coup d'état had created a full-scale civil war, most elements of the Loyalist defense were still at cross purposes through lack of organization and co-operation. This confused state of affairs was to continue throughout the war and to contribute, as significantly as the quantity of Rebel materiel, to the ultimate Loyalist defeat.

With communication to Madrid severed, at first each town was autonomous and everyone seemed to want to make war on his own initiative and for the benefit of his own group. Some of the events were preposterous examples of warfare, pathetically humorous. Any one of the militias in Madrid would send a truck to the grenade factory in Toledo (noted for its duds) to get grenades for its own men, but not for any other militia or for the government's arms depot. The unions and parties would buy war supplies in France and elsewhere by sending their own delegates in their own name, and not in the name of the Republican government. The Anarchists, mistrustful of the Communists, hoarded supplies everywhere they could; in fact, most of the parties maintained their own arsenals behind the lines while arms were desperately scarce at the front. In Catalonia, the CNT appointed itself to be the border guard and did not even recognize the passports issued by the Catalonian government. In the early stages of the war, the Madrid militiaman took the subway to the front and returned home when he had had enough fighting. The story is told that in the fierce, but fluid, fighting at the University of Madrid campus, it happened sometimes that opposing units occupied different floors of the same building; and there in the Clinical Hospital some Loyalists sent up a cargo of grenades, with pins pulled, in the elevator to a floor occupied by the enemy. Bombs were very scarce up in the Basque country and a small private airplane, which had been used for sightseeing prior to the war, dropped a cargo of stones on an enemy town. The Rebels besieged in the fortress of the Alcázar in Toledo were permitted to telephone their families in the city, thanks to the Loyalists, who controlled the telephone exchange. (Apropos of the Alcázar, André Malraux inserted this anecdote into his novel *Man's Hope*: Major Rojo went into the Alcázar for a parley with Moscardó, the commanding officer. The ceiling had been blown out of the office, but "on the back, which was undamaged, just above Moscardó's head, hung—would you believe it?—Azaña's portrait; they'd forgotten to take it down.") Fraternization across the trenches was common in some sectors, while in the cities no man's life was secure, especially if he lacked a trade-union card or party affiliation. To add to the terrorism in the big cities, the jails had been opened and looting was rife.

Only in Bilbao, with the exception of one tragic massacre of prisoners by enraged UGT[4] forces after an air raid, was the local government able to control the homicidal pandemonium from the start and to organize that city of 400,000 into an orderly co-operative effort. The

[4] UGT: *Unión General de Trabajadores* (General Workers' Union).

Basques are by tradition a democratic and well-disciplined people. They are also the most devoutly Catholic people in Spain, yet they fought against Franco and his banner of Catholicism. Basque support of the Republican government, however, was not so paradoxical as it might seem: the fact was that the Basques were attacked. Furthermore, the Fascist unitary philosophy of government was dedicated to eradicating the autonomous regional rights that the Basques were expecting to be granted, according to the example of Catalonia. Basque loyalty was finally rewarded with the Statute of Basque Autonomy, voted in early October, 1936, by the national Cortes transplanted to Valencia. Two days after the action by the Cortes, a vote of the mayors of the three Basque provinces elected José Antonio de Aguirre as President of the newly autonomous Basque country. The Basque summer-resort city of San Sebastián had already fallen (September 13, 1936) after a weak defense, but Bilbao built its *cinturón* of trenches and continued to give a good account of itself until the following summer. Perhaps the Basque government was determined to avoid a repetition of the events at the Basque border town of Irún, where the Anarchists had indiscriminately burned and destroyed everything in the city before they relinquished it to the Rebels on September 5, 1936.

Over in Barcelona the Catalonians proceeded to create their own Catalán army (as of December 7, 1936), independent of other Republican forces—and actually feared by the Valencia-based Republican government, which kept the Thirteenth International Brigade on hand in Valencia as protection against any possible movement from Catalonia. One seldom-considered fact of the early aspects of the war was that certain areas and certain units suffered from what the extremists described as the political discrimination of the central government in the allotment of airplanes and materiel. All weapons were very scarce, even for the central government, but maybe not so impossibly critical of supply as has been generally propagandized. If this is true, it explains partially the government's unwillingness to take the initiative during the first year of war, its feeble efforts at sea (Republican ships were manned largely by sailors who had murdered their officers) and on land, especially on the Aragón front, where the trade-unionist stronghold of Zaragoza might have been taken simultaneously from within and without. Because of the excesses of the uncontrollables, the government may have been reluctant to arm the militias other than for defensive and holding actions, as in the case of Madrid. Well-armed and all-conquering Anarchists, for example, might have been difficult to disarm upon the final formation of a new and more bourgeois state army. The Catalonians, who on their part owed so much to Madrid for their early Statute of home rule, did little to help Madrid in her crisis. It was not wholly attributable to a shortage of weapons that the halfhearted Catalonian "offensive" in Aragón fell short of Huesca, whose capture would have opened the way to Zaragoza; and the unsuccessful Catalonian expedition to Majorca was no more than a wild adventure. Until the concerted effort of November, 1936, in Madrid, the Loyalist defenders were too disorganized to block the continued Rebel advance in any sector. When the forces of Franco took Badajoz (August 14, 1936), near Portugal, he was able to link the Rebel armies of the south with those of the north very early in the war; and the likewise early capture of Irún several weeks later cut off the western French border to the Republic.

In Madrid itself, popular enthusiasm alone could not win the battle for the defense of the city. With the approach of autumn, things were not going well for the *madrileños*, and the government prepared to leave the city. Manuel Azaña departed from the National Palace (to which he had moved from the Casa del Príncipe at the very start of the war) on October 19, 1936, under circumstances announced by the press as a tour of the eastern and Catalonian fronts. Much has been written of his failure to visit the fronts and of his "cowardice" in leaving Madrid, although few Republicans at that time thought Madrid could hold out. Everything seemed to be disintegrating, and the rest of the government followed Azaña within three weeks. Little was left of the original diplomatic corps; many founders of the Republic and intellectuals like Marañón, Pérez de Ayala, Ortega y Gasset, and Madariaga either had left Spain already or were soon to make their exit; and though the local military organization was soon to show some improvement, Azaña was still unable to control the government with the authority inherent in his Presidential office.

On leaving Madrid, Azaña went to Barcelona. His enemies say he chose Barcelona so that he could be close to the French border in case of a Republican military collapse; his friends say he went to reside there in order, by his presence, to help keep Catalonia in tow. At first he was the guest of Companys in the Casa de Canónigos. Then he took up residence in the Catalonian Parliament building, where he was domiciled until after the short-lived Barcelona rebellion of May, 1937, during which the Parliament building was besieged and Azaña rightly feared for his life. Shortly after the May riots Azaña moved to the Capitanía General in Valencia, where he resided until February of 1938. Then he and the Presidential household moved back to Barcelona, having followed the shift of the government from Valencia. This time Azaña did not live in the city of Barcelona, but on a farm near Tarrasa, about forty kilometers northwest of Barcelona.

On the farm, named La Barata, the President led a tranquil existence. Though he was not unoccupied—there were always piles of documents to be signed, his ministers of government regularly visited him with reports, and he had to preside over frequent meetings in Barcelona—this period, like each of his previous eight-month stays

175

in Barcelona and Valencia, was an obscure one in Azaña's personal life, probably because he wished it to be so. Apprehensive of the mobs, and accompanied only by his wife (who contributed to the war effort as a nurse), by his private secretary, an occasional friend, a handful of guards, his military advisers, and the Treasurer of the Presidential Household (old friend Sindulfo de la Fuente), he lived from day to day increasingly irritated by news of Loyalist setbacks. Aside from his business of state in Barcelona, his principal sallies were visits to nearby places like Montserrat and Benicarló, and public appearances for his few wartime speeches. Because Azaña deplored the Communists and the Anarchists, and they had no use for him, his virtual seclusion was primarily a means of staying alive.

The rest of the government (the cabinet, that is) had given up Madrid for lost when on the evening of November 6, 1936, they left by auto for Valencia. Headed by Prime Minister Largo Caballero, they all traveled together, except Indalecio Prieto (then Minister of Air and Navy), who stayed on until the next evening when he left by airplane. The group traveling by car had a narrow escape before they arrived in Valencia: they were delayed on the way by a wildcat band of unsympathetic Anarchists. Although the original plan was for the government to be established in Barcelona, for a number of practical reasons Valencia instead became the improvised capital, and the seat of government activity was not moved to Barcelona until November of 1937. In a way it was unfortunate that Azaña chose to live in Barcelona while Valencia was the center of activity. His signature was sometimes urgently needed when it had to be got by mail, and he was unavailable for advice and decisions that should have been given and made on the spot.

Somehow the people of Madrid seemed to fight harder without the red tape and bureaucratic inefficiency. Only a handful of lower-echelon radio and censorship personnel remained behind. After the initial panic, the flight of the government had the opposite effect of erasing defeatism and rallying the people to a supreme effort of their own defense under orders of General José Miaja, who had been left to form and head a defense junta. In the present writer's opinion, four interdependent phenomena saved Madrid; no single one of them could have accomplished that result: (1) the leadership of strong-willed Miaja and his hastily organized General Staff—he knew how to demand obedience, and they knew how to respond; (2) the timely appearance of Russian technicians and materiel; (3) the arrival of three battalions of the Eleventh International Brigade at a critical juncture in the fighting, November 8; and (4) the people's collective will to resist. The last development had been solidified, although not created, by the first three. Men and women built parapets with ordinary builder's bricks and paving stones dug up from the streets. Barricades were improvised from furniture, mattresses, pillows, and other furnishings. The Plaza de España (where one can still see the statue of Don Quijote and Sancho Panza) grew a sandbagged trench, because from there it was only a short way down the hill to the Manzanares river and Casa de Campo where the Rebel attack was the strongest. The International Brigade had no sooner arrived than it went into action at Casa de Campo and around the nearby University City. All too quickly its ranks were halved by casualties in warfare as fierce as any battle had ever been. The besieging generals were confident of a quick ground victory that never came, nor did the ensuing and almost daily air raids of November and December break the will of the city. Gradually a stalemate developed that was to last in Madrid until the end of the war, which is to say that Madrid never surrendered.

Although the unquestionable bravery and tenacity of the International soldiers was instrumental in the rescue of Madrid, the Brigades were in the early part of the war as independent as the militias, and undeniably Communist dominated. They grew accustomed to a certain amount of deference from the grateful *madrileños*. A woman who had been a nurse in one of the Madrid hospitals told me that she had to give special treatment and extra food, including sugar which was so scarce, to the International Brigades' wounded, when the Spanish wounded did not even have enough to eat. Aside from the handful of idealists and intellectuals, who will inevitably appear in any Left-wing organization, the Brigades were populated with adventurers, riffraff, and Communist union-men from everywhere, who often subordinated military affairs to the propagandizing of Communist ideology. Even after the formation of the Peoples' Army later, the political committees and not the Republican government really directed the war. Each political group became increasingly intolerant of the others as the war progressed, and the Internationale was heard more often than the *Himno de Riego* (Republican national anthem). The International Brigades first went into action at Madrid and fought in Spain until September 28, 1938. By that time, the need for them was no longer desperate, and their withdrawal from the trenches was thought to have propaganda value. The Internationals officially left Spain on October 28, 1938, ten days after their farewell parade in Barcelona, although some of them found unofficial ways to return to fight for the Republic.

Interesting reading today are the now rare issues (May 24, 1937, to November 7, 1938) of *The Volunteer for Liberty*, organ of the English-speaking battalions of the International Brigades in Spain. This tabloid was published at weekly or longer intervals in a great variety of lengths and other dimensions, according to the availability of paper and presses, but always with the same general content. It was chiefly a pro-Russian and anti-capitalist propaganda sheet with an appeal directed to worker sentiment, despite its pretense at reporting world happenings and war news for the isolated soldier. A good strike in the U.S.A., for example, was always a worthy news item. Only once did the *Volunteer* speak of "our President," Don Manuel Azaña, with a biographical piece in the February 28, 1938, issue. Otherwise the attention went to the speeches and activities of Juan Negrín, whose Premiership of the Republic obviously was acceptable to the Communists.

Edwin Rolfe was a veteran of the Abraham Lincoln Battalion of the Fifteenth International Brigade and the second of three editors of *The Volunteer for Liberty*. In 1939 he published a book, *The Lincoln Battalion*, a history of that Battalion. On page 158 he described the first anniversary of the defense of Madrid (November 7–14, 1937) and spoke of the "gay flags and posters and decorations in celebration of the event and of the twentieth anniversary of the U.S.S.R., which all Madrid—all of Republican Spain—is commemorating with the warmth and spontaneity so characteristic of the people. Spanish flags wave from the electric poles of all street cars, huge signs and posters are plastered over all central buildings, even on the great arch in the Calle de Alcalá. Numerous huge pictures of the founder of Spanish Socialism, Pablo Iglesias, and of the well-loved and richly bearded (in the most fantastic colors) Carlos Marx." No atmosphere for Manuel Azaña!

On January 21, 1937, a little over two months after Madrid's most critical days, Manuel Azaña gave at the *Ayuntamiento* in Valencia the first of his four wartime speeches. One can still see him declaiming a part of this speech in the film *Spanish Earth*, produced in the first year of the war and narrated by Ernest Hemingway. The short scene in the film also gives a glimpse of Azaña's oratorical technique, although the confident pose is not typical of the President's four wartime speeches in general, which were more subdued and unsure than his previous ones. The old verve was replaced with a kind of warmth that had always been the one element lacking to a perfection of style in less melancholy days of public speaking. The whole Valencia speech was moderate in its appeal, and the tone was not defeatist, but neither did his words exude any unfounded faith in victory.

Azaña spoke of the re-establishment of order, in Spain and in Europe. Unlike most of his colleagues of government, Azaña never hoped for a general European war as the solution to the Spanish Republic's predicament. Such a solution would not be advantageous, he said, first because any war in itself "is always a catastrophe"; second, "because a general war, if it did break out, would rob the Spanish cause of its identity." As he paid homage to the *madrileños* for their magnificent defense of Madrid, a city "where nothing had ever happened," Azaña exhorted them to military discipline and obedience to the government as the only path to victory. With words of caution against the dangers of "Spanish spontaneity" and "personal initiative," he expanded his appeal to all Loyalists, in and out of uniform, for discipline and order.

The last lines of this discourse were pathos itself, and expression of deep regret and personal tragedy. "Peace will come (*vendrá la paz*), and I hope it overwhelms all of you with joy. But not me." The war has been torture, he continued, for someone in a position like his. "None of us has desired this awful fate . . . . We have fulfilled the terrible task of rising to the occasion." This is to say that he painfully continued in the Presidency only from a sense of duty. "Peace will come and with it victory, but the victory will be an impersonal one: the victory of the law [always the legalistic view], the victory of the people, the victory of the Republic . . . . It will not be a personal triumph, because when one has in his soul the Spaniard's grief that

I have, one does not gain a personal triumph over compatriots. And when your first magistrate raises the flag of victory, surely his heart will break, and no one will ever know who has suffered most for the liberty of Spain." Such were the words of a man who was more wounded than angry, more zealous of peace than of victory. Even though he made no concrete reference to possible defeat or compromise, the whole tenor of the speech gave the impression that Azaña would accept any government for Spain as long as it was based on national independence and individual liberties. Was this a disguised overture for an armistice, from a speaker experienced in rhetorical art of subtlety and suggestion? Surely the phrase "victory will come" typified the passiveness of his concept of victory.

In 1937 Azaña used certain devious diplomatic offices to work for a negotiated peace. His sending Julián Besteiro to London is still a mysterious affair. When the British government invited the Spanish President to attend the coronation of George VI on May 12, 1937, Azaña instead sent Besteiro, under circumstances which many people presumed to have been a peace mission, one which sought the aid of England as an intermediary in putting an end to the Spanish War. Apparently the effort was in vain, for Besteiro returned and nothing happened, nor did Besteiro ever make a report to anybody but Azaña.

Meanwhile Communist influence in Loyalist affairs was increasing day by day. Francisco Largo Caballero had been Prime Minister since September 4, 1936, when the moderate Giral government resigned after the fall of Irún and Talavera de la Reina. It was Largo Caballero who had accepted Communists in the government for the first time, and later regretted it. It was also he who, having assumed both the Ministry of War and the Prime Ministry, imagined himself to be a military strategist and made such a mess of things that the miraculous defense of Madrid in November owed nothing to him except its necessity, the result of his blunders. In two months, he had taken practically no steps to defend the city from either air raid or ground assault, while during this time his combined Minister of State and Chief of Political Commissars, the more-than-pink Julio Alvarez del Vayo, was very busy indoctrinating the armed forces. Largo Caballero was a hotheaded agitator and union man (head of the Socialist UGT) who had risen from the rank and file to insinuate himself into the government. This background, plus his support by a large segment of the workers, led Moscow to a wrong interpretation of his revolutionary tendencies. Largo Caballero was a "pure" kind of Socialist revolutionary, equally inimical to capitalists and Communists. When in typical Spanish fashion he proved to be not internationalistic, hence not subservient to Russian interests, means were found to replace him with Dr. Juan Negrín, who was installed as Prime Minister on May 17, 1937. As Minister of Finance under Largo Caballero, Negrín was the one who sent the Spanish gold to Moscow.

Professor of physiology at the University of Madrid, an intellectual, and outwardly a moderate type of Socialist, Negrín was to open the doors wide to Communist domination of the government and the armed forces. Prior to his ascent, the Communists had dominated principally the city that they had rescued at the end of 1936—Madrid. Negrín remains today one of the most controversial figures of the Spanish Civil War. Undeniably he was a strong leader, an indefatigable worker, and a fighter to the end. His courage, self-confidence, resourcefulness, and vigorous personality won him the perpetual praise of Herbert Matthews and certain other correspondents whose personal involvement with the Loyalist cause may have taken a measure of objectivity from their writing. Even Azaña accepted Negrín at first, and so did the non-Communist and non-Catholic Indalecio Prieto, whose key role as Negrín's Defense Minister lasted until April 5,

1938, when Communist pressure finally forced Negrín to remove Prieto. But few of the Negrín supporters in the press ever really knew this tactless, indecorous, disorganized, and unscrupulous man, whom even his friends admit to have been a kind of Rasputin-of-the-stomach-and-sex in his personal life. Was he secretly a Communist? Many think so. I doubt it. I should prefer to think that his close ties with the Communists were simply a matter of expediency, while in turn the Communists supported him because he was a man of action with little concern for parliamentary red tape. With time, Negrín became more and more Machiavellian. He lost sight of the cause and would have won the war at any cost, even at the cost of Republicanism itself. Meanwhile President Azaña continued to believe that no ideal was worth the destruction of Spain.

Having established himself firmly in the Premiership, Negrín soon showed a scorn for Azaña's plodding constitutionalism. Privately he often referred to Azaña as an *"hombre de cartón-piedra"* (papier-mâché man). To Negrín, Azaña represented weakness. These two men, so different in outlook, exasperated each other. Even though Negrín did keep up appearances, he would have preferred to ignore Azaña and Azaña's office of Presidency of the Republic. Negrín intimidated the Cortes, which under him met only seldom and did nothing, and he disregarded everybody else who failed to fall in line with his dictatorial policies. Eventually he had more power than any other Republican Minister had ever had, yet his constant complaint was that "they don't let me govern." But how did Negrín govern? His routine, or rather his lack of it, confused everybody. He was a tireless worker, but would work only in his own way. He could never be found when needed. He exposed himself to unnecessary danger by his frequent travels and visits to the various fronts. Then in the middle of the war, after first having consulted with Azaña, who presumably gave his approval, Negrín packed his bags and before dawn one morning enplaned for a convention of physiologists in Zurich! He returned from the convention disappointed, because he was hoping to exchange medical views with a certain American professor who did not attend. Such was life with Prime Minister Negrín in the midst of the Civil War.

In the summer of 1938, President Azaña lost his showdown encounter with Negrín. The Gestapo-like tactics of the Prime Minister's administration had bred the worst sort of terrorism, and Azaña made an attempt to utilize his constitutional prerogatives in order to replace Negrín. Inasmuch as Communist officers held two-thirds of the higher military commands, it was not difficult for the Communist party to persuade a majority of the senior officers to send to the President messages of unquestioned confidence in Negrín. Also a pro-Negrín parade of Russian tanks and airplanes was arranged to take place in and over Barcelona. Azaña found it impossible to act in face of such evidence that the army was behind Negrín; consequently, on August 16, 1938, Negrín went to see Azaña and emerged from the interview reconfirmed in the office of Prime Minister, which in reality was that of dictator, until the end of the war.

No one should deny that in the early months of the war the Communists helped save Madrid, or that the Communist units were the principal, if not the only, units fighting at the end of the war (in Catalonia, that is—all else was anticlimax). These two facts have led numerous observers to false conclusions, since it was the Communists who, in this writer's opinion, really lost the war for the Republic during the years of attrition between the beginning and end of the war. Despite the substantial German and Italian aid to the Insurgents, this was a war in which victory for the Loyalists was possible all along, after the first few months of utter chaos. Ironically, the Rebel uprising of July,

1936, against presumed Communist domination was what actually catapulted the Communists into a position of domination, unattainable before the war when even the Popular Front electoral victory of February, 1936, brought only fourteen Communist deputies to the Cortes.

The swiftness of the Republic's initial setbacks created an exceptional situation that required full utilization of makeshift defensive tactics, born of popular zeal. But that improvisation continued, despite the gradual buildup of what was called a Peoples' Army. Why? Because a weak government allowed military matters constantly to be subordinated to the imposing of ideologies. Many of the high Communist commanders under Negrín were stupid, even illiterate, individuals who continued in the same vein as in the early days of the war, when everybody was half-soldier and made war on his own account and in his own way. When the *Ejército Popular* was formed, a corps of professional officers might have been created, men not tied to the apron strings of any party. After the initial emergency in Madrid, the poorly organized militias and International Brigades and all their immense autonomy might more judiciously have been reserved only for such minor action as guerrilla warfare. After the confusion of the early days, the war was not lost by the soldier, but by the Loyalist military leaders' incapacity to utilize his qualities. In the entire two and one-half years of war, the Republican government made scarcely any progress in the development of intelligent and able officers.

To discover the exceptions to this is to reconsider always the regional nature of the war: that the combatants themselves fought for varying reasons and with varying means; that the areas of combat were largely isolated one from the other, each region with its own variety of Spanish provincial customs and temperament; and that the Spanish petty bourgeoisie in general wavered between a loyalty to its regional and national governments on the one hand, this loyalty diminishing in proportion as the proletarian revolution grew regionally and nationally, and on the other hand an awareness that it had less to lose to Fascist dictatorship than to a dictatorship of the proletariat, should the latter gain the upper hand in the event of a Republican victory. This is to reiterate that when proletarian violence makes democracy no longer possible, capitalism can turn to fascism as a last stand. All of these considerations created a Loyalist soldier who was difficult to define, because his first loyalty was frequently to his *patria chica,* or to his political party or trade union, or to whatever represented his own interests, rather than to the Republican government and to any collective ideal for which it stood. Since the issues of the war were never clear for either side, it is easy to understand why so much of a contradictory nature was written by on-the-spot soldiers and observers, who usually had only a worm's eye view of the war from the sector to which they were assigned. George Orwell wrote an absorbing narrative of the military action and political events in Catalonia (*Homage to Catalonia*), but he had no frame of reference to developments on the Basque or Central fronts. G. L. Steer recorded the entire course of the war in the Basque country (*The Tree of Gernika,* another excellent book), where the ideologies, the loyalties, and the fighting itself were so different from those of Catalonia that they might have been on another planet. Even the best of the correspondents who covered more than one front, like Hemingway, Herbert Matthews, Vincent Sheean, or Lawrence Fernsworth, sometimes tended to assume too much. When a writer did manage to perceive a coherent view of the war, that view was frequently fogged by his own political or religious bias. The best history of the Spanish Civil War will possibly be written some day by someone who was never in Spain.

Before Azaña presented himself in the halls of the University of Valencia to deliver his second speech of the war, on the occasion of its first anniversary, July 18, 1937, Málaga had fallen on February 8 of that year and Bilbao on June 19. Although things were going badly, they had not yet become hopeless, and Azaña was to give his only fighting speech of the war. He spoke of the German, Italian, and Portuguese aid to the Nationalists, aid without which the military rebellion would surely have failed. After he had reviewed the motives for the "foreign invasion," he turned his attention to the League of Nations, the Non-Intervention Committee, the proposal to give Franco belligerent rights, the miraculous formation of a Republican Army in one year, civilian morale, the origin of the war (hatred and fear), and, finally, the question of national unity. Again his words demonstrated his indignation, the word which best describes his reaction to the international treatment accorded the legitimate Spanish government.

Why had not England, France, or the U.S.A. helped the Spanish Republic? Undoubtedly their diplomatic reports had emphasized the unstable situation caused by proletarian extremism in Spain, and the democracies' demurral was based mainly on fear of involvement. Even though opinion was divided in the democratic countries, their governments probably would have come openly to the rescue of the Spanish Republic had it not been for a vain hope that non-intervention might prevent further ideological division of Europe by discouraging German and Italian aid to the insurgents. The democracies' continued failure to act, even when German and Italian aid became both ample and overt, presaged the coming spirit of appeasement, infamous in one word—Munich. In the case of Spain, non-intervention was equivalent to appeasement, because European status quo was to be achieved at the expense of the Spanish Republic, whose spasmodic aid from Russia (and trickle from Mexico) never matched that of the insurgents' assistance from Germany and Italy. Nor was Russia ever a real friend of the Spanish Republic. Russia not only sought to enrich herself with Republican gold, but coveted a position of advantage in international politics (like Germany and Italy) at the expense of Spanish lives. The first Russian materiel did not arrive, however, until October 15, 1936. By that time, non-intervention had already been proven a farce, for the Fascist dictatorships had supplied Franco uninterruptedly since almost the beginning.

France, in the person of its Premier, the Socialist Léon Blum, was more disposed than was England to help the Republic. He and his government had recently gained office on a *Front Populaire* program, like the Spanish government, and he personally not only wanted to help his fellow Socialists in Spain, but was convinced that a continuation of the present Spanish state was in the best interests of France. Yet the vehemence of the opposition from the Right, together with the fear of jeopardizing the friendship of England, vital in those troubled days, caused him to accede ultimately and reluctantly to the policy of non-intervention, a position conceived by the British in the very first week of the Spanish War. As early as July 21, 1936, the Spanish Prime Minister of the moment, José Giral, Azaña's old friend, had telephoned Paris to seek military supplies. This type of purchase was not only normal to a sovereign government under international law, but also guaranteed by a secret clause in the French-Spanish commercial treaty signed in December of 1935. Unofficially some French aid did reach the Spanish Republic—for example, the French Air Minister and friend of the Republic, Pierre Cot, did everything he could, over and under the counter—but ironically it was the early proven German and Italian intervention that persuaded the French to adopt a policy of avoiding an intervention contest. Blum's hands were tied; duty to his own France overrode the obligation he felt to Spain.

In the U.S.A. the master realist-politician, Franklin Roosevelt, envisaged internal political complications as a result of the religious factor if he acted in behalf of the Republic, this despite the fact that Americans who were awake to world affairs leaned largely to the Loyalists. Not enough people anywhere, however, really understood the Spanish situation; and the force of world opinion, major aim of all propaganda in the present atomic age, was not yet sufficiently developed in the 1930's to prevent the widespread vacillation in the matter of what to do about Spain. The non-intervention policy, result of that vacillation, became the most significant factor in the Loyalist military defeat, and the U.S.A. shared in the responsibility for it. Again this would have to assume that the Republic was salvageable and that the Loyalist state was worth saving, as Ambassador Bowers believed it was, though he was unable to convince Roosevelt until it was too late.

In Valencia in the early part of 1937, Manuel Azaña sat, or rather stood, for his only portrait in Presidential regalia. The artist was the well-known portrait painter, José María López Mezquita. A large quantity of this artist's canvases may be viewed in New York City at the Museum of the Hispanic Society of America. Born in Granada in 1883 (he died December 6, 1954), López Mezquita dedicated himself to portraiture at an early age and specialized in peasant types. Then in the late 1920's Archer M. Huntington, founder of the Hispanic Society of America, engaged López Mezquita to paint a series of portraits of prominent Spaniards and Spanish Americans. His is the well-known canvas of Alfonso XIII in hunting costume, of Juan Belmonte, and of the Infanta Doña Isabel de Borbón, of Ramón Pérez de Ayala, Unamuno, Baroja, and other Spanish intellectuals.

The Azaña portrait is a handsome work and the only known oil painting of Manuel Azaña. At this writing, the original portrait graces the mantel above the fireplace in the modest little apartment of Azaña's widow in Mexico City. Undoubtedly the painting will remain with her side of the family. Azaña himself held the canvas in great esteem, and now it is Sra. de Azaña's principal possession. On the occasion of one of my interviews with her, she gave me permission to bring my small camera in order to photograph the portrait. When I arrived, a feminine hand had adorned the mantel directly under the portrait with an elegant display of fresh carnations, whose red brilliance matched perfectly the bright red of the sash worn by the subject of the portrait. For the occasion, that same feminine hand had placed two specially bound copies of Azaña's books on the same mantel, one copy on each side of the flowers.

The portrait captures a characteristic pose, to which perhaps the large glasses or the slightly raised eyebrows endow a blank, slightly questioning—or is it stubborn?—expression. Though the eyes retain all their hauteur, they also have a hint of sadness, while the glossy forehead, double chin, and faintly disguised paunch announce the approach of the winter of life. The light of intelligence shines in this face; otherwise the exaggerated curve of the upper lip and its distinctive canal to the nose (a characteristic of all the Azañas) give the square physiognomy its only exceptional feature. Cover all of the portrait but the mouth and you will see the full, sensual, almost feminine lips.

The excessive flesh, which used to give him a squat appearance, disguised the fact that Azaña was slight of build. But the narrow and sloping shoulders are an accurate detail that distinguishes the original painting in Mexico from its copy, by the same artist, held in the Hispanic Society Museum in New York. This Museum claims to own only originals and was unaware, until I pointed it out to an official there (who, I think, did not believe me), that in this case their painting is a copy. Probably owing to a lack of public interest, the Museum's canvas of Azaña has not been on display in recent years, but is kept in a vault. The Society's records indicate that the picture was acquired (arrived at the Museum) on October 26, 1937. The original in Mexico, however, must have been painted very early in that year, because (1) the artist did not request permission to copy the painting until some time after he had finished the original and delivered it to Azaña, and (2) the copy now in the Hispanic Society Museum was reproduced in Republican Spain as early as February, 1937. Azaña himself did not want the copy to be made, for fear that the original would thus lose value; but according to Sra. de Azaña, "he owed López Mezquita a favor," and at length gave his permission. To the best of my knowledge, this was the copy which the artist sold to Huntington, who in turn presented it to the Hispanic Society.

The original painting remained hidden in France during the Second World War, along with an estimated six thousand books of all kinds remaining from Azaña's private library. The books are still there somewhere in France and, unfortunately, are not for sale.[5] After World War II, the exiled widow of Azaña made a trip to France in order to visit her husband's grave and to bring back to her apartment in Mexico City what she hoped would be the intact portrait. The painting was not only still safe, but its dimensions (which she had forgotten) fit perfectly on the wall for which it had been reserved in that "temporary" apartment of a second-class district in Mexico City. She has lived for many years now in that apartment, where she continues to nourish

---

[5] Azaña's only sister, Josefa (see page 9), had been deeded the family home in Alcalá de Henares by Manuel and Gregorio Azaña many years ago, and there she had lived until the early days of the Civil War when the Rebels held the city briefly. At that time she and her husband went to Murcia and then later to France. When Manuel Azaña relinquished his private residence at Serrano 38, he stored his books in a bookseller's basement in Madrid and later had them brought to Valencia during the war. From Valencia he sent the books to his sister in France. Reportedly numerous other personal and political documents were entrusted to another person in Toulouse whose domicile was raided by the Gestapo during the German occupation.

reminiscences of better days, though she is resolved never to return to Spain. I recall that she once reverently showed me an enlarged photograph of Azaña's right hand, the hand, she explained, which penned the books and signed the documents of state.

For two weeks at the end of April and beginning of May, 1937, that hand was writing its most telling analysis of the first year of the Spanish War, a sober statement of truths which relegates his 1937 speeches to the realm of forced optimism and the formal encouragement expected from the President of a people who were losing a war for, if not their questionable democracy, at least their independence. The Spanish title of this the most poignant of all Azaña's literary works was *La velada en Benicarló;* what is between its covers obviously could not be published during the war, at least from the pen of the President. Little unofficial publishing facility existed in wartime Republican Spain anyhow. Azaña took the manuscript with him when he crossed into France in 1939, and he allowed it to be published first in French as *La veillée à Benicarlo* (Paris, 1939) by the Gallimard firm, with French translation by Jean Camp. (By coincidence the work was published on the same day that France declared war on Germany.) Later in the same year, the Editorial Losada published in Buenos Aires the original Spanish text.

By intention or by coincidence, the title has symbolic importance. *Velada* can mean a soiree or evening party, but literally and etymologically (Azaña's diction is usually precise) it means a vigil or the act of watching something or watching over something. The book's vehicle of expression is a dialogue among some Loyalist professional and political types. Most of the conversation, about the Civil War, its causes, and its progress, takes place in the evening at an inn in Benicarló, where the travelers have stopped. Not only is the general discussion a kind of recorded *tertulia,* but interpreted in larger terms it is a wake for Spain, a *velada* which Azaña witnesses not only as the creator of these disputants, whom he "watches" while they argue their own opinions (mostly his own opinions), but as President, and thus, by obligation, the principal caretaker of what has become, to him, the corpse of Spain. Maybe Azaña did not intend such symbols; even so, their parallel is apt: he did conduct a *velada* during the whole of the Spanish Civil War.

Azaña wrote the dialogue two weeks before the CNT and POUM[6] insurrection of May 3–10, 1937, in Barcelona. In a foreword written in 1939 he tells how he dictated the rough copy during the four days of his siege in the Catalonian Parliament building, and he claims not to have added a word to the manuscript since. Maybe he needed these circumstances to impel him to vent his spleen, for the first time, in writing. The tempest of civil war within the Civil War put whitecaps of anger on Azaña's normally tranquil prose, now deep troughed with disillusionment. Keenly analytical, *La velada en Benicarló* reads like oratory given fictional form by the pressure of circumstances.

Azaña's premise, as always, is that what is moral and just is born of human reason. This conviction lay at the root of his variance with the church, for the Christian religion puts ultimate justice in another world. Now it is the whole war that lacks reason, because no possible outcome could justify the cost, nor does the war resolve anything. Azaña puts his own sentiment into the words of one of his discoursers: "If in '30 or '31, at the start of the Republic, its advent had depended on me, on the condition that Spain be plunged into a horrible war, I would have resigned myself not to see a Republic in my whole life."

As the group discusses the shortcomings of the Republic, someone comments upon the Spaniard's tragic capacity for quick-tempered violence. The atrocities of the Loyalists, however, are committed in

[6] POUM: *Partido Obrero Unificado Marxista* (Marxist Unified Worker Party).

spite of the government, "inert and impotent because of the rebellion itself," while those of the other zone are committed with the approval of the authorities. There are harsh words too concerning the undisciplined Loyalist militias, for the taking of street barricades is different from the planned strategy of a battlefield, where improvisation usually spells defeat. "Give a prize to the mess steward who prevents the insurrection of his battalion, but don't make him a colonel." And even of the regulars, "in our land—violent, intolerant, undisciplined— generals younger than sixty are a national threat." As to the war in Catalonia, "while others fight and die, Catalonia plays politics. There is almost no one at the front . . . . After eight months of war Catalonia still has not organized any useful force . . . . Catalonian affairs during the Republic have, more than any others, provoked the hostility of the army against the regime." Possibly the outburst against Catalonia can be attributed, in some degree, to the circumstances under which the polemic was written, for Azaña had been more than cordial to Catalonian aspirations when he was Prime Minister. But otherwise, what irony! Catalonia, which had counted on Azaña as its greatest champion in the days of the Constituent Cortes; Catalonia, to which Azaña had brought in person and in triumph the Statute of Autonomy—this same Catalonia was now the Republic's greatest liability.

Always a proponent of emancipation of women (in his essay "El Idearium de Ganivet" and elsewhere), Azaña now devotes lengthy and significant passages to a reappraisal of woman's role in the Republic. Her accountability in helping to bring about the war has disillusioned the emancipator. Spanish women did not take their newly granted responsibilities seriously, particularly their right to vote. Maybe the matron saw that numerically her single vote would always weigh less than the votes of her servants, but it is more likely that mistress and maids alike made a political program of Catholicism. During the time of the 1936 elections, a recommended Spanish catechism of the church had taught that it was a mortal sin to vote for or support the Republic, or any liberal government which espoused freedom of religion, press, or education.

Anyone who has lived in Spain knows that women form the very large majority of the parishioners who come out of nearly any church after mass, even in the deeply Catholic Basque country. Of all the Christian sects, Catholicism is the faith *par excellence* of sentiment. Catholicism also provides the most guarantees in exchange for obedience to its doctrine, which at the consumer level is usually reduced to simple ritual with a definite aesthetic appeal. If the male's outlook on life is an expansive one, woman must focus. He is most naturally at the tiller; she handles the anchor. She, the realist and the giver of life and continuity, needs constant reassurance, a fact which the church has exploited for centuries. Because patriotism is mostly an idealistic concept, patriotism belongs largely to a man's world; and this was so in the Spanish Republic, except for a few intellectuals like Victoria Kent (who, let it not be forgotten, at the start of the Republic opposed the immediate granting of female suffrage), or an unwomanish extremist like Dolores Ibárruri, *la Pasionaria* as she was called. Perhaps if the women of the Republic could have foreseen a long, brutal war, they might have given more attention to their political responsibilities. Instead their negligence helped to create an atmosphere favorable to a coup d'état, while some women actually kindled the flame of rebellion. The story is told how women used to cast grains of corn in the path of army officers: to identify them as chickens who were afraid to revolt. And once the war had begun, the rebels were quick to seize upon the propaganda value of their insurrection as a religious crusade, which had definite feminine appeal.

195

Unrelated to the causes of the Spanish War, but of unmistakable importance in its eventual outcome, was the already discussed non-intervention policy of England and France. This, more than anything else, evoked the wrath of President Azaña during the almost three years of war—in his private conversations, in his meetings of state, in his speeches, and in *La velada en Benicarló*, where he has an interlocutor named Pastrana make this observation: "If France and England had respected our right to buy arms in their markets, the military and political role of the U.S.S.R. would have been here equal to zero." This affirms the military and political role of the U.S.S.R. to have been pernicious, but necessary, and it demonstrates Azaña's awareness that Communist political influence was an inevitable part of the price for Russian military aid. Pastrana (Azaña) follows with a prophecy that came true: "If the Spanish Republic should perish at the hands of foreigners, England and France (especially France) would have lost the first campaign of the future war."

One by one the conversers go to bed. The *velada* is at an end. The inn and the town sleep in dark silence. Suddenly bombs fall, the town is on fire, and the inn is in ruins. All of the sympathetic characters of the *velada* are presumably wiped out by the raid. What good were all the words, Azaña seems to say, specks of dust in a maelstrom of destruction? What does the corpse care who was right and who was wrong? The sudden and well-calculated indifference of the ending dramatizes with eloquent irony Azaña's message—the senselessness of the Spanish Civil War.

La velada en Benicarló is a bitter book. Its shame, discouragement, frustration, and hopelessness are pathetic. Powerless to prevent the Civil War, or to alter its course, Azaña saw himself as the man who came either too soon or too late. Yet even in angry disappointment Azaña never resorts to personal vituperation in his speeches or published works; the name Franco is not mentioned here nor in any of Azaña's wartime speeches. Although Azaña was to resign the Presidency in 1939 in exile, *La velada en Benicarló* is really his political last will and testament. Here he relinquishes his claim to a place in public life, with the vain hope that some new leader (Negrín was not his man) should come forth to show the way.

In some of the "I accuse" pamphlet literature which followed the end of the Civil War, certain Spaniards who considered themselves loyal Republicans took the President to task for having written a defeatist work. Undeniably the book is a confession of personal insufficiency, veiled in a premise that neither side is worth the cost, that Azaña's countrymen were therefore dying stupidly. But it was an honest work, and Azaña did not publish it until he considered the war to have been irremediably lost for the Republic, and its lessons apparent. To the extent that any war can be useful, the Spanish Civil War did show that the Republic had taken root more than its opponents had believed; it did tear a lot of people from their lethargy; it did teach illiterates in the trenches to write (and all that this implies); it did instill in many Spanish minds some notion of a national conscience, where only a regional one had existed previously; and it did show to the world the unsuspected depths of Spaniards' convictions.

Both the writing of *La velada en Benicarló* (dictation of the definitive draft) and the installation of Negrín as Head of the Government date from May, 1937. By August 25 Santander had surrendered after offering only token resistance; Gijón fell on October 21. On the thirteenth of November, the same month in which the Republican government transferred its base from Valencia to Barcelona, Azaña made the third of his four wartime speeches, this time at the *Ayuntamiento* of Madrid.

His words are addressed to *"Señor alcalde, madrileños todos,"* whom he praises for the heroic defense of their city. It is a very good speech containing some interesting veiled references. One wonders how many of his audience knew that he was really speaking of his own situation when he told them that "the greatest achievement in the life of a man or of a people is to face up to one's fate, above all when that fate is undeserved and cruel . . . . " After he has commented on what he calls the return to discipline and authority, he says, and these are his exact words: "There is again a Republic, a Republic with its three colors and no more." And, as long as a democrat presides over the Republic, those three colors are "all there will ever be." He refers to the Republican flag (red, yellow, and purple), of course, but with the unmistakable warning that it cannot become all red (Communist), or black and red (Anarchist), or anything else. Consider the variety of political colors represented among his audience and his readers—the speech was reproduced in several languages—and imagine the mixed reaction to the words of this leader who, as he himself says, never relinquished from 1931 to 1939 a single principle of his concept of a Republic. "The goal of our war," he affirms, "is to re-establish a Republican peace and the Republic." He continues:

> I proclaim this once and a hundred times, because, my friends, the war and the rebellion have not overthrown any one of the moral principles which have made my public life, nor those which have sustained my personal life in the political sphere. No: not one of them has been overthrown, or yielded to any enemy. What seemed to me unjust in the month of July, 1936, still seems to me unjust today; and what seemed to me practical, urgent, and needful then, in the renovation of Spain, still seems so now. I do not wait for a rebellion, a revolution, or any insurrection to change all my personal and political sentiments. I am the same as I was in the year 1931, and in this spirit I preside over the Republic, and I believe that all Spaniards who love

their liberty and the independence of their country, in whatever party they may be (that is another question), must accept these fundamental principles.

In this speech, as in his other wartime addresses, one cannot help observing the frequency of the word *paz* used in preference to *victoria*. The judgment was clear; there could be no victory in a civil war. His opponents characterized as phlegm the honesty of a man who, as he had declared in his speech of January 21, 1937, still in his heart represented all Spaniards, and who therefore could not conceive of "victory" over any segment of them. He closes the speech with an expression of confidence in tomorrow (*"confianza en el mañana"*), which, like *peace*, is not a synonym for *victory*.

Azaña and the Republicans enjoyed brief elation when Loyalist troops managed to take the city of Teruel early in January of 1938.[7] This advance injected a feeling of renewed hope into the February 1, 1938, meeting of the Cortes at, of all places, the famous monastery of Montserrat. The meetings were brief, their only highlight being a speech read by Negrín. By February 22, Nationalist troops had recaptured Teruel. On March 9, a few days before Hitler invaded Austria, the Nationalists commenced their Aragón offensive, while Negrín flew to Paris to renew attempts at negotiating aid. Driving their wedge toward the Mediterranean, the Franco forces reached the sea on April 15 and cut the Republic in half. Barcelona, now isolated from the central sector of resistance, soon found its principal source of electric power to be in the hands of the enemy. On July 24 the

---

[7] The Republican commander at the victory of Teruel was General Hernández Sarabia, always a favorite of Azaña since the night of the inception of the Republic, when he had escorted Azaña into the War Ministry. During the war, Hernández Sarabia rose to be Under-Secretary of War, then Minister of War on August 7, 1936, for about a month until Largo Caballero succeeded him, and now he commanded all the Republican forces on the eastern front. Later, in France, he attended Azaña at Azaña's deathbed.

Loyalists undertook a desperate and briefly successful counterattack that has come to be known as the Ebro offensive, a surprise attack across the Ebro river. Fighting fiercely, the Republican forces won back territory that they were able to hold until mid-November. Those who know Azaña say that the early part of the Ebro offensive was the only period during the war when he exhibited any real optimism, perhaps because he saw in the gains some basis for negotiation. The offensive did bolster morale temporarily, but after the Loyalists had gradually retreated to their original positions, on December 23 the Rebel forces launched their own offensive on Catalonia. By now Franco had masses of imported men and materiel. His swift advance reached Tarragona on January 15, 1939, and culminated on January 26 in the fall of Barcelona, which did not know how to defend itself as heroic Madrid had done.

Something must be said, however, for Barcelona. Physically and culturally more the image of Paris than of Madrid, traditionally prosperous Barcelona has always had a solid core of thrifty bourgeoisie more orderly and less spontaneous than their counterparts in Madrid. The unruly element of Barcelona was mostly the trade-unionist class, larger and more powerful than that of any other large city in Spain, because Barcelona was and is the industrial hub of the nation. Regardless of class or political affiliation the people of Barcelona had been enervated by more than two years of hunger, privation, and political terrorism; and the force closing in on the city was between eight and ten times larger than the one that had threatened Madrid in her day of crisis. Then too, because of Communist domination and the purges even at the front, the will to resist was ebbing among both soldiers and civilians of all parties. All the evidence indicates that numerically the Communists were still the minority, had there been polls to prove it, but the Communists continued to control the Russian-made weapons and the whole military organization until it was too late. Even with a miraculous Loyalist victory, the future of democracy in Spain seemed doubtful, and this increasingly apparent fact had its effect on the civilian will to a doubtful sacrifice. As the enemy approached Barcelona, the fifth column within the city came out practically in the open. Accordingly the last-ditch battle planned for Gerona never came off. A contagion of defeatism had spread even to the rear guard, while in many sectors the exhausted main body of the army rivaled with its desertions the panic of the populace, because from that northeast corner of Spain the only escape route led to the sea or across the mountains to France. Coincident with these events of the last part of 1938 and the early months of 1939, British Prime Minister Chamberlain had been waving his umbrella around Europe, while Hitler was carving up Czechoslovakia.

The last public speech that Manuel Azaña ever made has elements of greatness. He gave the speech before the improvised Cortes assembled at the *Generalidad* building in Barcelona on July 18, 1938, the second anniversary of the outbreak of the war, and six days before the desperate Republican Ebro offensive. Later the speech was printed in pamphlet form, like his other wartime addresses. Unlike the others, there was a gilt-edged edition of exactly seventy-five handsomely bound copies. Copy number sixty-seven is today a treasured relic in the possession of Azaña's widow. The location of the remaining seventy-four copies is unknown. Undoubtedly some are privately held, but to my knowledge no library in the U.S.A. has a copy of the special edition.

In this speech, as ever, President Azaña showed himself to be more concerned with the salvation of his country than with any military victory of extermination. All of his wartime speeches had as their scope this larger view of things. Again he was speaking to all Spaniards and exhorting them to reconciliation. With his customary refinement of composition and delivery, Azaña's words of restraint continued to remind Republicans of their constitutional rights and duties to the very end. Most of what he had to say, therefore, was not new. He spoke of the reasons underlying the international aspects of the war. He reiterated that the war must be limited, for he still maintained that to limit it was to extinguish it. (Just prior to this speech, there had been some governmental discussion concerning the possibility of bombing Italian ports in retaliation.) He also reiterated his own Spaniard's shame at seeing foreigners fighting on Spanish soil. He mentioned again what he termed the Spanish disease of intolerance and fanaticism, and he reaffirmed that no one wins a civil war. His only new theme was a suggestion that after two horrible years the Spanish War had burned itself out, had run its course, that Spain and Spaniards of both sides were spent. The physical, economic, and moral destruction of Spain was the basis of his new appeal for peace, for he had never aspired to a victory of annihilation. The last sentence of the speech of July 18, 1938, is famous. It consists of sixteen printed lines (160 words) of exquisite declamatory prose, wherein he proclaims poetically that the dead, no longer angry, send the "message of the eternal fatherland, which says to all her sons: Peace, Pity, and Pardon." These three words, *Paz, Piedad y Perdón*, the last that Manuel Azaña uttered from the rostrum of state, have become known as the three P's of Azaña and have been quoted by everybody who has wished to discredit him.

The three P's surely indicated a readiness to negotiate, if not an admission of defeat, quite the opposite of Negrín's slogan of the three R's (*Resistir, resistir, resistir*). As it turned out, the war was lost anyhow, and without honor, but Azaña's speech was received badly by part of the government, and most especially by the Communists in attendance, who did not hide their abstention from applause after the President had finished. Azaña's advocacy of a negotiated peace was not lacking in support; it was what most Republicans favored privately. The controlling Communists, who now had the most to gain from a possible Loyalist triumph, were the principal voices demanding that the war be won at any cost. Oddly enough, if one can believe Julián Zugazagoitia (one of the Republican Ministers and director of the newspaper *El socialista*), not only did Negrín know about this speech in advance, but he approved of what Azaña said.[8]

Nevertheless, all the evidence indicates that from the spring of 1938 Azaña was a prisoner of Negrín's policies, and that during the last year of the war the President led a life of quiet desperation. It is a mystery why, in his political sequestration, Azaña was encouraged to make the speech of July 18, 1938. Maybe Negrín wanted a show of democratic appearances. Maybe the periodic public appearance of the Spanish President was essential to the pro-Republican segment of international opinion, to which Negrín was vulnerable. The President of the Republic had spoken on the first anniversary of the war, July 18, 1937, and the journalists and foreign correspondents would be quick to draw conclusions about his failure to address the nation on the second anniversary. In face of Franco's demand for an uncondi-

---

[8] Julián Zugazagoitia, *Historia de la guerra en España* (Buenos Aires, 1940), p. 440. Zugazagoitia quotes Negrín as follows, which I give in translation: "What Azaña said is in complete agreement with the aims of the Government. I saw the speech two days before it was given, and it was I who asked the president to reinforce that part which you think compromises the Government. Azaña himself was surprised that I accepted some parts of the speech, to the extent that when he expounded them to me he presumed they would not be to my liking. I did not reject them, because I found them to be all right, and I pronounced them suitable then and there. It was a job to convince him to give a speech. He turned down my invitation with these words: 'I just cannot speak unless I say what I feel and think. It would go against both my principles and my responsibility to address the nation and mince words.' That is, I explained to him, precisely what we wish of you: to tell the nation what you think. So, except for the pessimistic and gloomy tone, I subscribe to what the president said. Otherwise I could not have authorized the speech."

tional surrender, Negrín's famous Thirteen Points (announced May 1, 1938) for the cessation of hostilities had been another show of democracy. Since the Thirteen Points could be found in the Republic's Constitution anyhow, his proposing them as a basis for peace showed either naïveté or a lack of respect for the Constitution.

Why did not Azaña resign in 1938 when Communist domination became, under Negrín, an obvious reality? For the same reason that he had not resigned in 1936: pressure was brought to bear against him by various factions, this time especially by Indalecio Prieto with whom Azaña was always in close contact, as well as by the puppets of Moscow, previously Largo Caballero and now Negrín and Negrín's followers. For propaganda purposes at home and abroad, Azaña was still useful to both factions as the personification of a democratic Spain. Azaña in fact still lived with his fetish of legality and constitutionality, which from the start of the war he had reiterated to be the Republic's principal weapon and only hope of survival as a democracy, if by some chance the Loyalists did finally emerge victorious. The Cortes, already emasculated by 1938, was no longer the democratic symbol of former times, so the office of President remained in reality the only vestige of highly placed Republican legality. If the President were to resign voluntarily while a negotiated armistice was still possible, the responsibility for the end of the Republic could be laid at his door. Whatever the motivation, Manuel Azaña was still President when Barcelona fell on January 26, 1939.

The President and the rest of the Loyalist government were trapped in the fall of Catalonia. The main escape route was the Barcelona-Gerona-Figueras highway to the French border, where the national boundary bisects the town of Le Perthus, twenty-four kilometers north

Main route of the exodus from Catalonia.

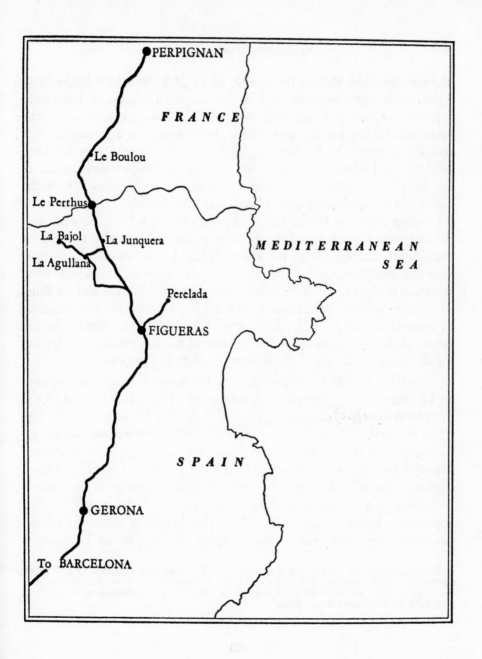

of Figueras. The road of the exodus of 1939 is the tourist highway of today, with signs in three or four languages, a plague of billboards, copious roadside lodging, and every kind of tourist service for the occupants of the foreign cars which speed along on a pavement that still leaves much to be desired. Figueras, dominating the flat farm land of the Llobregat River valley, became the improvised capital of the Loyalist government. North of Figueras the highway leaves the valley to traverse higher areas of oak and cork forests. Less than seven kilometers from the border the road passes through La Junquera, now the last tourist-goods stop (cheap pottery and reed purses) for French vacationers returning from the Costa Brava. On an unpaved side road near La Junquera, and respectively three and nine kilometers from the main highway, are the isolated villages of La Agullana and La Bajol (variantly spelled La Vajol). Less than ten kilometers from Figueras in another direction is Perelada, site of an old castle. Such obscure names as these, unnoticed by the traveler of today, provided the setting for the dramatic finale of the events of 1939 in Catalonia.

According to the Constitution, the Cortes was to go into session on October 1 and February 1 of each year. There in Figueras in the cavernous cellars of the historic Castillo de San Fernando, in a room formerly used as a stable, but now conveniently safe from bombs, on February 1 at about 10:30 P.M. Martínez Barrio (still the presiding officer of the Cortes) called to order the last meeting of the Republican Cortes in Spain.[9] He began by reminding the deputies of the historic and honorable nature of that final convocation of the people's representatives. Easily sentimentalized as the inspiring spectacle of democracy's last stand, the session convoked by Negrín on February 1

[9] Located on a hill overlooking Figueras, the Castillo de San Fernando would be an interesting tourist attraction nowadays, but with characteristic prudence Franco has foreseen that it might also be a shrine of martyrdom. The castle, therefore, is now a military post, with no admittance to civilians.

"according to the Constitution" was indeed laden with emotion, but it was also a convenient cloak for Negrín's unconstitutionality of the last six months. Except for reasons of sentiment and propaganda, why otherwise should the Cortes meet at such a time when it had been inactive since its last session on September 30 (one day early), 1938, when it had met briefly at the monastery of San Cugat del Vallés? And what affairs could those no less than fifty-six nor more than sixty-two (statements vary on the exact number present) of an original 473 deputies resolve at that critical juncture when all was confusion? Azaña for one, always the realist, did not attend, "to his eternal disgrace," wrote Herbert Matthews, intimating cowardice.

Actually this meeting of the deputies of the Cortes, whose bags were already packed, exemplified the main weakness of the Republic since its inception. The weakness was a zeal for oratory, organizations, meetings, and ineffectual lawmaking, rather than for action. Here while the Rebel airplanes strafed the escape routes, teeming with refugees, Negrín addressed a long speech to the mock Cortes in formal style and was rewarded by a vote of confidence. He had always been a poor speaker. On this occasion his talk was even more disjointed, especially the extemporaneous portion. He was a tired man, wholly exhausted from the strain of events. In his harangue he reasserted the legitimacy of the Republican government, whose own vote of confidence he observed to be symbolized by the flight of the civilian population from areas about to fall into Nationalist hands. He reviewed the whole military and civilian situation. He spoke at length on the refugee problem, which, till then, the French had refused to act upon. But the two most significant parts of Negrín's speech were (1) the decision to fight on in the Central Zone if Catalonia should fall, and (2) his Three Points for negotiating a peace, which represented an abridgment of his previous Thirteen Points. The Three Points were a guarantee of Spain's independence, a similar guarantee that the people would decide the government, and a guarantee against reprisals. The Three Points made no more impression than Azaña's three P's. Franco continued to demand, and did soon achieve, unconditional surrender.

Figueras was a nightmare. Jampacked with military and civilian officialdom, the town was bombed repeatedly by enemy aviation. The government was in utter confusion. The Castle lacked adequate electricity, and there were only a few telephones, not to mention the shortage of facilities for such basic things as bathing and natural functions. At night people slept on the stairways and in nearly every corridor; even this was preferable to the cold outside. Meanwhile an estimated four hundred thousand to one-half million refugees clogged the road northward from Figueras, hoping somehow to reach France. Old women, hysterical mothers, screaming children, wounded soldiers without medical attention—it was a spectacle of chaos that no eyewitness has ever found adequate words to describe fully. To the credit of the remaining Republican forces, defeated and physically spent, they managed to cover the retreat sufficiently well so that nearly everybody got out who wanted to get out. With streams of refugees pouring over the mountains everywhere, France finally had to face up to a situation that had become uncontrollable. By negotiation the border at Le Perthus was at last officially opened at 4:30 P.M. on February 5. A human tide surged past the Senegalese French border guards into France. Inundated, the best that France could offer was improvised concentration camps, whose unspeakable conditions later influenced many refugees to return to Nationalist Spain despite the reprisals that awaited them. But that is another story.

Azaña and all the high officials of the Republican government were in or near Figueras as the enemy approached. Prime Minister Negrín was lodged in a farmhouse in the vicinity of La Agullana. President

Azaña and his retinue had moved into the Castillo de Perelada, whose occupancy they had to share with paintings from the Prado stored in that castle prior to their removal to France and Switzerland. (Later Azaña saw the same collection on exhibition in Geneva.) Negrín visited Azaña there in Perelada before February 4, the date that the seat of government activity had to be evacuated from the Castillo de San Fernando in Figueras to—if the Loyalists could be said to have a capital any longer—La Bajol, in whose neighboring talc mines part of the government gold had been stored during the war. Azaña had moved to La Bajol before the fall of Figueras. Part way up a mountain is the sleepy village of La Agullana, whence a miserable road continues to the dead-end mountain top of La Bajol, an isolated settlement of a few dozen squalid dwellings and their few dozen wretched inhabitants, whose only earthly blessing must be the invigorating air and magnificent view. A rifle aimed northward from La Bajol would land a bullet in France.

One of the Presidential household who repaired to La Bajol was friend and brother-in-law Cipriano Rivas Cherif. A few weeks before the elections of February 16, 1936, Rivas Cherif and his wife had taken a theatrical company to Cuba and Mexico, having left their children to be cared for in Madrid. The youngest of the children went to live with the Azañas at the Casa del Príncipe when Manuel Azaña became President. Rivas Cherif heard the news of the uprising as he was boarding the "Cristóbal Colón" for Spain on July 18. Because of the events the ship changed course and went to Le Havre. From there he and his wife returned to Madrid via Paris, Barcelona, and Valencia. Don Cipriano had wanted to be Chief Propagandist for the wartime Republic but was offered instead the ambassadorship to Belgium. This he declined, preferring to become Consul General in Geneva, where his predecessor had deserted. In the spring of 1938 Rivas Cherif was removed from the consular post (more about this in the next chapter) and made official *Introductor de Embajadores* (Introducer of Ambassadors), a kind of receptionist of state and assistant to the President. This sinecure (in those times) put Don Cipriano under the Presidential roof and reunited the two friends on the farm near Tarrasa. Though Rivas Cherif's family remained in France, he too was to live midst the paintings in Perelada and accompany Azaña and his wife up to the mountain top of La Bajol.

The Presidential household moved from Perelada to La Bajol in a truck, supplied by General Rojo (Chief of Staff), and spent part of the first night in the open. La Bajol was cold, very cold. As Sra. de Azaña alighted from the truck she sprained her ankle painfully enough to increase the difficulty of the hike to France a few days later. The President finally found a warm hearth in La Bajol and on the next day was visited by Martínez Barrio and Luis Companys. Subsequently Negrín arrived with Alvarez del Vayo, Giral (then Minister without Portfolio), and again Martínez Barrio. At this second meeting Azaña echoed the opinion of General Rojo that it was pointless to go on fighting. Negrín, who must have concurred inwardly, would not let himself be convinced outwardly. As a result of their talk it was agreed that the Presidential party would pass over into France early the next morning on foot, two official cars and one personally owned Ford[10] to be loaded with personal effects and sent that same day to France, where the cars would pick up the party on the following morning. The truth is that Azaña did not join the mainstream to Le Perthus because he feared for his life. It has been said—and who knows with what veracity?—that the President refused the use of an airplane because he feared that Negrín might fly him back to the

---

[10] Some friends had given Azaña a Ford in 1933 when he ceased to be Prime Minister and no longer had a government car at his disposal. After Azaña finally resigned the Presidency, and thus again lost the official limousines, he and Rivas Cherif used the Ford a great deal in France.

Central Zone against his wishes. At any rate, the plan for the next morning was that Negrín would come to see the President safely across the border, whence, it was further agreed, Azaña would go to the Spanish embassy in Paris. There the President hoped to work through diplomatic channels to achieve a favorable peace. This was his only reason for not having resigned as soon as he reached France.

Accordingly Azaña and his party (including Sra. de Azaña, Rivas Cherif, Giral, Martínez Barrio, some army officers and bodyguards, a couple relatives, plus Epifanio the cook and Antonio the valet) were met by Negrín the next morning and started out from La Bajol while it was still dark, the border guards having been advised to expect them and allow them to pass. The group took the mountain path to Les Illes and walked into France just before dawn on Sunday morning, February 5. The cars were waiting and took the group to Le Boulou and then to Perpignan. The President remarked that he felt as if he had lived the first act of his play, *La corona*, wherein is pictured the end of a civil war, as Lorenzo and Diana are fleeing in the mountains.

After Azaña and Negrín had said their goodbye at Les Illes—it was their next-to-last meeting—Negrín walked back to Spain by the same path. As Negrín told others later, the surprise was mutual when he met Luis Companys and José Antonio de Aguirre,[11] the Catalonian and Basque Presidents, respectively, on their way out too. Negrín's reaction was supposed to have been one of disgust mixed with a feeling of good riddance. Some of the principals involved tell a different story. Angel Ossorio, who was in that second retinue, affirms that their departure was authorized by Negrín on February 4 and that Azaña was to go with them, but that Azaña left earlier than the prearranged

[11] Companys was apprehended later, tried by Nationalist court martial, and executed in October of 1940. Zugazagoitia fell victim to the same fate. Aguirre finally made his way to New York, where in 1941 he was appointed Lecturer in Spanish History and Law at Columbia University. With the liberation of France, Aguirre returned to Paris, where he died of a heart ailment on March 22, 1960, at the age of 56.

hour of 8:00 A.M. on February 5.[12] Whether by Negrín's oversight or by his intention or by their own unilateral action in leaving as they did, this second caravan was not expected by the French border guards at Les Illes and could not enter France until the following day, when their papers were finally accepted.

On February 8 Negrín and the remaining Loyalists were bombed out of La Bajol, which was then abandoned. Negrín and what was left of the government installed themselves in the last dwellings on the Spanish side of Le Perthus until it was unsafe to stay any longer. With emotions ill concealed, they watched the last Loyalist troops march into France. Rebel forces entered the Spanish section of Le Perthus a few minutes before 2:00 P.M. on February 9 and ran up their flag moments later. Less than three hours before, Negrín and his cortege had crossed the bridge into the French side of Le Perthus. From there Negrín went by auto to Toulouse. Apparently he did not leave any specific instructions with his generals or ministers, most of whom were still in France, when that same night of February 9 he flew from Toulouse back to the Central Zone with his Minister of State, Julio Alvarez del Vayo. During the last days of the retreat, Alvarez del Vayo had acted as messenger between the government and its consulate at Perpignan and, for all to see, had sped back and forth across the border in a big limousine while Azaña, the President of the Republic, was making plans to pass on foot unnoticed over the mountains.

Manuel Azaña left the Republic as he had entered it—obscurely. He never saw Spain again. Inasmuch as he had never disguised his feelings about the war, it was to his credit that he remained until the end of Catalonia, which might have been the end of the war.

[12] Angel Ossorio y Gallardo, *Vida y sacrificio de Companys* (Buenos Aires, 1943), pp. 254-55.

THE FRENCH AMBASSADOR TO SPAIN, Jules Henry, had set up his quarters in Perpignan and was urging the Loyalist government to surrender. On February 2 Henry had gone to Figueras and received an obstinate negative from Negrín and Alvarez del Vayo. As Azaña's sentiments were known, it was not hard for him to arrange with Henry that, given a couple days rest, he, the President, should go to the Spanish embassy in Paris in order to seek a more advantageous truce through diplomatic channels, the plan to which Negrín had acquiesced before the President left Spain.

The somber party came through Perpignan early on Sunday morning of February 5 en route to a chalet that Rivas Cherif had rented (and where his family had been staying) in Collonges-sous-Salève, a French hamlet on the edge of the Alps, close to Geneva and the Swiss frontier. The group ate a late supper in Montpellier and spent the night of February 5 in Nîmes before they reached their destination the next afternoon. Very soon after the group's arrival in Collonges, where they were met by the mayor, Azaña established contact by telephone with various individuals of the Loyalist cabinet and then phoned the embassy in Paris. One of his party, former Prime Minister José Giral, went to Paris to the embassy on February 6. (On February 7, the *New York Times* published an Associated Press dispatch to the effect that Azaña was staying with his brother-in-law, Alejandro [sic] Rivas Cheriff [sic], and printed a direct quotation from Azaña's nonexistent daughter!) Having received permission to enter Switzerland, Azaña and Rivas Cherif left for Paris via Geneva the night of February 8. The next day the President arrived in the French capital, where he was to remain at the Spanish embassy in the more or less constant company of Rivas Cherif, José Giral, and General Hernández Sarabia until nearly the end of February.

The *New York Times* had given Azaña one of its unaccustomed headlines on February 6. After February 9, dailies everywhere carried, as front-page news, rumors that Azaña was planning to resign, but the other Spanish War news varied a great deal according to whose dispatches one read. Each faction of the Spanish government—the Azaña realists and the Negrín die-hards—thought itself to be doing what was right and best. The controversy about how and when the war should have ended continues even today among the exiles in America and elsewhere.

As Azaña was arriving in Paris on February 9, the Rebel army reached Le Perthus. The next day the whole of the French frontier was thought to have been occupied, and the official end of Catalonia was reported in the press. Sizable numbers of Loyalist troops continued for some time, however, to hold isolated villages and conduct guerrilla warfare in the high mountains.

Back in the Central Zone, resistance continued even though the land area of the Zone comprised only about one-third that of Spain. Valencia held and so did Madrid, although Madrid was starving. To give them their due, Negrín and Alvarez del Vayo showed courage in returning to what was left of Loyalist Spain. There they intended to play for time and the European war, a course of action that Azaña had so often deplored. The chance that a general European war would save the Spanish Republic at the last moment was Negrín's real reason for refusing to surrender when the hopelessness of the Loyalist situation became manifest.

On February 14, Germans rejoiced at the launching of the battleship "Bismarck." Over in Paris, Azaña was consulting with various persons at the Spanish embassy and attempting to use the good offices of France and England to arrange a cease-fire in Spain that would guarantee no reprisals. Azaña's days at the embassy were not easy ones. He felt abandoned by Negrín, whose support he needed at the embassy, while at the same time Negrín and Alvarez del Vayo back in Spain felt that Azaña had deserted them. The President had to suffer also the slights and even insults of the subordinate personnel of the embassy who, because they had relatives still fighting in Spain, resented his presence there in the embassy. The ambassador himself, Marcelino Pascua, frowned upon the President's coming to the embassy and avoided him as much as possible.

On February 15, the Spanish President had an unexpected visitor at the embassy, Alvarez del Vayo, who had flown in from Madrid to try to persuade Azaña to return to Spain. Azaña refused, of course, and for this refusal Alvarez del Vayo takes him stoutly to task in his two books on the Spanish Civil War.[1] Azaña declined to return for precisely the same reason that his return was demanded: his repatriation might help prolong the war. Perhaps too the President would not have entrusted his life to Negrín and Alvarez del Vayo, once he were in Spain, for any reason other than to officiate at the signing of a peace treaty, for which his presence could conceivably be necessary.

[1] *Freedom's Battle* (London, Toronto, and New York, 1940) and *The Last Optimist* (London and New York, 1950).

No such settlement was imminent, despite subsequent efforts of all factions of the Republican government in and out of Spain, for Franco was then on the doorstep of victory and had even less reason to alter his demand for unconditional surrender. It seemed that nearly everybody of importance was in Paris—Azaña and his intimates, Basque President Aguirre, Catalonian President Companys, Martínez Barrio (still President of the Cortes), and most of the surviving Cortes itself— and none would go back to Spain to resume the puppet role which he had played during the last year in the interest of the common cause. That cause no longer had purpose; and continued warfare seemed irrational, because the people, starved and defenseless, did not want it.

The meeting between Alvarez del Vayo and Azaña was said to have been bitter, particularly in view of Azaña's undisguised receptiveness to any measure that might end hostilities, even to the possibility of a Presidential appeal to Republicans to defy Negrín and lay down their arms. The disaccord of this meeting and Azaña's formal resignation of the Presidency, later in the month, gave rise to epithets of "coward" and "deserter" by the Communists and the Francoists alike. Azaña was to become the scapegoat, for many of the fanatics on both sides failed to see clearly the political and military realities of the situation.

A considerable literature dedicated to the vilification of Azaña's character, by his so-called fellow Republicans, appeared in print after the war in short-book or pamphlet form. A couple typical titles are *Azaña. Combatiente en la paz. Pacifista en la guerra* (by Felipe Alaiz, Toulouse, n.d.) and *Después de la tragedia: La traición del señor Azaña* (by Jacinto Toryho, New York, 1939, printed in Cuba). These two diatribes describe Azaña as a megalomaniac, an anti-revolutionary, a coward, deserter, defeatist, a haughty, decadent Narcissus, and a thief. Perhaps the worst of all is that anyone should call this honorable man a thief, and say that he left Spain with millions in the bank. The truth is that when Azaña died in France, the Mexican government had to pay for the funeral; and from a personal knowledge, I can attest to the reduced circumstances of Azaña's widow today. Except for the Francoist-backed literature on the Republic, which accuses Azaña of everything, the diatribe by Toryho is one of very few commentaries of Republican origin that charge Azaña with financial dishonesty. Azaña's Republican opponents even on the highest levels of government would have admitted that honesty was his supreme attribute.

One particularly odious little book of very bad defamatory poetry is sufficient to demonstrate clearly the depth of degradation to which the memory of the Spanish President, and others, has been subjected in print. Entitled simply *Guerra civil,* and composed by a certain García Pradas, its 5,038 copies were printed at Vesoul (France) in 1947. The bitter poet, or poetaster, levels his barrage at all the enemies of the Republic, as he sees them. In a preliminary section he calls Azaña a "vile type," who was as much a traitor as Franco, and a coward. These four stanzas, entitled "Epitafio a un desertor," refer to Azaña, whom they characterize as having betrayed himself and his people, a vain incompetent so consumed during his lifetime by rancor and envy that he has cheated the appetite of the worms in his grave, who spit on him:

> Aquí yace, si en paz está consigo,
> quien murió de sí mismo envenenado
> cuando, al ser por su pluma desplumado,
> su vergüenza buscó en la fosa abrigo,
>
> Con soñar de su pueblo ser ombligo,
> fué el tiro a la barriga su dictado,
> y, en público su excelso magistrado,
> fué, a escondidas, su más vil enemigo.

Saltamonte de intentos en fracaso,
con la [sic] patas de atrás marcó su paso
y tembló aun del Poder en la alta cima.

De rencores y envidias carcomido,
bien poco que comer aquí ha traído
y eso es tal, que el gusano escupe encima.

To resume the narrative, Alvarez del Vayo went back to Spain with mission unaccomplished. Azaña, the man on whom (as the poet said) even a worm spits, stayed on in Paris. England and France had sent mediators to Burgos (Franco's capital); both Prime Minister Neville Chamberlain and Premier Edouard Daladier were preparing their respective peoples for a *de jure* recognition of Franco without conditions. Azaña was aware that Chamberlain and Daladier wanted him to resign first, so that they could claim their action to be the result, rather than the cause, of his action. When this recognition was imminent, twenty-some lesser powers having already recognized the Franco regime, Azaña made a decision. At about 10:00 P.M. on Sunday, February 26, Manuel Azaña picked up a terminal payment of salary and walked out of the Spanish embassy for the last time. For those who like symbolism, it was reported that an unusually large falling star dropped westward across the sky as he left the embassy and headed for the Gare de Lyon, to which José Giral,[2] Victoria Kent, and a few others had come to bid farewell to their President as he and Rivas Cherif boarded a train for Geneva.

[2] José Giral died December 23, 1962, in Mexico City. In accordance with his wishes, no public announcement of his death was made, not even to Spanish Republican organizations in exile, and he was buried without crucifix, rites, or speeches. Somehow the news of his death spread quickly, because hundreds of friends came to render silent homage to the ex-Prime Minister as his bier, covered with a large Republican flag, was lowered into Mexican soil.

The press did not know how to interpret Azaña's departure. At first it was thought he had resigned; there was talk of his having left a letter in the embassy. It seems, however, that Azaña was waiting for what did in fact become the formal recognition of the new regime by France and England on the next day, the twenty-seventh. Accordingly, back in Collonges, where he had arrived that morning, Azaña then drafted a letter of resignation without delay, his answer to a telegram just arrived from Negrín exhorting him to return to Spain. Azaña had postponed his resignation until the last legal prop in France, the Spanish embassy in Paris, was pulled from under him, though he must have resigned mentally after Negrín went back to Spain and appointed a Communist government.

The actual communication of resignation was in the form of a telegram to José Giral, addressed to him at 6 Rue du Chatillon, 4 gauche, to be transmitted to the President of the Cortes, Diego Martínez Barrio, at 89 Avenue Neuilly. Azaña sent the telegram from Collonges-sous-Salève on his tenth wedding anniversary, February 27, 1939. He composed it on the notebook paper of his godson, Enrique (son of Rivas Cherif), who is today a Mexican citizen, a Ph.D. in Spanish from the University of California, and was an instructor in Spanish literature at Mexico City College.

The letter of resignation of the Presidency was Azaña's last official act in the service of the Spanish Republic. Had he lived, his influence might have been a cohesive force for unifying the Republicans in exile in Europe and the Americas. Succinct in its details, yet characteristically rotund in its phrasing, a model of decorum (as one would expect of Azaña), the letter is more than a resignation; it is a statement of self-justification, but a document lacking in words of gratitude to anyone. I have translated the following text directly from the original:

Since the Chief of Staff charged with the direction of military operations informed me in the presence of the Prime Minister that the war was hopelessly lost to the Republic, a defeat in anticipation of which the government counseled and organized my departure from Spain, I have done my duty of recommending and proposing to the Government in the person of its Head, the immediate conclusion of a peace under humane conditions, in order to spare the defenders of the regime and the whole country new and sterile sacrifices. To that end I have worked personally as far as my limited means of action permit. I have attained no positive results. The recognition of a legal government in Burgos by the powers, specifically France and England, deprives me of the international legal representation necessary to communicate to foreign governments, with the official authority of my office, what is not only a dictate of my conscience as a Spaniard, but the profound yearning of the immense majority of our people. With the disappearance of the political apparatus of state—the Cortes, high party representation, etc.—I lack, inside Spain and out, the organs of counsel and action indispensable to the presidential function of guiding governmental activity in the manner that circumstances imperiously demand. Under such conditions it is impossible for me to retain, even nominally, a post which I did not resign on the very day of my departure from Spain because I was hoping to utilize this lapse of time advantageously to work for peace.

I place, then, in the hands of Your Excellency, as President of the Cortes, my resignation as President of the Republic, so that you may see it through the proper legal steps.

Manuel Azaña
Collonges-sous-Salève
February 27, 1939

The next day the Franco-controlled press shouted "coward," not only because of the resignation itself, but equally because the resignation did not emanate from Spain. Manuel Azaña, however, was conscious of legality to the end: when he had nothing left to represent, he resigned, and with the concluding exhortation that legal procedure be given to his resignation!

According to Article 74 of the Constitution, the President of the Cortes had to assume the interim Presidency of the Republic until the Cortes could take action on the resignation with at least one hundred deputies present. Such a quorum of the Cortes was quite impossible, with most of its deputies either dead or scattered to the four winds, but Martínez Barrio did what he could. He rang up all the deputies available in Paris and managed to assemble sixteen of the people's representatives at the Lapérouse restaurant on the Quai des Grands-Augustins. One of those who attended, Zugazagoitia, described the gastronomic order of the day as being by far more pleasant than the political one.

It has been reported inaccurately that Martínez Barrio refused outright to accept the interim Presidency. This is not the whole truth, even though by that time it made little difference who was President. Martínez Barrio was disposed to accept the post, as the group wanted him to, but only if he were given authority to end the war. His offer included a willingness to return in person to the Central Zone, provided he were assured freedom of action to carry out the authority that he demanded. All of this he telegraphed to Negrín and expected an early reply. No answer was ever given, though it is known that Negrín received the communication.

A few days later, on March 6, the group of deputies in Paris met again. Without a reply from Negrín, Martínez Barrio refused to act further. A government-in-exile was revived after the Franco victory, and still exists today with headquarters in Paris, but technically the Presidency of the Spanish Republic ended with the demurral of Martínez Barrio. In 1945, however, Martínez Barrio did allow himself finally to be confirmed in the Presidency by the remaining (but fewer than the quorum stipulated by the Constitution) members of the Cortes-in-exile meeting in Mexico City; and he was still President when he died of a heart attack in Paris on January 1, 1962, at the age of 78.[3]

Affairs back in the Central Zone were becoming more and more complicated. A situation developed which is not wholly clear even today, and which may have accounted for Negrín's inattention to Martínez Barrio. Negrín had problems more serious than the replacement of Azaña.

On March 1, Colonel Segismundo Casado, who commanded the Central army around Madrid, reviewed with Negrín the desperate nature of the military and civil situation. A few days later the army commanders met with Negrín near Albacete. In these talks, only Negrín and General Miaja favored a continuance of the war. General Miaja, it will be remembered, had been entrusted with the defense of Madrid early in the war after the withdrawal of the government from Madrid. Miaja had retained that command throughout the war and now was Commander in Chief of all Republican military forces.

On March 5, the remnants of the Republican navy revolted and put out to sea from Cartagena, while the honorable but till then unenterprising Colonel Casado attempted to set up a government in opposition to the Communist one. For this initiative, Casado was branded a traitor by Herbert Matthews and other writers. With victory impossible, Casado's aim was to end the war. With Julián Besteiro (another honest man) as the chief civilian, and Casado himself—soon replaced by Miaja—as the military leader, this self-declared government called

---

[3] With the death of Martínez Barrio, the next in line for the Presidency of the Republic is the first vice president of the Cortes elected in 1936, the Socialist Luis Jiménez Asúa. Though he prefers not to call himself President, he acts as such. Otherwise the empty chair would go automatically to the Communist Dolores Ibárruri, *la Pasionaria*.

itself the Junta de Defensa de Madrid (the Madrid Council of Defense). The fact that Miaja finally saw fit to join the coup ought to exonerate Casado and demonstrate that continued warfare was pointless. Since there was neither Cortes nor President, the Junta's claim to leadership was as good as Negrín's. When the Junta ordered the arrest of Negrín, he escaped by airplane with Alvarez del Vayo and a few dissident officers.[4]

By March 12, the Communists had lost power completely to the new Junta, whose representatives were received at the Nationalist capital of Burgos. No concessions were forthcoming. Instead Franco threatened a new offensive. After these facts had been broadcast by radio on March 26, there occurred, according to Colonel Casado, "what might be called the self-demobilization of the Republican Army, and it took place under such excellent conditions that in spite of the fact that 800,000 men were concerned, we did not have to regret one single act of violence, nor to contemplate the terrible sight of a disorderly retreat." On March 27 Madrid was defenseless; on the twenty-eighth only the Guadalajara front was still manned, while Nationalist troops entered Madrid unopposed. Casado continues: ". . . on the morning of the 29th, practically all the armies were dissolved. At eleven o'clock I gave instructions for the surrender, a surrender which naturally could not be made because none of the fronts were garrisoned." This is how the Spanish Civil War ended.

The only prominent Republican who by choice remained in Madrid to face the victors was Julián Besteiro, the old Socialist professor of logic and the first President of the Constituent Cortes. It was Besteiro whom Azaña had sent to England on the presumed peace mission in 1937. Sixty-nine years old in 1939, and of delicate health, Besteiro

[4] See Colonel Casado's book, *The Last Days of Madrid* (London, 1939), for his explanation of these events, refuted by Alvarez del Vayo and others in their books.

sacrificed himself in the role of final intermediary against reprisals. He knew well the risk involved: a Nationalist court-martial sentenced him to death. When this sentence was "commuted" to thirty years' imprisonment, Besteiro was confined to the prison-monastery of Carmona, where he died September 27, 1940. On June 28, 1960, his mortal remains were disinterred (the Spanish mania that Azaña abhorred) and secretly brought from Carmona to rest in Madrid, near the graves of Pablo Iglesias and Francisco Giner de los Ríos, as had been Besteiro's wish.

It remains to be said only that if Casado had been able to time his coup better, during the debacle in Catalonia, the coup might have effected a change in morale to continue the war for some time, mainly because the army of the Central Zone was stronger than the one in the north. At least some of the materiel scattered about France could have been got to the central island of resistance, along with the non-Communist professional officers and leaders who wanted only assurance that their services would be used properly. Coming when it did, Casado's coup could have been aimed only at peace.

Elsewhere in Europe, the German army was on the march. Hitler occupied Czechoslovakia on March 15, and on March 23 began pressure upon Poland to return Danzig and provide a corridor to East Prussia. Up in Collonges-sous-Salève, as the story goes, the ex-President posed for reporters and photographers on the balcony of his residence on a very cold day following his resignation. He spent the month of March in Collonges, except the few days when he and Rivas Cherif journeyed over to Paris to find a publisher for *La velada en Benicarló*, which they found, and for his memoirs, whose authorized publication was canceled by the German invasion of France. Azaña had been besieged with lucrative offers to publish the *Memorias* while he was at the embassy, but he considered their publication to be improper until he had resigned the Presidency.

Azaña kept a diary from 1931 through the years of the Republic and the war. Early in the Civil War he had given the books covering the first two years of the Republic to Rivas Cherif for safekeeping in Geneva, where Rivas Cherif was Spanish consul and secretary of the Spanish delegation to the League of Nations. One wonders how these two men, despite their intellectual interests and political convictions in common, were ever great friends. Although someone may object, the first analogy that comes to mind is (at least physically) Laurel and Hardy. On the basis of their differences in character, it was a case of attraction of unlike poles. Azaña was slow of movement, aloof, unemotional (to appearances), taciturn, blunt, moody, and somewhat introverted; Rivas Cherif was suave, gay, sprightly, nervous, even flighty, and given to banter. Don Cipriano regretted that banter in Geneva when, basking in the reflected glory of his illustrious friend, he let his guardianship of a sensational diary be known, whereupon his vice-consul Antonio Espinosa contrived to steal two of the notebooks and use them as a passport to defection. Soon thereafter, certain portions of the memoirs appeared in Nationalist newspapers. The fact that they were handwritten left no doubt concerning the authenticity of the photographic reproductions. In a short time the content of these intimate papers became well known even among the Republican officials, who had only to obtain and read a Nationalist newspaper. The theft of the memoirs weighed heavily on Azaña, and it was rumored that he had even suggested that a certain political prisoner in Republican hands be traded to the Nationalists in exchange for the two stolen notebooks. Whether this proposal was true or not, it bore no fruit, and Azaña had to endure the scandal, as well as the chilly treatment now accorded him by Indalecio Prieto[5] and other Republican statesmen whom he had treated badly in the memoirs.

Excerpts from the stolen portion of the diary were edited, with commentary, under the title *Memorias íntimas de Azaña* (see Chapter III, footnote one, above) and published in Madrid after the Civil War, as soon as the Nationalists controlled the printeries. The editor, Joaquín Arrarás, has also written a book on Franco, a history of the Second Republic, and a work on the siege of the Alcázar in Toledo. Although the "intimate" *Memorias* are genuine, since photocopies of certain handwritten sheets accompany the printed version, the redactor had the advantage of reproducing, and with his own interpretations, only the paragraphs and sections which could conceivably suit the ends of his publisher—the ruling regime. The main body of the *Memorias políticas y de guerra*, guarded carefully all these years by Azaña's discreet widow, will not suffer such a fate. Supposedly they are to be published with his complete works, and they may well reveal political aspects of the Spanish War which up to now have had to be surmised.

Perhaps the loss of portions of the diary was not the only indiscretion of Rivas Cherif in Geneva, although he vehemently maintains his innocence of the following incident. In May of 1938, London newspapers published stories that Rivas Cherif had lent his support to, if not originated, a movement whereby certain Spanish American nations would act as intermediaries to arrange an armistice in Spain. Presumably this intercessional movement lacked the sanction of Negrín but had the full approval of Azaña, for whom Rivas Cherif was supposedly acting. With or without Azaña's endorsement, the brother-in-law was exceeding his authority by acting unilaterally without the knowledge

[5] After having written prolifically and worked tirelessly for Spanish Republican causes in exile, Indalecio Prieto died from a heart ailment on February 12, 1962, in Mexico City at the age of 79.

or consent of the government. The incident enraged not only the Spanish ambassador to Switzerland but, among others, Negrín himself, who was quoted as being disposed to incarcerate Rivas Cherif as soon as the latter returned to Republican Spain. When Negrín did, in fact, remove Rivas Cherif from his post in Geneva on account of this unauthorized intrigue, Azaña took the dismissal of his friend as a personal affront and remonstrated violently with Negrín about the matter. Apparently the President's protection prevailed, and instead of going to prison Don Cipriano was made official *Introductor de Embajadores*. In this position Rivas Cherif succeeded none other than Amós Salvador, who in 1920 had helped Azaña and Rivas Cherif to found their journal *La pluma*. Perhaps Azaña's singular weakness in government was his persistent protection of a small group of his friends; in the case of Rivas Cherif, it was a question of nepotism as well.

After having resigned the Presidency on February 27, 1939, Azaña continued to live in Collonges with his wife until a couple months after World War II broke out on September 1 of that year. He was completely out of the news during this time and until his death the following year. In the first place, Azaña no longer held any official capacity, even had the Spanish War not ended; secondly, the prelusive rumblings of World War II—such as the Italian invasion of Albania (April 7), the German-Italian alliance (May 22), the German-Russian non-aggression pact (August 23), and finally the German invasion of Poland (September 1)—stole the headlines from any residual interest in the Spanish exiles. Many thousands of those expatriates were grouped in frightful poverty and abandon, which many continue to suffer to this day, in the area of southern France roughly between Bordeaux and Perpignan, including Toulouse.

Although Azaña was living comfortably, the strain of the last three years had weakened him physically. His coloring had never been good, and on the occasion described as Azaña's last interview, Lawrence Fernsworth noticed that the former President was not a well man. On pages 236-39 of his recent book, *Spain's Struggle for Freedom*, Fernsworth summarizes what was probably the last important statement that Azaña ever gave to the press, a statement that had never been published until Fernsworth's book came out in 1957. Fernsworth went over from Switzerland to ask Azaña what really had occurred within the government during the very first stages of the rebellion. In the course of the interview Azaña turned prophetic, predicting that the Falange would ultimately become corrupt and unpopular (which it has)[6] but that the army and the church would be "uppermost and have a good chance of holding on for a number of years because the people are more accustomed to that kind of combination. The generals and the bishops are again in the saddle—Spain has gone back one hundred years." Such was Azaña's final public statement on the future of Spain. Since he was then a political exile in a foreign country, the ex-President did not want to be quoted publicly on political matters at that time, and Fernsworth kept the bargain.

In November of 1939, two months after the European war had begun, the Azañas began their trek from Collonges through southern France. Originally they had thought of buying the chalet in Collonges, even though the house was not large enough for all of its occupants and visitors. After the outbreak of the European war, however, the Azañas imagined themselves to be in a dangerous zone and thought it

---

[6] "The Falange was accepted as the state party partly because it seemed the best bet for an authoritarian anti-Leftist military regime in an age of fascism. Franco conceived of the FET as the party of the state, but he never thought of his regime as a real party-state. The Falange, far from controlling the state, was no more than an instrument for holding the state together. Whenever its political pretensions threatened to disturb the internal equilibrium worked out by the Caudillo, he quickly cut the party down to size." Quoted from Stanley G. Payne, *Falange: A History of Spanish Fascism* (Stanford, Calif., 1961), p. 200.

228

best to leave. (Ironically Collonges was completely spared by the war, as the area around Geneva represented the farthest German penetration south on France's eastern frontier before the armistice of June 22, 1940, and also the anchor of the line that was to demarcate unoccupied France after the armistice.) On the recommendation of a friend, the ex-President, accompanied by Rivas Cherif, journeyed to the environs of Bordeaux in mid-October to see about renting a house there. In Pyla-sur-Mer, a beach suburb of Arcachon near Bordeaux, they saw a house so appealing that they decided to pool their remaining capital and buy the place, since it could not be rented. While the local agent went to Paris to negotiate with the owner, the two friends stayed in the vicinity of Arcachon to enjoy the peace of the ocean, the sand dunes, and the pines, not to mention the mild climate, and to anticipate the privacy and safety of the rustic dwelling that would soon be their new home.

The move to Arcachon in November was taxing, and there in Pyla-sur-Mer the ex-President began to look unwell. Physicians were summoned and diagnosed the cause of his difficult respiration and chest pains as a heart ailment. A photograph of Manuel Azaña taken in Arcachon shows that he had lost a great deal of weight and seemed to be the image of death itself; most noticeably the proud look had vanished. Actually Azaña had suffered from heart trouble for a long time without knowing (or admitting) his condition. Now, however, after various French heart-specialists had examined him and convinced him that the condition was serious, he began to limit his activity drastically, though he continued to receive occasional Spanish visitors.

In February of 1940 Azaña had a heart attack. Very close to death, he did not request any officiation of the church. Miraculously he recovered and by April was able to move about again. At that time Rivas Cherif began to think that the two families ought to try to obtain passage to the New World. From his new post in Chile the former U.S. ambassador to the Republic, Claude Bowers, tried unsuccessfully to pull the right strings for them, but German troops were overrunning France and all was confusion.

Midst the confusion Juan Negrín arrived unexpectedly at the Pyla-sur-Mer residence one night for a brief visit. He had come to offer the ex-President—and nobody else but him—a seat in a small boat that would take Azaña, Negrín, and a few others to England that very night. Though Azaña declined, he appreciated the offer and the last visit of the enigmatic Prime Minister, who, when he died at the end of 1956 in exile, sent to Franco the receipts for the Spanish gold that had been sent to Moscow during the Civil War.

The German advance southward meant that the Franco police could not be far behind. When France capitulated, the terms of the armistice of June 22 designated the Bordeaux-Arcachon region as an occupied zone. The sympathetic local prefect, recognizing that Azaña should leave the region, put an ambulance at the disposal of the sick man. Rivas Cherif and his family stayed in Pyla-sur-Mer, because Don Cipriano felt that the house should not be abandoned in those times, and perhaps also because he refused to believe that the German police and Spanish agents would arrest an ex-Introducer of Ambassadors.

Accompanied by a Spanish physician the Azañas rode the ambulance first to the outskirts of Périgueux, where they stayed several days in a certain castle. Then they went south to Montauban, a provincial town of some thirty thousand inhabitants, north of Toulouse. The patient arrived exhausted at what became his last stop.

Upper left: Azaña, May, 1940, Arcachon, France. *Center:* The grave of Azaña at Montauban. *Lower right:* The author, señora de Azaña, and Don Cipriano Rivas Cherif, Mexico City, 1959.

MANUEL AZAÑA
1880 – 1940

In Montauban the ex-President survived for about five months, bed-ridden, with his wife Dolores constantly at his side. They lived in a poor dwelling, but at least a shelter, obtained for them thanks to the kindness of Ricardo Gasset Alzugaray, deputy to the Cortes and Under-Secretary of Communications. Jammed with refugees, Montauban was part of the unoccupied zone, controlled nominally by the collabora-tionist Pétain government installed at Vichy by the Germans. One day Azaña received a visitor who was to play a significant role in the dying man's final weeks, Luis I. Rodríguez, the Mexican ambassador to Vichy.

Mexico, which to this day has no formal diplomatic ties with Franco Spain, was the Spanish Republic's staunchest friend during the Civil War, even though Mexican economic realities decreed that aid to the Republic be more in the form of moral support than materiel. After the war, Mexico threw open its doors wide to the Republican exiles,[7] among them the widow of Manuel Azaña. On June 23, 1940, the day after the armistice in France, the Mexican government instructed Rodríguez to negotiate with Vichy an agreement whereby Mexico might assume responsibility for the Spanish refugees in unoccupied France. The object of this move was to forestall a probable Nazi pres-sure upon the Vichy government to extradite the refugees to Spain, at the insistence of Franco, so that the refugees could be forced to stand trial for war crimes. The Gestapo and Franco's agents made a number of arrests, then and later, in spite of the agreement that Rodríguez did obtain.

One of those unfortunate "criminals" was Companys, former Presi-dent of Catalonia, who was taken back to Spain and executed. Another was Cipriano Rivas Cherif, who was arrested by German police and

---

[7] A good book on the subject is Lois E. Smith's *Mexico and the Spanish Republicans* (Berkeley, Calif., 1955). See also Mauricio Fresco's *La emigración republicana española* (Mexico City, 1950).

Spanish agents in Pyla-sur-Mer on July 10. The police confiscated the scant money and possessions of the Rivas Cherif family and shoved Don Cipriano into the jail at Pyla-sur-Mer. His wife and four children were ultimately released and allowed to leave France; they are in Mexico today. Don Cipriano was taken to the prison in Irún for two days. On the way from there to Madrid on July 13, his guards threatened to shoot him if he did not reveal the whereabouts of Azaña and of an imaginary fortune in state funds with which the ex-President was supposed to have absconded. The prisoner had nothing to say. Incommunicado in his cell in Madrid, Rivas Cherif received no news of the outside world for three months. Finally on October 21 he stood trial with other "war criminals" and comported himself nobly.[8] The military tribunal sentenced him to death. While he was awaiting execution, before foreign intervention helped to commute his death sentence to thirty years' imprisonment, on November 5 Cipriano heard a rumor of the death of Manuel Azaña. Who can describe that moment? —or the moment three days later when the rumor was confirmed as Don Cipriano was saying goodbye to Julián Zugazagoitia and Francisco Cruz Salido before their execution? In 1942 Don Cipriano was transferred to the penal colony of El Dueso, in the province of Santander, where long periods of solitary confinement were not unknown to him. After having served seven years of the sentence, parts of which he described in an article penned in the jaunty style of an unbroken spirit,[9] he was released in 1947 and now resides in Mexico City. There he is reunited with his sister, Dolores Rivas Cherif, widow of Azaña.

We were saying that one of Azaña's visitors in Montauban was Luis Rodríguez. After the latter had arrived in Montauban from Pau, two

[8] For interesting details of this trial, see Isabel de Palencia, *Smouldering Freedom: The Story of the Spanish Republicans in Exile* (New York and Toronto, 1945), p. 140. (There was also a London edition in 1946.)

[9] "O'Neill in a Franco Prison," *Ibérica*, Vol. IV, No. 4 (April 15, 1956).

former Loyalist officers, General José Riquelme and Colonel Arturo Mena, told Rodríguez of the whereabouts of Azaña and of his broken health. In his book Rodríguez describes the pathetic interview with Azaña,[10] who received him effusively: "Here I am, my illustrious friend," he said deeply moved, "turned into a human scrap"; and, says Rodríguez, Azaña's eyes became moist with tears. The two men talked for two hours, Azaña relating his odyssey through southern France and concluding: "And now I find myself without roots, exposed to every contingency; dying, without connections or money, without prospects or tranquillity, forgotten by friends and pursued by enemies. In no one, outside of my wife, who resignedly stays on with me, do I find another generous spirit capable of succoring me. Luckily you are here; I was hoping for your arrival with the same desperation with which a criminal awaits his pardon." Behold Azaña the suppliant, so ill that he speaks out of character (if Rodríguez's reconstruction of the conversation is accurate), having so far escaped from two wars only to be on the threshold of death in a shabby room in provincial Montauban. After shaking what he described as a feverish hand, Luis Rodríguez set about the task of improving the sick man's circumstances.

Rodríguez successfully petitioned the Mexican President to offer Azaña asylum in the Mexican embassy in Vichy, as Franco agents were known to be in Montauban. Sra. de Azaña was preparing to take her husband to Vichy when the local prefect decreed that they could not leave Montauban without an order from the French government, which was not forthcoming, so the Mexican emissary instead moved the Azañas on September 15 to better lodgings in the Hotel du Midi, an unpretentious provincial hotel but the best in Montauban. Rodríguez drove the patient and his wife to their new lodgings, put their room under military and diplomatic guard, and left funds for the

[10] *Ballet de sangre: La caída de Francia* (2d ed.; Mexico City, 1942), p. 212.

ex-President's maintenance. The next day Rodríguez started off to Vichy for further negotiation but was called back, still en route, when Azaña suffered another attack. Though this attack did not kill him, it left his speech impaired and his body partially paralyzed.

Having heard of Azaña's plight, General Hernández Sarabia arrived in October to stay with his ex-President until the end. On October 15 Azaña's Spanish physician died unexpectedly. As late as the end of October, Sra. de Azaña was still seeking authorization to take her husband to Vichy; all she could accomplish was a change of rooms in the hotel. Also at the end of October she read in a newspaper that her brother Cipriano had been condemned to death. Manuel Azaña, who never learned this news, was to live but one week more.

What may be the authentic version of his death has never been told, owing to the discreet refusal of Sra. de Azaña to engage in post-mortem polemics. She is a gentle soul anyhow, unsuited for the type of public debate that distinguished her husband. Because only one version of his death has ever appeared in print, a legend has grown up which says that Azaña died a penitent in the arms of the church. If this is so, then Azaña's *Garden of the Monks* fooled many people, his professed religious dissociation was hypocrisy, or at best self-deception, and the Spanish Republic's most brilliant orator was not the unswerving man of principle that even his enemies took him to be. Because of the eminent position from which he voiced his well-known hostility toward the church, or rather toward the temporal power of the Spanish church, in his case confession and repentance would have been equivalent to a repudiation of the Republic.

Despite the allegations of those who have criticized Azaña, he was never really irreligious; he merely insisted upon a lay republic. He was the product of a period in Spanish life when a man of good conscience had to become a revolutionary in order to be a patriot, if patriotism means the subordination of personal well-being to the welfare of the majority. All Spain knew Azaña's sentiments. He owed most of his political success not to his stand against the church per se, but to his honesty. He sincerely believed that the monk, even the simple Christian preoccupied with his own salvation and the hereafter, was an "anti-citizen." "Pure faith," reasoned Azaña in *El jardín de los frailes*, "is unsociable; it is not useful in the republic, whose sovereignty it neither strengthens nor defends." And what Spain needed most was responsible citizens.

At bottom, Azaña accepted the ethics of Christianity. He did not accept religious dogma or the Spanish church's intervention in public life in Spain. True, he was married by this church in 1929, according to custom and because his wife was a Catholic. Azaña was also a good husband who lavished loving care and understanding on his Catholic wife while he lived. Even after the fall of Catalonia and Azaña's escape from Spain, he used to take his wife to mass in France. Doña Dolores was then, and remains now, a practicing Catholic. He respected her convictions. She told me that she respected his until the end.

The tens of thousands of Spanish Republicans-in-exile are getting old. Whatever happens in Spain, nevermore will they pick up where they left off. But must one not admire their pride in the past, even though time tends to exaggerate their accomplishments (because nothing was ever really so good as is our happy recollection of it)? What if they have been convinced that Azaña, fugleman of the Republic, died repentant of his leadership and his pronouncements, of his and their lay Republic? Even more important, what will stand in the history books—not those of Franco Spain (for a retaliatory government can scarcely fail to tell fishy stories about the big fish that got away, even if only to die on the bottom), but the history books of a future Spain, or the histories of Spain published elsewhere today?

The repentance of great criminals is one of the triumphs that the church reserves for itself, a triumph that seldom misses its effect on the popular mind, as Balzac once observed. Therefore maybe it is less to Azaña's everlasting glory than to the church's own ends, as the church sees its duty, that a certain archbishop originated and circulated the tale (with or without the abetment of the Civil War victors) that Azaña called for extreme unction and confession before his death. It is a question of one person's word against another, so proof either way is impossible. We shall see both versions: the "unfavorable" one, and the other one with which Sra. de Azaña herself honored me. She was the only person who could know the facts as she described them to me. Without the slightest alteration or embellishment, they are herewith made public after more than two decades. But first the other version.

Soon after Azaña's death Spaniards, inside Spain and out, were asking one another, "Is it true that Azaña confessed?" A story had been circulated which was then, and is now, treated by pro-Franco writers in a manner so casual as to preclude its being anything but an accepted fact to anyone. One example of how it has been handed down can be found in a recent (1956) biography of Franco (one of many) entitled *Franco of Spain*, by S. F. A. Coles.[11] After the author has called Azaña a "pachydermous" homosexual earlier in the book, he refers to the death of the villain with these words (page 159):

> A compelling illustration of the innate Catholicism of the Spanish race was provided by Señor Azaña himself, an *Enciclopedista* and professed atheist, under whose Presidency hundreds of churches and

[11] The author demonstrates his gullibility and impropriety when on page 216, in a digression, he reverently cites a sensational fraud of a book, *Flying Saucers Have Landed*, by Desmond Leslie and George Adamski.

religious houses were burned and thousands of priests and religious [sic] murdered. When he lay dying at Bayonne [this is a 185-mile geographical error, by road] in 1940 he sent for the Archbishop . . . made a full confession, received Extreme Unction, and died in the bosom of the traditional faith.

The supposed voice of authority, however, was Eduardo Comín Colomer, whose "secret" history of the Republic has been cited above on page 117. A section of Volume II (pp. 450-53) on the death of Azaña gives the whole story, which may be summarized as follows:

On October 17, 1940, Monsignor Theas, Bishop of Tarbes and Lourdes, had just arrived at the seat of Montauban and was told that Azaña, quite ill, wanted to see him. The Bishop hastened to the Grand Hotel du Midi and went up to the room where Azaña, his face anguished and livid, was in bed. Azaña said, "I wish to die within the Catholic church." Convinced of his sincerity, the Bishop gave him his crucifix, which Azaña began to kiss saying, *"¡Jesús, piedad, misericordia!"* Then Azaña underwent confession, followed by the viaticum and extreme unction, although someone objected to the latter on the grounds that Azaña was a heart patient. A few days later, the official account goes, Azaña had a civil burial. (It was more than a few days—seventeen plus—if the Bishop confessed Azaña on or immediately after October 17, as the historian implies, for Azaña did not die until November 3.)

The ecclesiastic who was involved did, in fact, sign a statement dated March 7, 1952, which confirmed the original report that had appeared in the *Catholic Bulletin* of Montauban, November 6, 1940. An English translation of the affidavit reads as follows:

1. [Azaña] received in sound mind the Sacrament of Penitence, which I myself administered to him.

2. When I asked Sra. de Azaña's permission to administer the Viaticum to her husband I was certain that the sick man wanted to receive Communion. But I met with the obstinate refusal of N. [we do not know who this could be, and neither does Sra. de Azaña]. Five times I presented myself, and five times I had to go away: "That would affect him too much," I was told.

3. It was Sra. de Azaña who sent for me at midnight to administer Extreme Unction to the sick man, who received it *in extremis*, but in fully sound mind.

4. The Mexican consul, when he heard about this from Sra. de Azaña, arranged a civil burial for the president. The widow, afterwards, did not dare to protest, because Mexico was paying all the hotel expenses of the president and those who were with him.

5. What had happened with certainty was that the president either had preserved or had found again a very intense Christian faith.

Signed: Pierre Marie Theas,
Évêque de Tarbes et de Lourdes

All of this is surely *possible*, because it is not known that Azaña was ever officially excommunicated from the church. Catholics who join Masonry are automatically excommunicated if they know the serious nature of their action, but not many people were aware that Azaña had been initiated into Masonry. Even if he had been excommunicated, the absolution of a bishop was sufficient for reinstatement. In the eyes of the church, Azaña had surely committed sins equally egregious as murder or adultery, but even the murderer is still a member of the church so long as he does not deny a doctrine of Catholic faith.

After the Bishop had made his original statement in 1940, the account began to acquire embellishments as it passed from mouth to mouth. The tale even had a literary manifestation in the form of what is now a much-sought novel, an autographed copy of which came into my hands some time ago. Written by Daniel de Bois-Juzan and published in 1949 by the Amiot-Dumont house of Paris, its 308 pages of libelous copy bear the title *Celui qui fut Pedro Muñoz* (The Late Pedro Muñoz). The publisher did not have to state in a note on the back cover that Pedro Muñoz really lived and that he can be recognized as a contemporary statesman. It is without any doubt one man's version of the life of Azaña, its camouflage being only slight, and the whole *"vie secrète"* supposedly having been narrated to the author by an acquaintance of Azaña whose identity is not revealed. I am told that the novel was very much discussed in France, probably among the exiles, while at the same time nearly the whole edition vanished as if by magic shortly after its appearance in the book shops. Although it was not a bad novel, its arrival was hardly a literary event; and it would be interesting to know who bought up the copies, if indeed they were removed from the market in this way. Most of the Spanish exiles in France have hardly two francs to rub together. As for Sra. de Azaña, she expressed genuine surprise when I told her about the novel; besides, she was in Mexico at the time of its publication, and it would seem that she is scarcely in a financial position to defend her husband's honor by economic means.

Although the events of Azaña's life are easily discernible in the novel, one may disagree with their interpretation, with the motives or "secret life" behind them, and most especially with the characterization of Azaña. He is depicted as a *"garçon aux amours faciles."* He is an atheist with a blind faith in intelligence and an aimless, but consuming, ambition. He is a man who never really understands the people because he himself has never been hungry. We see the boy, then the student, the translator, writer, husband, prisoner, and statesman. As a semi-fictional creation this Pedro Muñoz, leader of men and governments, is a kind of cross between Valle Inclán's Tirano Banderas and

Pío Baroja's Silvestre Paradox; the whole work, in fact, is cast in the crisp style of Baroja. After Pedro Muñoz has consummated his anti-clerical programs, his military and agrarian reforms, and his plan for regional autonomy, he becomes President of the imaginary Republic of Turdénie, whose language, incidentally—and conveniently—is Spanish. (With *Turdénie*, does the author have in mind *Turdetania*, that ancient region of Spain inhabited by *turdetanos*? The conversion of other names in the novel is less subtle. The Model Prison is the Modern Prison; *Frente Popular* becomes *Frente Patriótico; Ciudad Leal* is an imitation, but not a designation, of *Ciudad Real; Pedro* and *Manuel* are both bisyllabic; and *Muñoz* and *Azaña* both bear an ñ.)

Civil war comes to Turdénie. President Pedro Muñoz sits down with his ministers, pistols on the table, to discuss strategy: offensive, defensive, war of position or of movement? Conditions deteriorate. Muñoz is spent, he who had assumed the Presidency as a refuge of solitude: *"Dégoût, lassitude, il a perdu la foi en l'action même, il laissera, de ce recoin, l'exécutif lutter, le législatif palabrer."* Finally this *"historien avisé, visionnaire inspiré, piètre politique"* is about to die, a total failure—and this is the part that interests us. He is pictured on his death bed murmuring that Dulcinea does not exist. A priest is summoned: the Bishop. "Repent, my son," says the Bishop after he has administered the sacrament. With his eyes fixed on the Bishop, Pedro manages to mutter *"Dulcinée n'existe . . . . "* as his last breath, whereupon the Bishop solemnly draws himself up and pronounces pardon: "The Peace of God be upon him, Don Quixote has confessed his error." Then, as the ecclesiastic leaves the room, he pensively quotes Santa Teresa: "God, consider that we do not understand ourselves, and that we do not know what we want, and that we withdraw ourselves far from what we wish for."

Now for a striking literary coincidence. If the events of Azaña's play, *La corona*, anticipated his escape from Spain on foot over the mountains, the circumstances surrounding his death bore an even more ironic similarity to those of a jaunty little short story that he had published in the very first issue (June, 1920) of his review *La pluma*. Entitled "A las puertas del otro mundo" (At the Gates of the Other World), and perhaps the best of Azaña's short fictional pieces, it depicts the decline and death of an aloof professor, a supposed intellectual like Azaña, who too (previous to 1920) was still enjoying his life of independence, contemplation, freedom from love and ambition.

The professor had a public post; he had also been in the 1869-73 Spanish Parliament as a member of an anti-Bourbon party. Afterward he had lived mostly with his books. "He did not go to mass; in the University and in the Academy he always voted with the opposition; he was held to be a man very much of the left." The young members of the Ateneo venerated him, although no one really knew him intimately. His spiritual life was a mystery.

Old age and the approach of death took the professor by surprise. He could conceive of the world without him, but not of himself without the world. His health improved for a while during the last summer, as in the case of the real Azaña, but with autumn he knew the end was in sight. With death near, he became serenely resigned, much to the chagrin of his wife. She was shocked by that impassiveness which, to a religious woman, seemed simply pagan. In order to avoid any risk of being moved or seeming sentimental, the professor forbade all talk about preparing his soul. He wanted only to be alone, in silence, "to count with melancholy the last beats of his heart." His wife, however, "neither was able nor wanted to respect the constraint of the dying man." After much thought, she remembered that her husband had been friendly with a certain priest, whom she at length summoned and introduced into the bedroom. The priest used all his professional wiles to extract a confession and reconciliation with the church, but the dying man stood his ground and took with him to the grave "the secret of his austerity." The priest could only pray over the corpse.

The church contested the professor's mortal remains with the freethinkers. His will, however, called for a simple civil burial in an unmarked grave. Thus was the professor buried on a windy March day, but not before his adherents had snatched the coffin and taken it on a tour of his favorite places in town. With this ironical note, the little tale came to an end, ready-made for the real-life variations on the theme.

According to Sra. de Azaña's version of her husband's death, at no time did she invite the Bishop to the hotel room. Neither did she encourage Soeur Ignace, the Sister of Charity (unmentioned in the Bishop's statement), who was the Bishop's coreligionist and who, according to Sra. de Azaña, ingratiated herself into the events at the hotel by means of repeated calls and persistent offers to be of service. When the patient heard of the Sister's interest in him, he received her just as he received refugees and other friends, for he was bedridden and lonesome. To occupy himself Azaña would also read the daily newspapers and, when he felt able, scribble a few more paragraphs of what was to remain his unfinished posthumous novel, *Fresdeval*, which is supposed to be included in his complete works when they are published.[12]

[12] Azaña invented *Fresdeval* as a shortened form of "Fresdelval," the name of a crumbling monastery in northern Spain which he and Rivas Cherif had visited before the advent of the Republic. The plot of the novel, set in a nineteenth-century atmosphere, reportedly centers about events in three generations of a family that lives in the region of that monastery.

Gradually the calls of the Sister became excessive and unwelcome, the Sister having at first sought Sra. de Azaña's diplomatic connections to aid the flight of certain Jewish families from fallen France. Even when the calls became bothersome, Doña Dolores' innate cordiality and courtesy prevailed. A Catholic herself, she would avoid rudeness to a representative of the church.

Imagine the wife's plight when, already distraught with it all—the flight from Spain, the retreat through France, the isolation, the lack of funds, their homeless state but for that dilapidated hotel, her husband sought by the police and quite obviously dying—in the midst of all this, she received word that her brother Cipriano had been taken and was condemned to death. (Azaña himself probably would have been apprehended too, had not his death ended the vigil of the police.) At the moment Sra. de Azaña's only immediate recourse to negotiation on behalf of her brother was to enlist the Bishop's help. Soeur Ignace took her to the Bishop, who obligingly composed two telegrams: one to Franco and another to Rome. Sra. de Azaña herself dispatched the telegrams. As no reply had come from Spain by the next day, the Bishop called at the hotel. While he was there he talked for the first time with the sick man, who was unaware of the circumstances of the visit. By the time of another subsequent visit from the Bishop, Azaña was failing fast. In order to discourage callers Sra. de Azaña henceforth kept the door locked to all except Hernández Sarabia and the servant Antonio, who had faithfully remained in service to the Azañas.

Even before the end came, Manuel Azaña scarcely recognized anybody and did not know what was happening. Sra. de Azaña told me that neither she nor her dying husband requested any officiation of the church. If the rites were so administered—and well they might have been, for Sra. de Azaña found it hard to recount the last hours, so great were her grief and confusion—Azaña, semicomatose, was either unaware of what was occurring or he was powerless to oppose it.[13]

Manuel Azaña's physicians said that the cause of death was an expanded heart, of the kind that some athletes are supposed to have. Here was a mental athlete, whose habitually pallid aspect always disguised a man of not little emotion, which he had learned to dominate, much to the displeasure of his foes who called him cold. That he had suffered from heart trouble before was a fact unknown to most of his colleagues.

There was no autopsy, no will. He had no children and the name Azaña died with him, since the only son of his deceased only brother (beyond childhood) was killed during the Civil War.

Manuel Azaña, who had fled Spain on a Sunday, February 5, 1939, died on Sunday, November 3, 1940. His body lay in state under Mexican protection. Republican flags had been prohibited, so it was the flag of Mexico that draped the coffin. He is buried in Montauban in a cemetery where cypress trees preside over the dead. Engraved on his tomb are a cross and the laconic inscription of his name and lifespan—and nothing more. Throughout the years a voluntary committee of Republicans-in-exile has maintained perpetual care of the grave, which is their symbol of a lost Spain. The stone never lacks a wreath

[13] This account differs from the description of Manuel Azaña's last moments given in Rivas Cherif's *Retrato de un desconocido*, which has appeared as this manuscript goes to press. Rivas Cherif describes the last days of Azaña in the form of a letter received from Doña Dolores. Though it is not definitely stated, the reader is given the impression that Azaña did receive the last rites of the church, and at the behest of his wife, for Doña Dolores speaks of having sent the servant Antonio for the nun and the Bishop, who, conforming to Hernández Sarabia's and her wishes, arrived just before the ex-President died. But that is all she says: that they did arrive, and moments later Azaña died. I cannot explain the discrepancy in the two accounts, since both have the same source. I can indeed recall having asked Sra. de Azaña very specifically whether her husband requested confession and extreme unction. Her answer was a resounding *no*. We can no longer ask General Hernández Sarabia; he died of a heart attack in Mexico City on May 3, 1962, at the age of eighty-one. And were a servant named Antonio still alive, who would know where to find him?

of flowers, and each year a delegation of exiles visits the tomb on the anniversary of the President's death.

In the days when England seemed ready for her own epitaph, the London *Times* of Tuesday, November 5, 1940, found space for a last tribute to Manuel Azaña. The long résumé of his career characterized him as a man "of high ideals, noble intentions, and of great force and industry." On the same day that Londoners read their final news of one President, across the seas Americans were going to the polls to elect another President to an unprecedented third term in office.

What happened to Dolores de Azaña? The Mexican ambassador took her to Vichy. The rest of the story has already been told:

> After great difficulties Señora de Azaña and her sister were reunited. Later they crossed the ocean on a liner chartered for the transportation of European refugees.
>
> Señora de Azaña was in the same cabin with eight other women and children. I muttered something to the effect that she should have been made more comfortable. With a sad look she said:
>
> "What does anything matter now?"
>
> The loss of her husband has indeed been a terrible blow to this fair, blue-eyed woman whom the president surrounded with the tenderest care and love.[14]

[14] Isabel de Palencia, *op. cit.*, p. 131 (1945 edition).

AFTER Don Quijote had been knighted at the inn, and as he was returning home to provision himself with money, clean shirts, and a squire, the knight of La Mancha met with his first adventure, the one which sets the tone of his entire career. Bound to an oak tree, the young boy Andrés is suffering the corrective blows of his master, the farmer whose sheep he had lost. Upon superficial inquiry, Don Quijote frees Andrés and exacts from the farmer assurance that he will pay the back wages claimed by the lad. In Chapter XXXI when Don Quijote and Andrés meet again, the knight receives not the gratitude he had expected, but curses, for Andrés had got only a doubly hard lashing and a worsened situation as a result of Quijote's intervention. "The word of a peasant is not regulated by honor," muses the knight. "A curse upon you and all knights-errant that were ever born," cries Andrés. By the unavailing acts of Don Quijote, maybe Cervantes tries to tell us that good intentions are not enough. They can be tragic, in fact, unless the well-intentioned person investigates the consequences beforehand, for the essence of tragedy is to fail despite the best of intentions, which were wrong, misplaced, or misguided.

Good intentions are the tragic story of Manuel Azaña and of the Spanish Republic. Consider now the epigraph to this book and its parody: to know what is right is not the same thing as to know how to defend what is right. Azaña freed too many Andreses and trusted too many masters with whips in their hands. The Republic fell apart because of rash words and mad deeds.

Manuel Azaña found it impossible to instill in others his own clear vision of a new and democratic Spain. He knew that the success of the Republic depended upon the creation of a responsible citizenry. Yet the whole history of that Republic was a crescendo of public disorder. Many people say that the Republic had insufficient time to solve its problems, but these people forget that things never got better; they always got worse, and there was never any rapport between the Right and Left wings of the government itself. When the shouts became acts, the Civil War erupted.

Good intentions are the plague of the Spanish people, whose strength in individual instincts creates a weakness in collective ones, and a consequent political history of incontinuity. Primo de Rivera began with good intentions, so did Negrín, and even Franco. If nearly every Spaniard feels himself to be the potential savior of the fatherland, it is not a wonder that, as Madariaga once observed, the leaders of Spain rise from sea level and bring to their office all the "peculiarities, singularities, and angularities of their isolated growth." The men of the Republican governments, mostly well-intentioned and quixotic egotists, never learned the virtues of self-subordination, moderation, and collaboration—the middle-term entities so necessary to democracy, which is the system of government best suited to develop the solid middle class envisaged by Manuel Azaña.

How does one judge Manuel Azaña, particularly with respect to the Civil War years and his conduct in France in exile? Can a man be judged by any except his equals in condition? Even the opponents of Azaña's policies and methods respected his intellectual and moral honesty, which perhaps in some subtle way attracted more followers than his great oratory. Although he was a leader of enormous talent and erudition, Azaña acquired most of his knowledge from books, and he never really knew "life" nor people well. He was a detached spirit, to be sure, but beneath the hauteur was disguised an unsuspected softness and emotionality. At bottom, perhaps Azaña was a weak and shy individual who hid these qualities with a show of strength through a fetish of unbending legality.

Whatever its origin, and howevermuch it failed him, that fetish was his greatness. He personally represented the Constitution, as some statesman or group of statesmen must do in every nascent republic. If he made one tragic mistake, it was the way he handled the church, which in Spain you can either protect or kill—but not kick, as he did. Even this, however, he tried to do honestly and legally. Though the background changed, Azaña always acted the same role and espoused the same ideals. Accordingly, his unvarying strict parliamentary approach to good government was called authoritarian by an undisciplined peacetime Cortes, and termed cowardly by an authoritarian wartime government and a nation given to violence.

Because Spaniards are an impressionable people, easily aroused, and even more easily deceived than their more *au courant* Latin brothers in France and Italy, Spanish politics tend to be inconsistent. Few people would suspect that the avowed liberal José Ortega y Gasset, who was to become one of the main voices of the 1931-36 Republic,

249

had welcomed the advent of the Primo de Rivera dictatorship in 1923 with a public statement in *El sol*, or that the general who was to become Franco's voice of Radio Seville during the Civil War, General Queipo de Llano, publicly declared himself in opposition to a military dictatorship at the outset of Primo de Rivera's coup. The unique trait of Manuel Azaña, however, was an unflagging consistency in both domestic and international political philosophy from beginning to end, from before the Primo de Rivera days until the last word of the telegram by which he resigned the Presidency.

If this book serves any purpose, let it be above all else the public reinstatement of a noble soul who tried and failed. Maybe there was some Sancho Panza at his deathbed who knows that Dulcinea does exist; otherwise there is little hope for a liberal and democratic Spain.

THESE hitherto unpublished letters, the first by Azaña's lawyer, the second by Azaña, concern Azaña's imprisonment in Barcelona in 1934.

From Angel Ossorio to Gregorio Azaña, Brother of Manuel Azaña

2 de Noviembre de 1.934

Muy distinguido Sr. mío:

Hace dos o tres días el Sr. Alvarez Ugena me comunicó por teléfono el deseo que Vd. tenía de conocer la verdadera situación del proceso iniciado contra su hermano D. Manuel y el encargo de que me preguntara sobre el particular. Estimó—y yo también—que sería mejor que yo le escribiera a usted directamente en lugar de transmitirle las referencias por su conducto. Me dispuse a hacerlo sin perder momento pero las circunstancias no me lo han permitido hasta ahora.

Detenido D. Manuel, fué conducido a una comisaría de Vigilancia, a la residencia del General de la División después y al barco "Uruguay," más tarde. Desde allí fué llevado dos o tres días después al "Ciudad de Cádiz" y desde ayer está en el destructor "Alcalá Galiano," completamente solo. El me dice que se siente *más preso,* pero su carta revela mucho mejor humor y yo estoy más tranquilo, porque en la actual situación están mejor salvaguardadas su dignidad y su seguridad.

El General Pozas practicó unas diligencias de tipo gubernativo, de aquellas que autoriza el Código de justicia militar antes de que se forme el proceso. De ellas no resultaba cargo alguno y me cuentan que tanto el instructor como el Auditor dijeron que, si por ellos fuera, le pondrían en libertad.

El Auditor elevó las diligencias al Presidente del Tribunal Supremo. Este, que naturalmente no sabía qué hacer con ellas, las pasó al Fiscal. Y el Fiscal redactó una querella bastante inconsistente, pues según me refieren—yo no lo he visto—se limita a sostener que es verosímil que D. Manuel tuviera algo que ver con el movimiento de la Generalidad, porque tuvo una reunión en el Hotel Colón con 20 o 30 amigos, porque había visitado en días anteriores la Generalidad, porque estaba en Barcelona y porque había aparecido oculto en otro domicilio. La Sala dictó providencia negándose a admitir la querella, por juzgarse incompetente. El motivo era que si los hechos de Azaña (y de Bello, pues también se refería a él) guardaban relación con el movimiento político de la Generalidad, era natural que si no se había de dividir la continencia de la causa, el fuero de los Consejeros de la Generalidad arrastrase a los otros ante el Tribunal de garantías. Me aseguran que los Magistrados Sres. Iglesias, Crespo y Antón Oneca reservaron su voto en el sentido de estimar la competencia de la Sala.

Contra esa providencia interpuso el Fiscal recurso de súplica. Al mismo tiempo yo presenté un escrito diciendo que D. Manuel estaba preso sin que se supiera por orden ni a disposición de quién, por lo cual procedía que la Sala telegrafiase al Auditor diciéndole que no era cierto que D. Manuel estuviese a disposición de ella como se aseguraba en Barcelona. Con esto creían en Barcelona que el Auditor decretaría la libertad. La Sala proveyó que como todavía no era firme su anterior providencia, había de esperar la resolución del recurso de súplica y entonces se proveería.

Inmediatamente se resolvió ese recurso, reformando su anterior proveído. Admitió la querella, elevó suplicatorio al Congreso para poder procesar (con lo que da por prejuzgado el asunto antes de que se practique una sola diligencia), mandó instruir sumario, delegando en el Magistrado de Barcelona Sr. Lecea y dispuso que continuara la detención del querellado. Dícese que contra este último extremo han formulado voto particular los mismos tres magistrados que antes menciono.

Frente a ese extremo de la detención, propuse recurso de súplica. La copia del mismo que remito a Vd. adjunta, me releva de entrar ahora en otras explicaciones.

La Sala se desentendió fácilmente de tramitarlo diciendo que no éramos parte en la causa, lo cual procesalmente es verdad, pero humana y jurídicamente tiene otra explicación muy distinta. Ante esta actitud yo he hecho dos cosas: presentar un escrito advirtiendo a la Sala, en los términos más respetuosos, de lo irregular de su conducta; y hacer que su hermano de usted pida la libertad en nombre propio, sin valerse de abogados ni de procurador. Doy por descontado que también de esto se desentenderá la Sala con cualquier pretexto liviano. Vea usted por donde un Juez instructor, y no un instructor cualquiera, sino el Tribunal Supremo nada menos, niega al Diputado a Cortes el derecho de quedar en libertad a las 72 horas sin estar procesado. La suspensión de garantías es para la elasticidad de movimientos de la autoridad gubernativa, mas no para que la judicial prescinda de los cánones a que tiene que estar sujeta. Tesis tan clara ha quebrado en este caso.

Según las noticias que recibo de Barcelona, no se logra que aparezca cargo alguno contra don Manuel. Companys y Lluhí han declarado la verdad de la actitud de aquél frente al desvarío en que ellos se metieron. Numerosos y calificados elementos de izquierdas republicanas han atestiguado de la misma manera los esfuerzos de su jefe para contrarrestar la locura catalanista. Ahora mismo he redactado un escrito pidiendo que declaren en Madrid los señores Sánchez Román, Domingo, Barcia, Zulueta, Giral y Salvador, que pueden dar fe de los esfuerzos enormes que su hermano de usted hizo para evitar lo que ocurrió. Llegó hasta encargar que fuesen en avión los jefes de otros partidos para ver si entre todos conseguían reducir a los exaltados barceloneses. Pero hoy por hoy, aunque el sumario resultase un expediente de beatificación, todo sería inútil. El Congreso concederá el suplicatorio. El Supremo procesará, la detención continuará y en fin, la cadena de dislates y de vejaciones será muy larga. Las armas de la ley y la presunta serenidad de los Tribunales no juegan para nada en este asunto. Estamos ante un problema político y políticamente será tramitado. Mientras la tempestad no se calme todos los esfuerzos serán inútiles. Su única eficacia consistirá en ir formando una larga cadena de injusticias y violencias que el día de mañana servirá para la reparación.

Porque yo fío en la reparación y aun en la apoteosis. Como yo me he batido ya frente a las pasiones desbordadas en los casos del "Maura no," de la explosión dictatorial, de la persecución de Santiago Alba, etc., estoy acostumbrado a no alarmarme excesivamente ante los griteríos inconscientes. La distinción de don Antonio Maura entre la opinión y el ruido está muy presente en mi memoria.

Yo no tengo miedo en este instante más que a un golpe militar que pudiera consumar en don Manuel una ferocidad. Aparte de esto, me parece que lo mejor que le puede ocurrir ahora es que le tengan como le tienen. Si estuviera en la calle, sería muy difícil que se librara de un atentado. Y si, asqueado, se marchaba de España, probablemente habría terminado su vida política. Una persona de la calidad moral de Don Manuel Azaña, de la injusticia vuelve, de la fuga, no.

Por otra parte, el magistrado Sr. Alarcón, está haciendo los más vivos esfuerzos para complicar a Don Manuel en el proceso del contrabando de armas. De esto no tengo sino referencias privadas y simples rumores. Pero todo lo doy por averiguado. Espero de un momento a otro que le acusen de las niñas desaparecidas, del asesinato del cura Merino y del "affaire" Stawinski.

Frente a todo esto no hay más armas que la razón y la serenidad. Yo me esfuerzo de usar de las mías y en sugerirlas a los demás. El viaje será malo pero el destino resultará agradable. Esto, si no se atraviesa el peligro antes aludido y que es el único que me inspira temor hoy por hoy.

Pregúnteme cuanto Vd. quiera, porque me hago cargo de la situación de su ánimo. Sugiérame las ideas que se le ocurran, porque viniendo de Vd. serán acertadas. Y, en fin, disponga de mi buen deseo con igual confianza que tendría con un viejo amigo.

Téngame por suyo y reciba un saludo afectuoso.

Angel Ossorio (Rubricado)

November 2, 1934

Dear Sir

Two or three days ago Mr. Alvarez Ugena telephoned me and told me of your wish to know the true status of the case brought against your brother, D. Manuel, and of your request that he ask me about the matter. He judged— and I do too—that it would be best for me to write to you directly instead of sending the report through him. I was prepared to do so right away, but circumstances have prevented me until now.

After having been arrested, D. Manuel was taken to a police station, afterward to the office of the Major General, and later to the ship "Uruguay." From there he was taken two or three days later to the "City of Cádiz" and yesterday removed to the destroyer "Alcalá Galiano," where he is completely alone. He tells me that he feels *more like a prisoner,* but his letter reveals a much better frame of mind and I am more at ease, because his dignity and safety are better safeguarded under the present conditions.

General Pozas performed certain administrative formalities authorized by the Code of Military Justice before suit is brought. No accusation was formulated, and I am told that the government attorney as well as the judge advocate would set him free if it were up to them.

The judge advocate referred the proceedings to the chief justice of the Supreme Court. The latter, who naturally did not know what to do with them, passed them on to the attorney general. The attorney general drew up quite an inconsistent charge, since, as told to me—I have not seen it—it is confined to upholding that it is likely that D. Manuel had something to do with the movement of the Catalonian government, because he met with 20 or 30 friends at the Hotel Colón, because on previous days he had visited the Catalonian parliament building, because he was in Barcelona, and because he had been found in hiding in another dwelling. The court pronounced judgment by refusing to admit the charge on grounds of its incompetency. The reason was that if the acts of Azaña (and of Bello, since he was referred to also) had any relevancy to the political movement of the Catalonian government, it was natural that if there was not going to be any division of consistency

255

in prosecution, the jurisdiction of the Counselors of the Catalonian government would drag the others before the Tribunal of Constitutional Guarantees. I have been assured that the magistrates Messrs. Iglesias, Crespo, and Antón Oneca held back their vote in order to appraise the competency of the court.

The attorney general then filed an appeal for reconsideration against that decision. At the same time I presented a writ saying that D. Manuel was under arrest without its being known by whose order or under whose jurisdiction; consequently the court should telegraph the judge advocate telling him of its uncertainty that D. Manuel was within its jurisdiction as affirmed in Barcelona. As a result of this, they thought in Barcelona that the judge advocate would decree his freedom. The court decided that inasmuch as its previous verdict still was not definite, it would necessarily await the decision on the appeal and then reach a verdict.

That appeal was granted immediately, with a consequent return to the previous decision. The charge was admitted, letters rogatory were referred to the Congress for arraignment (which means that the matter is prejudged before the initiation of any proceedings), an indictment was drawn up delegating authority to the Magistrate of Barcelona, Mr. Lecea, and the continued detention of the defendant was ordered. It is said that the same three aforementioned magistrates have cast a special vote against this last demand.

I confronted that demand for detention by filing an appeal. My enclosure of a copy of it in this letter relieves me from entering into other explanations at this time.

The court easily renounced responsibility for handling this appeal by saying that we were not party to the case, which procedurally is true, but which humanly and legally has a very different explanation. Confronted by this attitude I have done two things: presented a writ advising the court, in the most respectful terms, of the irregular nature of its conduct; and instructed your brother to request his freedom in his own name, without having recourse to lawyers or to counsel. I take for granted that the court will find some slight pretext for rejecting this too. Observe the extent to which a trial judge, and not just any judge, but none less than the Supreme Court, denies to a deputy to the Cortes the right of freedom after 72 hours without being indicted. The suspension of guarantees is for the government to wield its authority with latitude, but not for the judiciary to disregard the precepts to which it must be bound. Clearly there has been such a violation in this case.

According to what I hear from Barcelona, no proof can be brought against Don Manuel. Companys and Lluhí have testified to his opposition to the wild schemes in which they were involved. Numerous and competent Left-wing republicans have also testified to their leader's efforts to oppose the Catalonian madness. I have just drawn up a petition requesting that Messrs. Sánchez Román, Domingo, Barcia, Zulueta, Giral, and Salvador in Madrid sign an affidavit certifying the enormous efforts that your brother made to prevent what occurred. He even urged the heads of the other parties to come by airplane to see whether, by group action, they could manage to dissuade the exalted politicians of Barcelona. But right now, even though the indictment should turn out to be a means of beatification, all would be useless. The Congress will grant the letters rogatory. The Supreme Court will prosecute, the detention will continue, and, in short, the vexatious chain of absurdities will be prolonged. The arm of the law and the supposed impersonality of the courts count for nothing in this matter. We are faced with a political problem which will be processed in a political manner. Until the storm calms, every effort will be in vain. The only silver lining lies in the fact that some day the growing chain of injustices and violations will require redress.

Because I am confident in redress and even in his apotheosis. Since I have already struggled against unbridled emotions in the cases of "Maura no," the dictatorial explosion, the persecution of Santiago Alba, etc., I am accustomed to not becoming inordinately alarmed in the face of senseless uproar. I can still see the honorable figure of Antonio Maura very clearly midst the accusation and shouting.

At this moment my only fear is that a military coup could light a fire of wrath in don Manuel. Aside from this, it seems to me that the best thing that can happen to him right now is to be held where he is. If he were on the street, it would be very hard to protect him against assault. And if he were to leave Spain in disgust, this would probably end his political career.

The Tragedy of Manuel Azaña

A person of the moral stature of Don Manuel Azaña can make a comeback from injustice, but not from flight.

In addition, Judge Alarcón is making the most intense efforts to implicate Don Manuel in the traffic of contraband arms. In this matter I have only private reports and plain rumor. But nothing surprises me. Any moment I expect him to be accused of the missing girls,[1] of the assassination of the priest Merino, and of the Stawinski affair.

Reason and calm are the only arms to combat all this. I am forcing myself to adopt this attitude and to suggest the same to others. The road will be rough, but the destination will be rewarding. Yes, unless we get involved in the aforementioned threat, which is the only thing that breathes fear into me at present.

Ask me all you wish, for I can imagine your state of mind. If you have any ideas, tell me, because coming from you they should be good ones. And, in short, rely upon me with the same confidence as you would upon an old friend.

Cordially and affectionately yours,

Angel Ossorio (signature)

From Manuel Azaña to His Friend, Pedro Vargas, Lawyer in Valencia

Barcelona, 11 de Noviembre 1.934

Sr. D. Pedro Vargas

Mi querido amigo:

Parece que es corresponder mal con quien profeso tanta amistad y estimación dejar transcurrir varias semanas sin contestar a una carta como la suya. En realidad, aparte de otros enojos, solamente desde que estoy en el "Galiano" dispongo de tiempo y de medios para cumplir con los amigos el grato deber de agradecerles sus buenos recuerdos.

---

[1] The "missing girls" were some little girls who had disappeared in Madrid at that time, and of whose disappearance nothing has ever been learned. It is a classic unsolved case.

Había que entregar las cartas abiertas (todavía las recibo así), y aunque no tenía que decirle a nadie cosas graves, ya soy demasiado talludo para someterme a un régimen de colegial. Aquí en este barco me encuentro a gusto, y no tengo ninguna prisa por salir. Tanto más, cuanto que sería inútil tenerla. Las derechas, en efecto, se ensañan conmigo como Vd. dice, pero no se ensañarían si los republicanos de ahora no me hubieran puesto indefenso entre sus colmillos. Tengo la sospecha de que, Alfonso XIII, retornado, no se hubiera arrojado contra mí con más furor.

Debo decirle, además, que nada de lo que hacen conmigo ni de lo que intentan hacer, me sorprende. Me bastaba conocer a las personas para pronosticar que aprovecharían cualquier ocasión para destruirme, si pueden. Allá ellos.

De todos los amigos recibo diariamente conmovedoras palabras de afecto a las que no sé cómo responder. La de Vd. se encuentra entre las más estimadas. Le quedo muy obligado y le reitero mi afectuoso saludo de correligionario y amigo, q.e.s.m.

M. Azaña (Rubricado)

Barcelona
November 11, 1934

My dear friend:

When I let several weeks go by without answering a letter like yours, it would seem to be poor treatment of a person for whom I profess so much friendship and esteem. Actually, aside from other annoyances, only since my arrival on the "Galiano" have I had the time and means to attend to the pleasant duty of thanking friends for their kind messages.

I was required to transmit letters unsealed (I still receive them that way), and though I had no weighty things to tell anybody, I am too old now to submit myself to schoolboy regulations. Here on this ship I am comfortable and am in no hurry to leave, especially since impatience would be futile. You are correct when you say the Right wing is taking its vengeance on me, but they would not do so if the present republicans had not rendered me defenseless in their clutches. A reinstated Alfonso XIII could hardly have attacked me more frenziedly.

I should tell you, moreover, that I am not surprised by any part of what they are doing to me or are trying to do. To know the people involved was enough to predict that they would seize any chance to destroy me if they could. So much for them.

From all my friends I receive, daily, touching words of affection which I hardly know how to answer. Your words are among those that I hold most dear. I remain obligated to you and reiterate the affectionate regards of a coreligionist and friend.

M. Azaña (signature)

Bibliography

IT IS NOT possible at present to compile a complete list of Azaña's myriad speeches in single editions, published in various languages, or his many articles in newspapers and magazines published in Europe and in Spanish America.

BOOKS BY MANUEL AZAÑA

La corona. Madrid: Compañía Iberoamericana de Publicaciones Mundo Latino, 1928, and La Farsa, 1932. The *Entremés del sereno* is appended to the 1928 edition and was also published in Italian as *Intermezzo madrileno* in *Collezione del teatro comico e drammatico*, Vol. XXXIII (Florence: Casa Editrice "Nemi," 1933).

Discursos en campo abierto. Madrid, Bilbao, and Barcelona: Espasa-Calpe, 1936.

En el poder y en la oposición (1932-34). 2 vols. Madrid, Bilbao, and Barcelona: Espasa-Calpe, 1934.

Estudios de política francesa contemporánea. Vol. I: *La política militar.* Madrid: Editorial "Saturnino Calleja," n.d. (prologue signed October, 1918). The projected additional two volumes were never published.

La invención del Quijote y otros ensayos. Madrid: Espasa-Calpe, 1934.

El jardín de los frailes. Madrid: Sáez Hermanos, 1927.

Mi rebelión en Barcelona. Bilbao, Madrid, and Barcelona: Espasa-Calpe, 1935.

La novela de Pepita Jiménez. Madrid: Imprenta Ciudad Lineal, 1927.

Pepita Jiménez, by Juan Valera. Notes and prologue by Manuel Azaña. ("Clásicos Castellanos" series, Vol. XXX.) Madrid: Ediciones de "La Lectura," 1927.

Plumas y palabras. Madrid: Compañía Iberoamericana de Publicaciones, 1930.

Una política (1930-32). Bilbao, Madrid, and Barcelona: Espasa-Calpe, 1932.

Valera en Italia. Amores, política y literatura. Madrid: Editorial Páez, 1929.

La velada en Benicarló. Buenos Aires: Editorial Losada, 1939. Published originally in French as *La veillée à Benicarlo.* Translated from Spanish into French by Jean Camp. Paris: Gallimard, 1939.

"Vida de Don Juan Valera." Unpublished manuscript, Spanish National Prize of Literature, 1926.

TRANSLATIONS BY MANUEL AZAÑA

From the French

Cendrars, Blaise. *Antología negra.* Madrid: Editorial Cenit, 1930.

An odd collection of animal fables, folklore, anecdotal and moral tales, proverbs, legends of the creation of mankind, allegory, and personification of natural phenomena.

Erckman, Emile, and Chatrian, Alexandre. *Historia de un quinto de 1813.* 1921. A novel.

Giraudoux, Jean. *Simón el patético.*

A *"fragmento"* of Azaña's translation of this novel appeared in the March 29, 1924, issue of *España;* at that time it was "about to be published by Editorial Calpe."

Montfort, Eugène. *La Niña Bonita o El amor a los cuarenta años.*

A novel published by Azaña's magazine *La pluma,* which carried Rivas Cherif's book review of this translation in the February, 1922, issue.

René, Benjamin. *Los soldados en la guerra. Gaspar.* 1921. A novel.

Bibliography

Staël-Holstein, Anne Louise Germaine de. *Diez años de destierro*. Madrid: Espasa-Calpe, 1919 and 1931.

Voltaire. *Memorias de su vida*. Madrid and Barcelona, 1920.

From the English

Borrow, George. *Los Zíncali (Los gitanos de España)*. Madrid: Ediciones "La Nave," 1932.

First published in 1841, this is one of Borrow's books on gypsies. Normally Azaña's books were painstakingly proofread, but this is an exception. The errata sheet at the end lists 118 errata. Perhaps he was busy with affairs of state; the publication date is 1932.

———. *La Biblia en España*. 3 vols. Madrid: Colección Granada, 1921.

Chesterton, Gilbert K. *La esfera y la cruz*. Place and date of publication unknown.

Chesterton's *The Ball and the Cross* and Borrow's *The Bible in Spain* obviously held more than an intellectual appeal for Azaña, because these otherwise unrelated books—the first a novel and the second a personal narrative—have in common a religious theme wherein Catholicism is attacked by an atheist (in *The Ball and the Cross*) and by a former atheist turned evangelist (Borrow himself). It would seem that even in the work that he selected for translation, Azaña was attracted to erudition that could expose what he considered to be the intolerance of the Roman Catholic church.

Some of these translations were mentioned in the text. Others cannot be identified completely because they were printed in small editions, copies of which are hard to find today. It is possible that there were still other Azaña translations. One and another of the listed translations can be found in various libraries in Spanish-speaking countries. None but the following ones have been located in U.S. libraries, and they only at the one place indicated: *Antología negra*, Johns Hopkins University; *La Biblia en España*, Duke University; *Los Zíncali*, Library of Congress.

Borrow's *The Bible in Spain* is the most important of all these works. Although first published in 1842, the book had never been translated into

Spanish, which seems inconceivable in view of its wealth of firsthand data on mid-nineteenth-century Spain. In England it was an enormously popular book that saw many editions and reprintings. Azaña translated from the definitive revised edition of 1896, the U. R. Burke text with glossary (incorporated into Azaña's footnotes), which was the eighteenth edition and the one that has been reprinted so often since 1896.

George Borrow had once been a hardened atheist. With his total conversion, he became as persistent and fanatical in his new-found faith as he had been in his former disbelief. He had already traveled and written a great deal before the British and Foreign Biblical Society sent him to Spain to print and disseminate the New Testament there. Ostensibly *The Bible in Spain* is an account of his evangelical activities in Spain, but actually it is an excellent travelogue on the regions, customs, and language (Borrow was a linguist) of Spain as they were at that time. Although Borrow was interested primarily in the everyday types which represent collective Spanish traits, the narration is a valuable key to the personality of high political, literary, ecclesiastical, and civil figures of that epoch. One meets, for example, the Duque de Rivas and the colorful figure of Mendizábal, the Jewish Prime Minister who was one of Spain's ablest statesmen. Much can be learned of the Jews and Moors, of the Carlist Wars, and of the prisons, to which Borrow was not a stranger.

Azaña was always drawn to books on Spain's political history, especially those which emphasized the role of the church. Here he was fascinated also with Borrow as a person: the persistent Protestant missionary who fought both the government and the church—the latter more than the former—in order to print an unannotated 5,000-copy edition of the New Testament in Spanish. To publish the edition without notes was the real obstacle. Having been frustrated at every turn, Borrow lambasted the intolerance of the Catholic church throughout his narrative: "the Popish system, whose grand aim has ever been to keep people's minds as far as possible from God, and to centre their hopes and fear in the priesthood." Because the book contains a number of outbursts like this one, Azaña's translation must have had difficulty reaching the bookstands in Madrid when it was published in 1921.

In a preliminary note to the Spanish translation, Azaña praises Borrow for his tenacity, his *"razón"* and *"serenidad,"* and most of all for his struggle for a minimum of hospitality, liberty, and tolerance. Evidently Azaña's purpose in translating the work was at least partly didactic, for he summarizes: "Borrow's book is a beautiful document for the history of tolerance, not in laws, but in the mind of Spaniards." To Azaña the book was a work of art, without caricature or false statement, a creation wherein things and places and customs were painted with an exactness that was not only true, but revealing—even to Spaniards.

Azaña was a more than competent translator. *The Bible in Spain* was not easy to translate. Widely interspersed with expressions from gypsy and other dialects, Borrow's already wordy style was rendered even more difficult by a lexicon that is archaic to the twentieth-century reader, be he Englishman, American, or Spaniard. Azaña's translation, however, is accurate and smooth, even where Borrow's prose reads like a legal document. If the inexperienced translator tends to increase verbiage, Azaña's art lay in reducing it while at the same time accounting for every word of the original English prose.

Selected Works on Manuel Azaña, the Spanish Republic, and the Spanish Civil War

Alaiz, Felipe. *Azaña. Combatiente en la paz. Pacifista en la guerra.* Toulouse, n.d.

An anti-Azaña diatribe in pamphlet form.

Alcalá Zamora, Niceto. *Los defectos de la Constitución de 1931.* Madrid, 1936.

Published after Alcalá Zamora was deposed from the Presidency of the Republic.

Alvarez del Vayo, Julio. *Freedom's Battle.* London, Toronto, and New York, 1940.

Republican Minister's view of the Spanish Civil War; pro-Negrín.

———. *The Last Optimist.* London and New York, 1950.

Mostly autobiographical. Interesting pages on Azaña.

Arrarás, Joaquín. *Francisco Franco.* Translated from Spanish into English by J. Manuel Espinosa. Milwaukee, 1938.

A Catholic book from a Catholic press, Bruce of Milwaukee. Derogatory references to Azaña.

————. *Memorias íntimas de Azaña*. Madrid, 1939.

The stolen portions of Azaña's memoirs, carefully edited for the desired effect, together with caricatures of Azaña.

————. *Historia de la Segunda República Española*, Vol. I. Madrid, 1956.

Published by the Spanish government. Profusely illustrated.

Atholl, Katharine (Duchess of). *Searchlight on Spain*. London, 1938.

Pro-Republican, day-by-day account of the Civil War, particularly as it affected the British Empire.

Aznar, Manuel. *Historia militar de la guerra de España* (3d ed.), Vol. I. Madrid, 1958.

Published by the Spanish government. Profusely illustrated.

Bahamonde y Sánchez de Castro, Antonio. *Un año con Queipo de Llano. Memorias de un Nacionalista*. Mexico City, 1938.

One of the few accounts of life under the Nationalists in southern Spain during the Civil War.

Barea, Arturo. *The Clash*. Translated from Spanish into English by the author's wife, Ilsa Barea. London, 1946.

The Clash is really Book III of the trilogy *The Forging of a Rebel*, New York, 1946. One of the best first-person narratives to come out of the Civil War. Eyewitness account of the defense of Madrid. A very personal document.

Baroja, Pío. "The Mistakes of the Spanish Republic," *The Living Age* (Boston), January, 1937, pp. 422-27. Translated from an article of unknown date in *La Nación* of Buenos Aires.

Insight into the political disenchantment of one of Spain's leading novelists.

Bauer, Eddy. *Rouge et Or: Chroniques de la "Reconquête" Espagnole, 1937-1938*. Paris, n.d. (signed 1938).

Pro-Franco account of the first two years of the Civil War.

Bibliography

Benavides, Manuel D. *Guerra y revolución en Cataluña.* Mexico City, 1946.

Pro-Republican account of the war in and around Barcelona. Pages on Azaña.

Berenguer, Dámaso. *De la Dictadura a la República.* Madrid, 1946.

Self-justification by Primo de Rivera's successor. Covers the period from the fall of the dictatorship to the first few days of the Republic. Author's prologue is signed 1935.

Bertrand, Louis, and Petrie, Sir Charles. *The History of Spain.* London, 1956 (rev. ed.).

Anti-Republic, pro-Franco.

Bessie, Alvah. *Men in Battle.* New York, 1939.

A soldier's view of the Civil War by an International Brigadist. Pro-Communist.

Bois-Juzan, Daniel de. *Celui qui fut Pedro Muñoz.* Paris, 1949.

Fictionalized version of the life of Azaña. A novel.

Bollati, Ambrogio, and del Buono, Giulio. *La guerra di Spagna.* Torino, 1937.

Pro-Franco.

Bolloten, Burnett. *The Grand Camouflage: The Communist Conspiracy in the Spanish Civil War.* New York, 1961.

English journalist's minute documentation of the rise of communism in Spain up to the overthrow of the Largo Caballero government.

Borkenau, Franz. *The Spanish Cockpit.* London, 1937.

A good account of the Republic and of the war, as far as it goes, which is to the first part of 1937.

Bowers, Claude G. *My Mission to Spain.* New York, 1954.

A well-intentioned but blindly pro-Republican work by the U.S. ambassador to the Spanish Republic, 1933-39. Contains numerous errors of detail, some of them with reference to Azaña, to whom the author is generously sympathetic.

The Tragedy of Manuel Azaña

Brenan, Gerald. *The Spanish Labyrinth.* London, 1943, 1950, 1960.

A scholarly book, one of the best on events leading to the Civil War, with an outstanding chapter on anarchism. Pages on Azaña.

Buckley, Henry. *Life and Death of the Spanish Republic.* London, 1940.

A pro-Republic book written by a Catholic British journalist, now a standard work on the Civil War. Scattered, but extensive, material on Azaña. Excellent analysis and original photographs of the main Republican personalities.

El Caballero Audaz (pseudonym of Carretero, José María). *De Alfonso XIII a Lerroux pasando por Azaña.* Madrid, 1933.

Defamation of Azaña.

———. *Secretos y misterios del terrorismo en España.* Madrid, 1933.

More defamation of Azaña.

Casado, Segismundo. *The Last Days of Madrid.* Translated from Spanish into English by Rupert Croft-Cooke. London, 1939.

One of the few accounts of the disintegration of the Republican army in the Central Zone during the last months of the Civil War. A condemnation of the policies of Negrín and Alvarez del Vayo. Generally sympathetic toward Azaña.

Casares, Francisco. *Azaña y ellos. Cincuenta semblanzas rojas.* Granada, 1938.

A vitriolic scandal sheet. Libelous material about Azaña, Rivas Cherif, and many other Republicans. Published in Nationalist territory during the war.

Cattell, David T. *Communism and the Spanish Civil War.* Berkeley and Los Angeles, 1956.

Documents the growth of Communist influence upon the Republic during the Civil War. Thorough, accurate, unbiased.

———. *Soviet Diplomacy and the Spanish Civil War.* Berkeley and Los Angeles, 1957.

Further documentation of one aspect of *Communism and the Spanish Civil War.*

Bibliography

Chabás, Juan. *Literatura española contemporánea, 1898-1950.* Havana, 1952.
One of the few histories of Spanish literature which give space to an analysis of Azaña's works.

Clérisse, Henry. *Espagne 36-37.* Paris, 1937.
A French journalist's view of the early part of the war. Abundant horror photographs.

Coles, S. F. A. *Franco of Spain.* Westminster, Maryland, 1956.
Superficial, inaccurate. Maligns Azaña.

Colodny, Robert Garland. *The Struggle for Madrid: The Central Epic of the Spanish Conflict (1936-1937).* New York, 1958.
The only extensively documented military history of the battle of Madrid. Unbiased, but pro-Republican in spirit. Interestingly presented. Numerous typographical errors.

Comín Colomer, Eduardo. *Historia secreta de la Segunda República.* 2 vols. Madrid, 1954 and 1955.
A treatise on Masonry in the Republic. Many exaggerations and inaccuracies. Pages on the death of Azaña.

———. *La República en el exilio.* Barcelona, 1957.
More on Spanish Masonry and much repeated from the previous book.

La Constitución Española de 9 de diciembre de 1931, with glosses by Antonio Royo Villanova. Valladolid, 1934.

Conze, Edward. *Spain To-Day: Revolution and Counter-Revolution.* New York, 1936.
Unreliable.

Cot, Pierre. *Triumph of Reason.* Chicago and New York, 1944.
French Air Minister's explanation of the reasons for the French defeat in World War II. Chapter X deals with the Spanish Civil War and the French policy toward the Republic. Reliable data, well written.

Del Portillo, Eduardo M., and Primelles, Carlos. *Horas del cautiverio* Madrid, n.d.

An account of the whereabouts of important Republicans in the months preceding the overthrow of Alfonso XIII. Two chapters on Azaña, the second of which is inaccurate.

Díaz Doin, Guillermo. *El pensamiento político de Azaña*. Buenos Aires, 1943.

Not a study of Azaña; gleanings from his writings.

Domenchina, Juan José. "Un entendimiento ejemplar: Don Manuel Azaña, escritor y político," *Universidad de La Habana; publicación bimestral,* Año 17, Nos. 100-103 (1952), pp. 238-72.

A rambling and disorganized article by Azaña's former private secretary.

Domingo, Marcelino. *La revolución de octubre: Causas y experiencias.* Barcelona, 1935.

Exposé of the *Bienio Negro,* chiefly its origin. Pro-Azaña, anti-Lerroux.

Falcón, César. *Crítica de la revolución española (Desde la Dictadura hasta las Constituyentes).* Madrid, 1931.

Prophetic. Pages on Azaña.

Fernsworth, Lawrence. *Spain's Struggle for Freedom.* Boston, 1957.

An anti-Franco book by a Catholic-turned-Unitarian who was a correspondent in Spain during the Civil War. Valuable pages on Azaña. An authentic work whose data are more reliable than its Spanish orthography.

Ferrándiz Alborz, F. *La bestia contra España.* Montevideo, Uruguay, 1951.

Socialist propaganda, plus personal narrative, by a prominent Republican who went into hiding in Franco Spain. One of the few accounts of conditions in Spain immediately after the end of the Civil War. A good narrative.

Fresco, Mauricio. *La emigración republicana española: Una victoria de México.* Mexico City, 1950.

Lists all the prominent Republican exiles who emigrated to Mexico.

Bibliography

García Pradas, J. *Guerra Civil.* Vesoul, France, 1947.

Defamatory poetry, aimed at all "enemies of the Republic," including the "vile" Azaña.

Giménez Caballero, E. *Manuel Azaña (Profecías españolas).* Madrid, 1932.

Defamatory biography by a fanatical Falangist organizer.

Góngora Echenique, Manuel. *Ideario de Manuel Azaña.* Valencia, 1936.

A tribute to Azaña, published before the outbreak of the Civil War.

González Ruiz, Nicolás. *Azaña. Sus ideas religiosas. Sus ideas políticas. El hombre.* Madrid, 1932.

Inimical to Azaña, though moderate in attack. Undercurrents of religious fanaticism.

Hardin, Floyd. *The Spanish Civil War and Its Political, Social, Economic and Ideological Backgrounds: A Bibliography.* Denver, 1938.

An important list of titles. An indispensable source of hundreds of magazine articles. Topical index.

Hayes, Carlton J. H. *The United States and Spain: An Interpretation.* New York, 1951.

Hayes, a Catholic, was former U.S. ambassador to Spain. Pro-Franco, anti-Republic, the book is well written, but it contains numerous half-truths and some untruths.

Hernández, Jesús. *Yo, ministro de Stalin en España.* Madrid, 1954.

An exposé of communism in Spain during the Civil War.

Jellinek, Frank. *The Civil War in Spain.* London, 1938.

A good account of the war up to August, 1937. Pro-Republic. Material on Azaña.

Jones, Hugh Parry. "The Spanish Civil War: A Study in American Public Opinion, Propaganda and Pressure Groups." Unpublished Ph.D. dissertation, University of Southern California, 1949.

A fine work which should have been published.

Juventud Republicana Española. *Azaña: Una vida al servicio de España.* Mexico City, 1942.

A pamphlet, with articles by sixteen prominent Republicans, in homage to the memory of Azaña.

La Mora, Constancia de. *In Place of Splendor.* New York, 1939.

Womanish, Communistic, and anti-Azaña.

Langdon-Davies, John. *Behind the Spanish Barricades.* London, 1936.

Pro-Republic, this book covers only the early months of the Civil War.

Largo Caballero, Francisco. *Mis recuerdos: Cartas a un amigo.* Mexico City, 1954.

Self-justification of Largo Caballero's political role during the Republic and Civil War. These memoirs, written in epistolary form, show that he was an uncompromising revolutionary, but not a Communist. Loosely written.

Last, Jef. *The Spanish Tragedy.* Translated by David Hallett from the Dutch (published in Holland in 1938). London, 1939.

This work, by a Dutch journalist who became a Communist and fought in the famous Fifth Regiment during the battle for Madrid, covers the Civil War only through 1937. The author claims (page 252) that "the Soviet Union has no imperialistic aspirations."

Lerroux, Alejandro. *La pequeña historia. España 1930-36. Apuntes para la historia grande vividos y redactados por el autor.* Buenos Aires, 1945.

Machinations of the men of the Republic. A back-room view by the head of the government during the Black Biennium, Azaña's archenemy.

Lojendio, Luis María de. *Operaciones militares de la Guerra de España, 1936-39.* Barcelona, 1940.

The standard work from the Nationalist point of view.

Longuet, Jean. "Interviewing Premier Azaña," *The Living Age* (Boston), February, 1933, pp. 506-9.

Translated from *Vu,* a Paris illustrated weekly, no date given. (Azaña spoke French fluently.)

Bibliography

Madariaga, Salvador de. *Spain: A Modern History*. New York, 1958.

A revision and extension of earlier editions, the first one *(España)* having been published in 1930, this indispensable work covers the whole twentieth century, with point of reference in the nineteenth. The author discusses the shortcomings of the Republic and the irresponsibility of the succeeding regime. Generally sympathetic to Azaña.

————. *Anarchy or Hierarchy*. New York, 1937.

A work mostly of political theory, written with Spain in mind.

Malraux, André. *Man's Hope*. New York, 1938.

Panorama of the early part of the Civil War. One of the few narratives to include a view of the Republican air force.

Manuel, Frank E. *The Politics of Modern Spain*. New York, 1938.

Scholarly. Emphasis on 1931-36.

Marañón, Gregorio. *Liberalismo y comunismo. Reflexiones sobre la revolución española*. Buenos Aires, 1938.

A pamphlet, hostile to the wartime Republican government.

Marcus, James S. "The Personality of Manuel Azaña." Unpublished honors essay, Harvard University, 1951.

Immature but thoughtful.

Martínez Barrio, Diego. *Orígenes del Frente Popular español*. Buenos Aires, 1943.

One of the few books on this subject.

Matthews, Herbert L. *The Education of a Correspondent*. New York, 1946.

First-hand data on the fall of Catalonia.

————. *The Yoke and the Arrows*. New York, 1957.

Reminiscences. Pages 198-99 on the event at the Toledo Alcázar, written on hearsay, were corrected in the second edition (1961).

Maurín, Joaquín. *Hacia la segunda revolución: El fracaso de la República y la insurrección de octubre* (2d ed.). Barcelona, n.d. (prologue signed April 14, 1935).

An interesting work, despite its extravagant schemes for implementation of social reform. Material on Azaña, with special reference to his army reforms.

Mendizábal, Alfredo. *The Martyrdom of Spain: Origins of a Civil War.* New York, 1938.

The author, a Spanish Catholic professor, concludes that all parties, classes, and groups (including Azaña's) shared the responsibility for the Civil War but those who started the war bear the greatest blame. A thoughtful work by a Republican moderate.

Merin, Peter. *Spain between Death and Birth.* Translated from the German by Charles Fullman. New York, 1938.

Passionately anti-Franco, pro-Republican. Good photographs.

Mola Vidal, Emilio. *Lo que yo supe . . . (Memorias de mi paso por la Dirección General de Seguridad).* 3 vols. Madrid, n.d. (Vol. I signed February, 1932; Vol. II signed April, 1932; Vol. III signed March, 1933).

Memoirs of the advent of the Republic, by Franco's literary general.

————. *El pasado, Azaña y el porvenir.* Madrid, 1934.

Included, along with the previous book, in Mola's *Obras completas,* Valladolid, 1940, this volume deals—in its psychopathic way—with Azaña's army reforms and Mola's military theory in general.

Mori, Arturo. *Crónica de las Cortes Constituyentes de la Segunda República Española.* 13 vols. Madrid, 1932.

A day-by-day account of how the Republic's Constitution was framed, with many speeches. Biased to the Left.

Morrow, Felix. *Revolution and Counter Revolution in Spain.* New York, 1938.

Communistic, anti-Azaña.

Orwell, George. *Homage to Catalonia.* New York, 1952.

One of the great personal narratives to come out of the Civil War, but a view of the war whose validity is limited largely to one sector of military and political activity.

Ossorio y Gallardo, Angel. *Vida y sacrificio de Companys*. Buenos Aires, 1943.

Azaña's lawyer, a former Monarchist who offered his services to the Republic at the outbreak of the Civil War and was appointed ambassador first to Belgium, then to France, and finally to Argentina, writes in defense of the memory of Luis Companys. Pages on the exodus from Catalonia.

————. "Azaña y las derechas," *Revista de las Indias* (Bogotá, Colombia), December, 1944.

Pages of homage. Disorganized.

————. *Mis memorias*. Buenos Aires, 1946.

Opinions on the Republic and the Civil War.

————. *La guerra de España y los católicos*. Buenos Aires, 1942.

The last chapter is a fictional dialogue between Azaña and Neville Chamberlain, who died within a few days of each other.

Palencia, Isabel de. *Smouldering Freedom: The Story of the Spanish Republicans in Exile*. New York and Toronto, 1945; London, 1946.

Sentimental, unreliable, pro-Negrín. Kind pages on señora de Azaña.

Payne, Stanley G. *Falange: A History of Spanish Fascism*. Stanford, California, 1961.

The definitive work on the Falange to date. Excellent analysis of the character of José Antonio Primo de Rivera.

Peers, E. Allison. *The Spanish Tragedy: 1930-1936*. New York, 1936.

A middle-of-the-road analysis of why the Republic failed. Tendency to overlook the shortcomings of the Right.

————. *Catalonia Infelix*. London, 1937.

An objective analysis of Catalonia's role in the Republic.

Pérez Salas, Jesús. *Guerra en España (1936 a 1939)*. Mexico City, 1947.

An unpolished but highly significant work by a regular army officer who remained loyal to the Republic. Strongly anti-Communist. The author's honesty and common sense make this work one of the most genuine accounts of the war. Pérez Salas sees Negrín as a dictator and Azaña as Negrín's virtual prisoner. The book should be better known.

Pla, José. *Historia de la Segunda República Española.* 4 vols. Barcelona, 1940 and 1941.

A poor example of what a work of history should be. Anti-Republic.

Prieto, Carlos. *Spanish Front.* London, Edinburgh, Paris, Melbourne, Toronto, and New York, 1936.

The book makes frequent reference to Miguel [sic] Azaña.

Prieto, Indalecio. *La tragedia de España: Discursos pronunciados en América del Sur.* Buenos Aires, 1939.

Six speeches given in South America in defense of the Republic.

————. *Palabras de ayer y de hoy.* Santiago de Chile, 1938.

Four speeches given in Spain on Republican affairs. In the speech dated May 1, 1936, Prieto predicts that if there were a rebellion, Franco would be the man to lead it.

————. *Cómo y por qué salí del Ministerio de Defensa Nacional: Intriga de los rusos en España.* Paris, 1939.

A speech, given in Spain, in which Prieto tells how and why he was dismissed by Negrín.

Ramos Oliveira, Antonio. *Politics, Economics and Men of Modern Spain, 1808-1946.* Translated from Spanish into English by Teener Hall. London, 1946.

The best general book on those aspects of Spanish life delimited by its title; also the most incisive chapter that has been written on Azaña. Antitotalitarian, but points out the weaknesses of the Republic.

Ratcliff, Dillwyn F. *Prelude to Franco.* New York, 1957.

A brief study of Primo de Rivera.

Regler, Gustav. *The Great Crusade.* Translated from the German by Whittaker Chambers and Barrows Mussey, with a Preface by Ernest Hemingway. New York and Toronto, 1940.

A good novel of the Civil War, though somewhat choppy. Regler fought in the International Brigades. There is a good description of the battle for Madrid and of the Republican victory at Guadalajara. Exaltation of the proletariat.

Bibliography

Rivas Cherif (Rivas-Xerif), Cipriano. *Retrato de un desconocido (Vida de Manuel Azaña)*. Mexico City, 1961.

This life of Azaña is not objective, is excessively autobiographical, and contains numerous minute errors of fact and of typography, but it is the first book of its kind, though weak on Azaña's early years (to age thirty-four).

Rodríguez, Luis I. *Ballet de sangre: La caída de Francia* (2d ed.). Mexico City, 1942.

Valuable material on the Republican exiles in France, including Azaña.

Rojo, Vicente. *¡Alerta los pueblos!* Buenos Aires, 1939.

A source of information on the fall of Catalonia by the Republican general who was Chief of Staff.

Rolfe, Edwin. *The Lincoln Battalion*. New York, 1939.

Published by the Veterans of the Abraham Lincoln Brigade.

Romanones, Conde de. *Obras completas*. 3 vols. Madrid, 1949.

Much twentieth-century history by an important political figure of the Monarchy.

Sender, Ramón. *Counter-Attack in Spain*. Boston, 1937.

Good material on the defense of Madrid by a great Spanish liberal, a widely known novelist and professor at the University of New Mexico.

Sevilla Andrés, Diego. *Historia política de la zona roja*. Madrid, 1954.

Typical Fascist view of the Republic: all red. Published by the Spanish government.

Smith, Lois Elwyn. *Mexico and the Spanish Republicans*. Berkeley and Los Angeles, 1955.

This documentation of Mexico's efforts to aid the Republic during the Civil War and to assimilate the Spanish exiles after the war shows the impact of the *émigrés* upon Mexican politics and society from 1940 to 1955.

Smith, Rhea Marsh. *The Day of the Liberals in Spain*. Philadelphia, 1938.

This study is restricted to the formation and evolution of the 1931 Constitution. Scholarly, but contains some errors.

Steer, G. L. *The Tree of Gernika*. London, 1938.

An apologia for the Basques. One of the best books on the Civil War and the only good one on the fighting in the Basque provinces. War maps and photographs.

Taylor, F. Jay. *The United States and the Spanish Civil War*. New York, 1956.

Well documented.

Thomas, Hugh. *The Spanish Civil War*. New York, 1961.

Because this history, a best-seller, may come to be considered the definitive work on the Spanish Civil War, it deserves more than just brief commentary. Thomas' 720-page political and military history is a masterpiece of organization, the first work of its kind to integrate in detail and with impartiality the views of the government and the war of both sides, and the second work (Madariaga's *Spain* was the first) to bring the chaos of the entire 1931-39 period into narrative order for readers of the English language. Reviews in the most prestigious newspapers and magazines lauded the author's literary style as well as his grandness of scope and his gift for synthesis. The book is a milestone—let there be no mistake about that—but the historian will see two obvious procedural faults: (1) the author's extensive reliance upon the facts and figures of Nationalist military operations as presented by the Francoist historians Lojendio, Aznar, and Villegas, whose lengthy military histories are largely state-subsidized works of sycophantic propaganda; and (2) the author's fondness for apocryphal anecdotes and undocumented conversations reconstructed from strictly hearsay evidence. Unfortunately the book contains numerous errors of fact and much questionable interpretation of facts. Pablo de Azcárate, one-time Deputy Secretary-General of the League of Nations and ambassador of the Republic to England during the Civil War, exhibited fifty-some such errors in the July 21, 1961, edition of *España libre*, a Spanish Left-wing newspaper of New York. Eventually both the Leftist and Rightist presses will cull and list publicly all the inaccuracies in this important book which affect their point of view. Inasmuch as Thomas has dealt harshly and somewhat unfairly with Manuel Azaña, I wish to take exception to the following (page numbers refer to Thomas' book):

Bibliography

Page 23. Though Azaña did translate George Borrow, mentioned by the author, and, unmentioned, Gilbert Chesterton, Voltaire, Eugène Montfort, Jean Giraudoux, Blaise Cendrars, and others, I know of no translation of Bertrand Russell or Stendhal.

Page 24. The author says that Azaña was accused of being a homosexual: "There is a possibly apocryphal story which well illustrates his character. It was said that a journalist once asked Don Manuel how he had come to embark upon this sexual eccentricity. 'Just like you,' replied Azaña, 'asking questions.'" If this anecdote is "possibly apocryphal," why print it in a history? Apocryphal or not, this story was told of the dramatist Jacinto Benavente, not of Azaña.

Page 24. Azaña married at the age of forty-nine, not forty-six.

Page 24. Azaña was secretary of the Ateneo, yes, but why omit the fact that he was also later its president?

Page 25. This statement is doubly misleading: "A very hostile study is given by Arrarás in his introduction to Azaña's Memoirs." Naturally Arrarás' study is hostile since it was published in Franco Spain in 1939 expressly to discredit Azaña and since Ararrás edited only selected parts of the stolen portions of Azaña's memoirs.

Page 79. With reference to the October, 1934, revolution in Barcelona, the author admits that Azaña was not a participant in the plot, but he continues: "On the other hand, I think Professor Peers is right in suggesting that Azaña was perfectly ready to accept the Presidency of a new federal Spain, if such a crown had been offered to him." This speculation is wholly unfair and not founded upon anything the legalistic and constitutional Azaña ever said or wrote or intimated. With further statements on pages 86 and 88, the author implicates Azaña in the Barcelona affair by not fully exonerating him. All the evidence shows that Azaña tried to *prevent* the Barcelona uprising rather than to condone it with his support or silence.

Page 308. Azaña did not flee from Madrid in the autumn of 1936 "without even telling the Cabinet."

Page 308. Although Azaña did visit Montserrat during the Civil War, the author is wrong in affirming that he *lived* there, "conveniently far from likely aerial attack and conveniently near the French frontier in case of a general collapse."

Page 352. Rather than doing nothing to prevent the execution of José Antonio Primo de Rivera, according to my information Azaña did all he could—unsuccessfully—to prevent that execution.

Page 619. "Azaña died in 1940 in Aquitaine. The Bishop of Montauban gave him supreme unction. The old anti-clerical thus returned in the end to the faith which he had so much attacked." Azaña died in 1940 in Montauban; that of his own volition he died in the arms of the church is by no means certain.

Toryho, Jacinto. *Después de la tragedia: La traición del señor Azaña.* New York, 1939.

Impassioned and vitriolic.

Trotsky, Leon. *La revolución española.* Madrid, 1931.

Prophetic: the book was written almost three months before the proclamation of the Republic.

———. *The Spanish Revolution in Danger.* Translated by Morris Lewitt. New York, 1931.

A guide for Spanish revolutionaries.

———. *The Lessons of Spain—the Last Warning.* Colombo, Ceylon, 1956. Originally written in 1937.

Explains the mistakes of the Spanish proletariat. Incisive, intuitive. Disparages Azaña.

Unamuno, Miguel de. "Anarchy in Spain," *The Living Age* (Boston), March, 1934, pp. 22-24.

On the fanaticism and destructiveness of the Anarchists.

Villanueva, Francisco. *Azaña (el gobierno).* Mexico City, n.d. (but post-1940).

Restricted to the period 1931-34. Generally sympathetic to Azaña.

Wallace, Lillian P., and Askew, William C. (eds.). *Power, Public Opinion, and Diplomacy.* Durham, North Carolina, 1959.

Contains a notable essay on the policy of non-intervention by J. Bowyer Bell entitled "French Reaction to the Spanish Civil War, July–September, 1936."

Bibliography

Zugazagoitia, Julián. *Historia de la guerra en España.* Buenos Aires, 1940. Though its nearly six hundred pages are dense and poorly organized, this history of intrigue and conflict among the wartime Republican personalities is invaluable. Many pages on Azaña, to whom the author is generally sympathetic. The author was one of the Republican Ministers executed by the victors.

Index

Index

Dante, 23
Danzig, 224
De la dictadura a la República, 78
Deactivation Law, 105-7
Declaration of the Rights of Man, 19
Defectos de la Constitución de 1931, Los, 88
Después de la tragedia: La traición del señor Azaña, 216
Diario of Manuel Azaña; see *Memoirs of Manuel Azaña*
Díaz, Josefina, 7, 10
Díaz Cobeña, Luis, 13
Díaz Gallo, Josefa, 11
Díez-Canedo, Enrique, 47, 70
Dirección General de los Registros, 15, 62
Dirección General de Seguridad, 79
Discursos en campo abierto, 93, 145
D'Olwer; see Nicoláu d'Olwer, Luis
Domenchina, Juan José, 166, 176
Domingo, Marcelino, 72, 73, 130, 253, 257
Don Quijote, 4, 6, 9, 11, 24, 32, 49, 55, 62, 64, 65, 136n, 177, 240, 247
Doré, Gustave, 11
Du Midi, Hotel, 233, 234, 237, 243
Dulcinea, 240, 250
Duque de Rivas, 23, 31, 70

Ebro offensive, 200, 201
Echevarría, Juan, 47n
Ejército Popular; see Peoples' Army
El Dueso, 232
Emigración republicana española, La, 231n
En el poder y en la oposición, 93, 99
"Enabling Act," 125
England, 16, 149, 164, 181, 187, 188, 196, 215, 218, 219, 220, 223, 230, 245
Entremés del sereno, 45, 47
Escorial, El, 11, 26, 41, 42, 44, 79, 160
España, 26-29, 37, 47, 54, 58, 62, 64, 136n, 166n

Espina, Antonio, 47
Espinosa, Antonio, 27, 225
Esquerra Party, Catalonian, 153
Estudios de política francesa contemporánea, 14, 16, 18, 19, 31, 59, 69
European Movement Congress, 161n
European War; see World War II
Existentialism, 59, 63

FAI, 168; see also Anarchism
Falange, 108, 125, 128, 171, 228; see also Fascism
Falange: A History of Spanish Fascism, 228n
Fantasías, 25
Fascism, 68, 108, 125, 128, 129, 130, 134, 137, 140, 159, 160, 161n, 165, 168, 173, 186, 188; see also Falange
Fascist(s); see Fascism
Federación de Anarquistas Ibéricos; see FAI
Fedra, 24
"Fénix de las Españas, El," 29
Fernández Almagro, Melchor, 47
Fernando III, 25
Fernsworth, Lawrence, 154, 165, 166, 186, 228
Figueras, 204, 206, 208, 209, 213
Finca de los Barrancos, 7
Fioretti, 23
First Spanish Republic, 6, 88, 156
First World War; see World War I
Fogazzaro, Antonio, 23
Forja de los sueños, La, 8
Foscolo, Ugo, 23
France, 16, 17, 18, 59, 64, 69, 72, 74, 79, 149, 171, 174, 175, 187, 188, 191, 192, 196, 199n, 201, 204, 206, 207, 208, 209, 210, 212, 215, 217, 218, 219, 220, 224, 228, 229, 230, 232, 233, 235, 239, 243, 249

Index

Index

Universidad Central; *see* Madrid, University of

Universidad Complutense; *see* Alcalá, University of

University City; *see* Madrid, University of

"Uruguay," 251, 255

Uruguay, 47

U.S.S.R.; *see* Russia

Valencia, 8, 77, 84, 88, 95, 111, 145, 173, 175, 176, 179, 180, 189, 191n, 197, 209, 214

Valencia, University of, 187

"Valera," 136n

Valera, Carmen, 30, 31

Valera, Juan, 30-35, 48, 54, 136n

Valera en Italia: Amores, política y literatura, 31

"Valera en Rusia," 30

Valladolid, 53, 75, 120, 121

Valle Inclán, Ramón del, 24, 27, 47n, 51, 52, 59, 67, 69, 83, 136, 239

"Vanidad y la envidia, La," 29

Vargas, Pedro, 258, 259

Vatican, the, 102, 243

Veillée à Benicarlo, La, 192; see also *Velada en Benicarló, La*

Velada en Benicarló, La, 55, 98, 164, 170, 192-97, 224

Vera de Bidasoa, 127

Verga, Giovanni, 23

Verne, Jules, 10

"Vicario de Durón, El," 12

Vicario Sanz, José María, 11, 12, 14, 15

Vichy, 231, 233, 234, 245

Vida de Don Juan Valera, 30, 31, 35

Vida y sacrificio de Companys, 212

Villalba de los Alcores, 53

Villegas, General Rafael, 90

Virgen del Val, 4

Viriato, 74

Voltaire, 22, 44

Volunteer for Liberty, The, 178, 179

Washington, 84

Weimar Republic, 84, 107, 125

Where Dreams Are Forged, 9

Wilson, Woodrow, 29

World War I, 16, 17, 18, 21, 22, 63

World War II, 191, 192, 196, 215, 227, 228, 229, 230, 231

Xirgu, Margarita, 46, 47, 65

Y sucedió así, . . . , 78

Zaragoza, 7, 11, 139, 174

Zugazagoitia, Julián, 203, 211n, 221, 232

Zuloaga, Ignacio, 160

Zulueta, Luis de, 253, 257

Zurich, 184